W9-BTM-475

CCNA Self-Study

CCNA Flash Cards and Exam Practice Pack

Second Edition

Eric Rivard

Jim Doherty

Cisco Press

Cisco Press
201 West 103rd Street
Indianapolis, IN 46290 USA

CCNA Flash Cards and Exam Practice Pack
Second Edition

Eric Rivard and Jim Doherty

Copyright© 2004 Cisco Press

Published by:
Cisco Press
201 West 103rd Street
Indianapolis, IN 46290 USA

Printed in the United States of America 1 2 3 4 5 6 7 8 9 0

First Printing July 2003

Library of Congress Cataloging-in-Publication Number: 2002105412

ISBN: 1-58720-079-1

Warning and Disclaimer
This book is designed to provide information for CCNA candidates looking for hands-on study. Every effort has been made to make this book as complete and accurate as possible, but no warranty or fitness is implied.

The information is provided on an "as is" basis. The authors, Cisco Press, and Cisco Systems, Inc. shall have neither liability nor responsibility to any person or entity with respect to any loss or damages arising from the information contained in this book or from the use of the discs or programs that may accompany it.

The opinions expressed in this book belong to the authors and are not necessarily those of Cisco Systems, Inc.

Feedback Information
At Cisco Press, our goal is to create in-depth technical books of the highest quality and value. Each book is crafted with care and precision, undergoing rigorous development that involves the unique expertise of members of the professional technical community.

Reader feedback is a natural continuation of this process. If you have any comments on how we could improve the quality of this book, or otherwise alter it to better suit your needs, you can contact us through e-mail at feedback@ciscopress.com. Please be sure to include the book title and ISBN in your message.

We greatly appreciate your assistance.

Publisher	John Wait
Editor-in-Chief	John Kane
Executive Editor	Brett Bartow
Acquisitions Editor	Michelle Grandin
Cisco Representative	Anthony Wolfenden
Cisco Press Program Manager	Sonia Torres Chavez
Manager, Marketing Communications, Cisco Systems	Scott Miller
Cisco Marketing Program Manager	Edie Quiroz
Production Manager	Patrick Kanouse
Development Editor	Marc Fowler
Project Editor	Marc Fowler
Copy Editor	Gayle Johnson
Technical Editors	Andy Barkl
	Drew Rosen
	Tim Sammut
Team Coordinator	Tammi Barnett
Book Designer	Gina Rexrode
Cover Designer	Louisa Adair
Composition	Mark Shirar

Trademark Acknowledgments

All terms mentioned in this book that are known to be trademarks or service marks have been appropriately capitalized. Cisco Press or Cisco Systems, Inc. cannot attest to the accuracy of this information. Use of a term in this book should not be regarded as affecting the validity of any trademark or service mark.

CISCO SYSTEMS

Corporate Headquarters
Cisco Systems, Inc.
170 West Tasman Drive
San Jose, CA 95134-1706
USA
www.cisco.com
Tel: 408 526-4000
  800 553-NETS (6387)
Fax: 408 526-4100

European Headquarters
Cisco Systems International BV
Haarlerbergpark
Haarlerbergweg 13-19
1101 CH Amsterdam
The Netherlands
www-europe.cisco.com
Tel: 31 0 20 357 1000
Fax: 31 0 20 357 1100

Americas Headquarters
Cisco Systems, Inc.
170 West Tasman Drive
San Jose, CA 95134-1706
USA
www.cisco.com
Tel: 408 526-7660
Fax: 408 527-0883

Asia Pacific Headquarters
Cisco Systems, Inc.
Capital Tower
168 Robinson Road
#22-01 to #29-01
Singapore 068912
www.cisco.com
Tel: +65 6317 7777
Fax: +65 6317 7799

Cisco Systems has more than 200 offices in the following countries and regions. Addresses, phone numbers, and fax numbers are listed on the **Cisco.com Web site at www.cisco.com/go/offices.**

Argentina • Australia • Austria • Belgium • Brazil • Bulgaria • Canada • Chile • China PRC • Colombia • Costa Rica • Croatia
Czech Republic • Denmark • Dubai, UAE • Finland • France • Germany • Greece • Hong Kong SAR • Hungary • India • Indonesia
Ireland • Israel • Italy • Japan • Korea • Luxembourg • Malaysia • Mexico • The Netherlands • New Zealand • Norway • Peru
Philippines • Poland • Portugal • Puerto Rico • Romania • Russia • Saudi Arabia • Scotland • Singapore • Slovakia • Slovenia
South Africa • Spain • Sweden

About the Authors

Eric Rivard, A+, MCSE, CCDA, CCNP, CCSE, is a Senior IT Specialist and IT Manager at Valley Center Municipal Water District. He is the author of the first edition of the *CCNA Flash Card Practice Kit.* He also teaches Microsoft classes at National University. In his spare time, he volunteers with the Boys Scouts of America. He lives with his wife, who is expecting their first child, in Oceanside, Calif.

Jim Doherty is employed with Cisco Systems as a solutions marketing manager with responsibility for Routing and Switching and Security. He has served as project manager on IP Telephony and Call Center Solutions. Over the past several years he has taught professionals in both academic and industry settings on a broad range of topics, including electric circuits, statistics, economics, and wireless communication methods. Before joining Cisco, he worked for Ericsson Mobile Phones. Jim co-authored *Cisco Networking Simplified,* published by Cisco Press. He also served in the U.S. Marine Corps, where he earned the rank of sergeant before leaving to pursue an education. He holds a BS in electrical engineering from North Carolina State University and an MBA from Duke University.

About the Technical Reviewers

Andy Barkl, CCNP, CCDP, CISSP, MCT, MCSE+I, MCSA, CNA, A+, CTT+, i-Net+, Network+, Security+, Server+, has more than 19 years of experience in the Network+IT field. He owns MCT & Associates LLC, a technical training and consulting firm in Phoenix, Ariz. He spends much of his time in the classroom but has also been responsible for many Microsoft Windows 2000, Exchange 2000, and Cisco networking deployments for clients across Arizona. He's also the online editor for MCPMag.com, TCPMag.com, and CertCities.com, and he's a contributing author and editor for Sybex and Cisco Press. He hosts a multitude of exam preparation chats monthly on MCPmag.com, TCPmag.com, and CertCities.com. You can reach him at abarkl@WeTrainIT.com.

Drew Rosen, CCIE No. 4365, is a product marketing manager in Cisco's Internet Learning Solutions Group. He has been involved in the production and launch of numerous ILSG products, including Building Scalable Cisco Internetworks (BSCI), Configuring BGP on Cisco Routers (CBCR), Configuring Cisco Routers for IS-IS (CCRI), Advanced MPLS VPN Solutions (AMVS), Building Metro Optical Networks (BCMON), and Implementing QoS. He lives in Florida with his wife, Meredith, and daughter, Chelsea.

Tim Sammut, CCIE No. 6642, is a senior network consultant for Northrop Grumman Information Technology. He has served in key project roles involving technologies from LAN switching to security to SNA integration. He has helped many organizations, ranging from 100 to 130,000 users, make the most of their network investment. He holds CISSP, CCIE Security, and CCIE Communication and Services certifications.

Dedications

Eric Rivard–

I dedicate this second edition to my wife, Tammy, and my family. I am the man I am today because of your example and love. Thank you for everything.

Jim Doherty–

To Samantha and Conor.

Acknowledgments

Eric Rivard–

First, I want to thank my Father in Heaven for giving me everything I have: my family, my health, the freedoms I enjoy, and the continued opportunity to work with Cisco Press. I love you and owe everything to you.

To my wife, Tammy: Wow—we are going to be parents! I am so excited for this child and am so honored that you are going to be the mother of our children. You have been such a big part of my life for so long, and I cannot imagine life without you. I love you, honey. Thank you for understanding when I could not be there for you because I was occupied with meeting deadlines. To my family, my mother and father, thank you for the unconditional love you have given me. I truly have the best parents in the world. To my brothers, Alain, Clint, Byron, and Richard, you guys are my best friends. I love spending time with you and remembering our childhood. Alain, thanks for the good example you set for me when I was younger. Clint, you are at the right place at the right time. Continue to serve the Lord, and return with honor. Byron, you are growing to be a fine young man. Always put the Lord first, and everything will turn out fine. Richard, my baby brother, keep on practicing your kung fu, and always honor your mother. I love you guys. To my father and mother-in-law, you are truly my second parents. Thank you for accepting me as a son, for your love, support, and the great example you have been to us. I love you. And to the rest of my family, Patrick, Wendy, Big Jake, Marianne, Justin, Becky, Nathan, Little Jake, Megan, Jared, and Tyler, I love you guys. Thanks for everything.

Thank you to the team at Cisco Press for giving me the continued opportunity to work with you. Michelle Grandin, thanks for understanding about the deadlines and for being such a good friend. I look forward to working with you in the future. Jim Doherty, it's great working with you again. And finally, thank you to all the employees at Cisco Press who worked so hard behind the scenes to make this book possible.

Jim Doherty–

I would like to thank Neil Anderson, Mike Gremer, and Ric Chavez for letting me use them as guinea pigs while we studied for the CCNA exam; my technical reviewers, Tim Sammut, Andy Barkl, and Drew Rosen, for their diligent work; all the contributors to *Interconnecting Cisco Network Devices,* from which this material was boiled down, and the fine people at Cisco Press, especially Michelle Grandin and John Kane, whose advice, encouragement, and council have made this a positive and rewarding experience.

I would also like to give special thanks to my friend Paul Della-Maggiora, who encouraged me to publish these notes and provided guidance throughout the entire process.

Table of Contents

Foreword   ix

Introduction   x

Part I: INTRO   3

Chapter 1   Introduction to Networking   5

Chapter 2   Network Devices and Network Topologies   37

Chapter 3   Local Area Networks and Wide Area Networks   53

Chapter 4   Network Media   79

Chapter 5   Switching Fundamentals   95

Chapter 6   Interconnecting Networks with TCP/IP   123

Chapter 7   Routing   149

Chapter 8   WAN Technologies   175

Chapter 9   Operating and Configuring Cisco IOS Devices   199

Chapter 10   Managing Your Network Environment   241

PART II: ICND   277

Chapter 1   Configuring Catalyst Switch Operations   279

Chapter 2   Extending Switched Networks with VLANs   351

Chapter 3   Determining IP Routes   389

Chapter 4   Managing IP Traffic with Access Lists and   457
            Network Access Translation

Chapter 5   Establishing Serial Point-to-Point Connections   489

Chapter 6   Frame Relay   521

Chapter 7   ISDN   549

Chapter 8   Last-Minute Exam Tips   577

PART III: STUDY SHEETS   581

INTRO Study Sheets

ICND/CCNA Study Sheets

Foreword

CCNA Flash Cards and Exam Practice Pack is a late-stage practice tool that provides you with a variety of proven exam preparation methods, including physical and electronic flash cards, study- and practice-mode assessment tests, and review-oriented Quick Reference Sheets. Together, these elements help you assess your knowledge of CCNA concepts and focus your practice on those areas where you need the most help. This book was developed in cooperation with the Cisco Internet Learning Solutions Group. Cisco Press books are the only self-study books authorized by Cisco for CCNA exam preparation.

Cisco and Cisco Press present this material in a text-based format to provide another learning vehicle for our customers and the broader user community in general. Although a publication does not duplicate the instructor-led or e-learning environment, we acknowledge that not everyone responds in the same way to the same delivery mechanism. It is our intent that presenting this material through a Cisco Press publication will enhance the transfer of knowledge to a broad audience of networking professionals.

Cisco Press will present existing and future practice test products through these *Flash Cards and Exam Practice Packs* to help achieve Cisco Internet Learning Solutions Group's principal objectives: to educate the Cisco community of networking professionals and to enable that community to build and maintain reliable, scalable networks. The Cisco Career Certifications and classes that support these certifications are directed at meeting these objectives through a disciplined approach to progressive learning. To succeed on the Cisco Career Certifications exams, as well as in your daily job as a Cisco certified professional, we recommend a blended learning solution that combines instructor-led, e-learning, and self-study training with hands-on experience. Cisco Systems has created an authorized Cisco Learning Partner program to provide you with the most highly qualified instruction and invaluable hands-on experience in lab and simulation environments. To learn more about Cisco Learning Partner programs available in your area, go to www.cisco.com/go/training.

The books Cisco Press creates, in partnership with Cisco Systems, meet the same standards for content quality demanded of the courses and certifications. Our intent is that you will find this and subsequent Cisco Press certification and training publications of value as you build your networking knowledge base.

Thomas M. Kelly
Vice President, Internet Learning Solutions Group
Cisco Systems, Inc.
May 2002

Introduction

Ever since the Cisco Systems career certification programs were announced, they have been the most sought-after and prestigious certifications in the networking industry. For many, passing the CCNA exam is a crucial step in building a rewarding career in networking or obtaining career advancement.

Notorious for being among of the most difficult certifications in the networking industry, Cisco exams can cause much stress to the ill-prepared. They are so difficult because, unlike other certification exams, Cisco's exams require the student to truly understand the material instead of just memorizing the answers. This pack is best used after you have used another, primary method of test preparation, and need a mode of self-assessment and review to bring you confidently to test day.

CCNA Enhancements: INTRO, ICND, and the New CCNA Exam

In June 2003, Cisco Systems announced three enhancements to the CCNA program. These include a new two-step exam and training path for candidates just entering the networking field, revisions to the existing CCNA exam, and the option for candidates to apply the ICND exam for CCNA recertification.

The two certification paths for CCNA include:

- Passing the CCNA 640-801 exam

- Passing the INTRO 640-821 exam and ICND 640-811 exam

Note that the two-step approach *does not replace* the existing one-exam option, but merely allows candidates to achieve the CCNA certification in two stages, if preferred, by passing a new Introduction to Cisco Networking Technologies (INTRO) exam and a new Interconnecting Cisco Network Devices (ICND) exam.

Note also that the new ICND exam now qualifies for recertification.

The revised CCNA 640-801 exam replaces existing CCNA 607-607 exam and is designed to better suit the networking needs of entry level candidates.

The *CCNA Flash Cards and Exam Practice Pack* is designed to help you work through the final stage of preparing for the INTRO, ICND, and CCNA exams. As such, it contains review, testing, more review, and more testing. This book contains flash cards that assist you in your memorization, Quick Reference Sheets to provide convenient condensed exam information, and a powerful exam engine with more than 500 questions that test your exam knowledge, with simulations to help you prepare for all question types on the actual Cisco exam.

Study Paths for INTRO, ICND, or CCNA

The materials in this book will serve you whether you are preparing for the INTRO exam, the ICND exam, or the new CCNA exam. Simply follow the plan laid out below.

Preparing for the INTRO Exam

If you are preparing for the INTRO exam, you should be sure that you have a solid grounding in basic internetworking, by either enrolling in the INTRO course with a Cisco Learning Partner, or reading *CCNA Basics Self-Study Guide* or *CCNA INTRO Exam Certification Guide*. Once you are ready to measure your level of knowledge and readiness for the INTRO exam, use this pack in the following way:

- Review all flash cards in Part I (available in the physical version of this book and on the CD)

- Review the INTRO Quick Reference Sheets, which appear at the end of this book (these are also available in printable PDF on the CD)

- Take the practice test for the INTRO exam, included on the enclosed CD

Preparing for the ICND Exam

If you are preparing for the ICND exam, either as a follow-on to the INTRO exam or as your CCNA recertification exam, you should be sure that you have a solid grounding in basic internetworking, by either enrolling in the ICND course with a Cisco Learning Partner, or by reading *Interconnecting Cisco Network Devices Self-Study Guide* or *CCNA ICND Exam Certification Guide*. Once you are ready to measure your level of knowledge and readiness for the ICND exam, use this pack in the following way:

- Review Chapter 9 of Part I and all flash cards in Part II (available in the physical version of this book and on the CD)

- Review the ICND/CCNA Quick Reference Sheets, which appear at the end of this book (these are also available in printable PDF on the CD)

- Take the practice test for the ICND exam, included on the enclosed CD

Preparing for the CCNA Exam

If you are preparing for the CCNA exam, you must have a solid grounding in basic internetworking. First, either enroll in the ICND course with a Cisco Learning Partner, or read *Interconnecting Cisco Network Devices Self-Study Guide* or *CCNA ICND Exam Certification Guide*. Once you are ready to measure your level of knowledge and readiness for the CCNA exam, use this pack in the following way:

- Review all flash cards in Part II and Chapters 1, 2, 3, 5, 7, 10, and 11 in Part I (available in the physical version of this book and on the CD)

- Review the ICND/CCNA Quick Reference Sheets, which appear at the end of this book and also in printable PDF on the CD

- Take the practice test for the combined versions of the INTRO and ICND exams, included on the enclosed CD

The Purpose of Flash Cards

For years, flash cards have been recognized as a quick and effective study aid. They have been used to complement classroom or coursebook training and significantly boost memory retention.

The flash cards in this book are intended to serve as a final preparation tool for the INTRO, ICND, and CCNA exams. They work best when used in conjunction with an official study aid for the exams. They might also be useful to you as a quick desk or field reference guide.

Who These Flash Cards Are For

These flash cards are designed for network administrators, network engineers, Network Academy students, and any professional or student looking to advance his or her career through achieving Cisco CCNA certification.

How to Use These Flash Cards

Although these flash cards are designed to be used as a final-stage study aid (30 days before the exam), they can also be used in the following situations:

- **Pre-study evaluation**—Before charting out your course of study, read one or two questions at the beginning and end of every chapter to gauge your competence in the specific areas.

- **Reinforcement of key topics**—After you've completed your study in each area, read through the answer cards (on the left-hand pages) to identify key topics and reinforce concepts.

- **Post-study quiz**—By flipping through this book at random and viewing the questions on the right-hand pages, you can randomize your self-quiz to be sure you're preparing in all areas.

- **Desk reference or field guide to core concepts**—Junior networking professionals, sales representatives, and help-desk technicians alike can benefit from a handy, simple-to-navigate book that outlines the major topics aligned with basic networking principles and CCNA certification.

Review one section at a time, reading each flash card until you can answer it correctly on your own. When you can correctly answer every card in a given chapter, move on to the next chapter.

These flash cards are a condensed form of study and review. Don't rush to move through each section. The amount of time you spend reviewing the cards directly affects how long you'll be able to retain the information needed to pass the test. A couple of days before your exam, review each section as a final refresher.

What These Flash Cards Cover

In addition to covering every topic outlined on the INTROP, ICND, and CCNA exams, these flash cards cover additional concepts to assist you when you implement Cisco devices in the field. This book also includes a chapter that gives you last-minute tips to help assist you in your preparation for the CCNA exams.

Quick Reference Sheets

At the back of this book, you will find a batch of Quick Reference Sheets, which serve as a study guide for the CCNA exams and as a companion reference to the *Interconnecting Cisco Network Devices* book. If you are seeking CCNA certification, these study sheets are well suited to reinforcing the concepts learned in the text rather than as a sole source of information. If you have either already obtained CCNA certification or simply need a basic overview, these sheets can serve as a standalone reference. The notes can also be printed from the enclosed CD-ROM.

The operating systems used in the study sheets are Cisco IOS software Release 12.0 for the routers and Cisco Catalyst 1900/2820 Enterprise Edition Software Version V8.01.01 for the switch. The configuration commands used in these notes might or might not be valid on other routers and switches currently available. You are cautioned to read the user manual before using any equipment. Failure to do so can result in damage to your equipment, network, and career outlook.

Conventions Used in This Book

Some of the flash cards and study sheets contain important Cisco IOS commands used in that chapter. Because the CCNA exam might test your knowledge of IOS commands, it's crucial that you understand the function of every command. The conventions used to present these commands are the same conventions used in the IOS Command Reference:

- Vertical bars (|) separate alternative, mutually exclusive elements.

- Square brackets ([ ]) indicate an optional element.

- Braces ({ }) indicate a required choice.

- Braces within square brackets ([{ }]) indicate a required choice within an optional element.

- **Bold** indicates commands and keywords that are entered literally as shown.

- *Italic* indicates arguments for which you supply values.

What Is Included on the CD-ROM

The CD-ROM enclosed with this pack will reinforce your study by providing the following features:

- An electronic version of the flash cards that runs on Windows and Palm platforms. You may shuffle the flash cards to randomize your study, review pre-defined sets ("just the basics," "tough terms," and "final exam"), and create your own custom sets for focused practice.

- A powerful practice test engine designed to simulate the INTRO, ICND, and CCNA exams. The practice test engine includes simulation questions types introduced to the CCNA exam in 2002, and helps you become familiar with the format of the CCNA exam and reinforces the knowledge you need to pass the exams.

- A complete set of printable study sheets for the INTRO, ICND, and CCNA exams for quick reference and review in a graphical format.

Part I

INTRO

Chapter 1
Introduction to Networking

Chapter 2
Network Devices and Topologies

Chapter 3
Local-Area Networks and Wide-Area Networks

Chapter 4
Network Media

Chapter 5
Switching Fundamentals

Chapter 6
Interconnecting Networks with TCP/IP

Chapter 7
Routing

Chapter 8
WAN Technologies

Chapter 9
Operating and Configuring Cisco IOS Devices

Chapter 10
Managing Your Network Environment

Part I

Chapter 1

Introduction to Networking

This chapter reviews the fundamentals of internetworking, including PC basics, data conversions, the Cisco hierarchical model, the OSI model, and data encapsulation. The purpose of this chapter is to help refresh your memory of key concepts and topics covered on the INTRO and CCNA exams. Mastery of the topics in this chapter is important for passing both exams and also is a prerequisite for a successful career in the networking industry.

The Cisco hierarchical model is a vital blueprint to follow when designing networks. Following this model helps you create a fast, efficient, reliable, expandable network. The OSI reference model was developed in the early 1980s as a guideline for creating interoperable networks. Imagine if different vendors incorporated their own standards for every product they created! The networking industry would be full of devices that were compatible only with the vendor that created it.

After you have mastered the concepts inherent in the OSI reference model, you will have the troubleshooting knowledge to identify most network errors and define within what layer the error is occurring.

Question 1

What PC component is considered the "brains" of the computer?

Question 2

What is the PC bus?

Question 1 Answer

The CPU is considered the "brains" of the computer. It is the PC component where most calculations take place.

Question 2 Answer

The PC bus is a collection of wires through which data is transmitted from one computer component to another. The bus connects all the PC's internal components to the CPU and RAM. Think of the bus as "highways" on which data moves from one component to another.

Question 3

What is the main function of a PC motherboard?

Introduction to Networking

Question 4

What is the main function of a Network Interface Card (NIC)?

Introduction to Networking

Question 3 Answer

The motherboard provides a bus and data path that connect all components to it. Everything plugs into the motherboard and depends on it to communicate with other devices. It is the nerve center of the computer system.

Question 4 Answer

The main function of a NIC is to connect a computer to a network. A computer NIC plugs into the motherboard and connects to the network through a network cable.

NOTE

Most motherboards today have onboard NICs.

Question 5

How many bits (b) are in a byte (B)?

How many bytes (B) are in a kilobyte (KB)?

How many bits (b) are in a megabyte (MB)?

How many bits (b) are in a nibble?

Introduction to Networking

Question 6

Convert the decimal number 167 to binary.

Introduction to Networking

Question 5 Answer

There are 8 bits in one byte. Most computer coding schemes use 8 bits to represent each number, letter, or symbol; 1 byte represents a single addressable storage location.

There are 1000 bytes in a kilobyte and 8 million bits in a megabyte.

There are 4 bits in a nibble.

Question 6 Answer

Binary (base 2) uses only two symbols (1 and 0) instead of ten symbols like decimal (base 10). In binary, 1 signifies on, and 0 signifies off. When you convert a decimal number to binary, each digit represents the number 2 raised to a power exponent based on its position. The following table helps you convert decimal to binary:

Base exponent	2^7	2^6	2^5	2^4	2^3	2^2	2^1	2^0
Place value	128	64	32	16	8	4	2	1

To convert a decimal number to binary, first find the largest power of 2 that fits into the decimal number. With the decimal number 167, 128 is the largest power of 2 that fits into it, so 128 is considered on. Subtracting 128 from 167 leaves you with 39. The largest power of 2 that fits into 39 is 32, so 32 is considered on. Subtracting 32 from 39 leaves you with 7, so 4, 2, and 1 are considered on. This leaves you with the following binary number:

10100111

Question 7

Convert the binary number 01100100 to decimal.

Question 8

Convert the binary number 0101011011000010 to hexadecimal.

Question 7 Answer

Converting a binary number to decimal is the reverse of converting a decimal number to binary. When converting from binary, look at the numbers that are considered on, and then find their place value. In the binary number 01100100, the place values 64, 32, and 4 are on. If you add together these place values, you get the decimal number 100.

Question 8 Answer

Converting binary to hexadecimal is easier than it looks. No matter how large the binary number, always apply the following conversion: Break the binary number into groups of four, starting on the right and moving left. If the binary number is not divisible by 4, add 0s to the leftmost group end until there are four digits in every group.

Using this conversion, 0101011011000010 is broken into the following groups: 0101 0110 1100 0010. After you have the groups, you can convert the digits to hex. 0101 is 5 in hex, 0110 is 6, 1100 is C (the 2 bits that are on are 8 and 4; adding them together produces 12, which is C in hex), and 0010 is 2. Therefore, 0101011011000010 is 0x56C2 in hex.

NOTE

Remember that hex is a base 16 numbering system. It uses the symbols 0 to 9 and A to F. Anything greater than 9 (10 to 15) is A to F (10 = A, 11 = B, and so on).

Question 9

What are the three layers of the Cisco hierarchical model?

Question 10

In the Cisco hierarchical model, what is the function of the access layer?

Question 9 Answer

The three layers of the Cisco hierarchical model are

- The access layer
- The distribution layer
- The core layer

Question 10 Answer

Sometimes referred to as the desktop layer, the access layer is the point at which users connect to the network. Some functions of the access layer include

- Connectivity into the distribution layer
- Shared bandwidth
- MAC address filtering (switching)
- Segmentation
- Provides a point at which users connect to the network
- Security by allowing access lists to further optimize user needs

Question 11

What is the function of the distribution layer in the Cisco hierarchical model?

Question 12

What is the role of the core layer in the Cisco hierarchical model?

Question 11 Answer

Also known as the workgroup layer, the distribution layer is the demarcation point between the network's access and core layers. Its primary function is to provide boundary definition, and it's where packet manipulation takes place. Routing, route summarization, filtering, and WAN access also occur at the distribution layer. The distribution layer determines how packets access the core, so it is the layer at which policy-based connectivity is implemented. Some of the distribution layer's functions are as follows:

- Collection point for access layer devices

- Broadcast and multicast domain segmentation

- Security and filtering services such as firewalls and access lists

- Provides translation between different media types

- Inter-VLAN routing

- Address or area aggregation

Question 12 Answer

The core layer is the backbone of the network. Its main function is to switch traffic as fast as possible. The core layer ensures that every device in the network has full reachability to all other devices. Because its function is to switch traffic as fast as possible, it should not perform any filtering to slow down traffic.

Question 13

What are key reasons why the OSI reference model was created?

Question 14

The ISO's OSI reference model contains seven layers. What are they? Include the layer number and the name of each layer in your answer.

Question 13 Answer

The OSI reference model was created for the following reasons:

- To create standards that enable vendor interoperability by defining functional guidelines for communication between networked applications

- To clarify general internetworking functions

- To divide the complexity of networking into smaller, more manageable sublayers

- To simplify troubleshooting

- To let developers modify or improve components at one layer without having to rewrite an entire protocol stack

Question 14 Answer

The seven layers of the OSI model are as follows:

- **Layer 7**—Application layer
- **Layer 6**—Presentation layer
- **Layer 5**—Session layer
- **Layer 4**—Transport layer
- **Layer 3**—Network layer
- **Layer 2**—Data link layer
- **Layer 1**—Physical layer

Question 15

What does the application layer (Layer 7) of the OSI model do? Give some examples of this layer.

Question 16

In the OSI model, what are the responsibilities of the presentation layer (Layer 6)? Give some examples of this layer.

Question 15 Answer

The application layer is the layer closest to the user. This means that it interacts directly with the software application. The application layer's main function is to identify and establish communication partners, determine resource availability, and synchronize communication. Some examples include the following:

TCP/IP applications such as Telnet, FTP, Simple Mail Transfer Protocol (SMTP), and HTTP

OSI applications such as Virtual Terminal Protocol; File Transfer, Access, and Management (FTAM); and Common Management Information Protocol (CMIP)

NOTE

An application must have a communicating component such as FTP to be relevant to internetworking.

Question 16 Answer

Also known as the translator, the presentation layer provides coding and conversion functions to application layer data. This guarantees that the application layer on another system can read data transferred from the application layer of a different system. Some examples of the presentation layer are

- Compression and decompression
- Encryption
- JPEG, TIFF, GIF, PICT, QuickTime, MPEG
- EBCDIC and ASCII

Question 17

What are the functions of the session layer (Layer 5)? Give some examples.

Question 18

What is the transport layer (Layer 4) responsible for? Give some examples of transport layer implementations.

Question 17 Answer

The session layer is responsible for creating, managing, and ending communication sessions between presentation layer entities. These sessions consist of service requests and responses that develop between applications located on different network devices. Some examples include SQL, RPC, X Window System, ZIP, NetBIOS names, and AppleTalk ASP.

Question 18 Answer

The transport layer segments and reassembles data from upper-layer applications into data streams. It provides reliable data transmission to upper layers. End-to-end communications, flow control, multiplexing, error detection and correction, and virtual circuit management are typical transport layer functions. Some examples include TCP, UDP, and SPX.

NOTE

Not all transport protocols perform error detection and correction. For example, UDP does not perform error detection or correction.

Question 19

What is flow control, and what are the three methods of implementing it?

Question 20

Describe the function of the network layer (Layer 3), and give some examples of network layer implementations.

Question 19 Answer

Flow control is the method of controlling the rate at which a computer sends data with the intention of preventing network congestion. The three methods of implementing flow control are

- Buffering
- Source-quench messages (congestion avoidance)
- Windowing

Question 20 Answer

The network layer provides internetwork routing and logical network addresses. It defines how to transport traffic between devices that are not locally attached. The network layer also supports connection-oriented and connectionless services from higher-layer protocols. Routers operate at the network layer. IP, IPX, AppleTalk, and DDP are examples of network layer implementations.

Question 21

Are network layer addresses physical or logical?

Question 22

What is the responsibility of the data link layer (Layer 2)?

Question 21 Answer

Network layer addresses are logical addresses specific to the network layer protocol being run on the network. Each network layer protocol has a different addressing scheme. They are usually hierarchical. They define networks first and then hosts or devices on that network. An example of a network address is an IP address, which is a 32-bit address often expressed in decimal format. 192.168.0.1 is an example of an IP address in decimal format.

Question 22 Answer

The data link layer provides the establishment, maintenance, and release of data-link connections among network entities and for the transfer of data-link service data units. The data link layer translates messages from the network layer into bits for transport onto the physical medium, and it lets the network layer control the interconnection of data circuits within the physical layer. Data-link specifications define different network and protocol characteristics, including physical addressing, error notification, network topology, and sequencing of frames. Data-link protocols provide delivery across individual links and are concerned with the different media types, such as 802.2 and 802.3. The data link layer is responsible for putting 1s and 0s into a logical group. These 1s and 0s are then put on the physical wire. Some examples of data link layer implementations are IEEE 802.2/802.3, IEEE 802.5/802.2, packet trailer (for Ethernet, FCS, or CRC) FDDI, HDLC, and Frame Relay.

Question 23

The IEEE defines what two sublayers of the data link layer?

Question 24

For what is the LLC sublayer responsible?

Question 23 Answer

The two sublayers of the data link layer are

- The Logical Link Control (LLC) sublayer
- The MAC sublayer

These two sublayers provide physical media independence.

Question 24 Answer

The Logical Link Control (802.2) sublayer is responsible for identifying different network layer protocols and then encapsulating them to be transferred across the network. There are two types of LLC frames: service access point (SAP) and Subnetwork Access Protocol (SNAP). An LLC header conveys to the data link layer what to do with a packet after it is received.

Question 25

What functions does the MAC sublayer provide?

Question 26

What are some network devices that operate at the data link layer?

Question 25 Answer

The MAC sublayer specifies how data is placed and transported over the physical wire. It controls access to the physical medium. The LLC layer communicates with the network layer, but the MAC layer communicates downward directly with the physical layer. Physical addressing (MAC addresses), network topologies, error notification, and delivery of frames are defined at this sublayer.

Question 26 Answer

Bridges and switches are network devices that operate at the data link layer. Both devices decide what traffic to forward or drop (filter) based on MAC addresses. Logical network addresses are not used at this layer. Data link layer devices assume a flat address space.

Question 27

What is the function of the OSI model's physical layer (Layer 1)? Give some examples of physical layer implementations.

Question 28

How do the different layers of the OSI model communicate with each other?

Question 27 Answer

The physical layer defines the physical medium. It defines the media type, the connector type, and the signaling type (baseband versus broadband). This includes voltage levels, physical data rates, and cable specifications. The physical layer is responsible for converting frames into electronic bits of data, which are then sent or received across the physical medium. Twisted pair, coaxial cable, and fiber-optic cable operate at this level. Repeaters and hubs are network devices that operate at the physical layer.

Question 28 Answer

Each layer of the OSI model can communicate only with the layer above it, below it, and parallel to it (a peer layer). For example, the presentation layer can communicate with only the application layer, session layer, and presentation layer on the machine it is communicating with. These layers communicate with each other using SAPs and protocol data units (PDUs). The SAP is a conceptual location at which one OSI layer can request the services of another OSI layer. PDUs control information that is added to the user data at each layer of the model. This information resides in fields called headers (the front of the data field) and trailers (the end of the data field).

Question 29

What is data encapsulation?

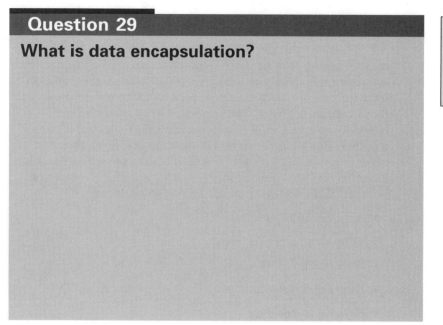

Question 29 Answer

A PDU can include different information as it goes up or down the OSI model. It is given a different name according to the information it is carrying (the layer it is at). When the transport layer receives upper-layer data, it adds a TCP header to the data; this is called a segment. The segment is then passed to the network layer, and an IP header is added; thus, the data becomes a packet. The packet is passed to the data link layer, thus becoming a frame. This frame is then converted into bits and is passed across the network medium. This is data encapsulation. For the CCNA test, you should know the following:

- **Application layer**—Data
- **Transport layer**—Segment
- **Network layer**—Packet
- **Data link layer**—Frame
- **Physical layer**—Bits

Chapter 2

Network Devices and Topologies

Network topology refers to the way in which network devices are connected in a network. It describes the layout of the wire and devices as well as data transmission paths in a network.

This chapter covers the various network devices that operate on Layers 1, 2, and 3 of the OSI model and the different network topologies.

Although most of the information included in this chapter is required for the INTRO exam, you will find some of the topics covered here on the CCNA exam as well.

Question 1

What are two types of Layer 1 network devices?

Network Devices
and Topologies

Question 2

What are some network devices that operate at the data link layer (Layer 2)?

Network Devices
and Topologies

Question 1 Answer

Two types of Layer 1 network devices are

- **Repeaters**—Repeaters regenerate and retime network signals, amplifying them, which allows the signal to travel a longer distance on a network medium.

- **Hubs**—A hub is also known as a multiple-port repeater. It also regenerates and retimes network signals. The main difference between a hub and a repeater is the number of cables that connect to the device. A repeater typically has two ports, whereas a hub has from four to 48 ports.

Question 2 Answer

Bridges and switches are network devices that operate at the data link layer. Both devices decide what traffic to forward or drop (filter) based on MAC addresses. Logical network addresses are not used at this layer. Data link layer devices assume a flat address space.

Typically, a bridge is designed to create two or more LAN segments and is usually implemented in software.

A switch is a high-speed multiport bridge that is typically implemented in hardware. Switches are designed to replace hubs while providing the filtering benefits of bridges.

Question 3

What are collision domains?

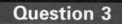

Network Devices
and Topologies

Question 4

What devices are used to break up collision domains?

Network Devices
and Topologies

Question 3 Answer

A collision domain defines a group of devices connected to the same physical medium.

A collision occurs when two packets are sent at the same time and collide with each other (electronically). When a collision occurs, a jam signal is sent by the workstation detecting the collision to clear the segment. A jam signal affects all the machines on the segment, not just the two that collided; when the jam signal is on the wire, no workstations can transmit data. The more collisions that occur in a network, the slower it is, because the devices have to resend the packet.

Question 4 Answer

Switches, bridges, and routers are used to break up collision domains. They create more collision domains and fewer collisions. Each port on a bridge, switch, and router creates one collision domain. For example, a switch with 24 ports has 24 separate collision domains.

Question 5

At what layer of the OSI model do routers and multilayer switches function?

Network Devices and Topologies

Question 6

In addition to learning the remote network and providing a path to the network, what other functions do routers carry out?

Network Devices and Topologies

Question 5 Answer

Routers and some multilayer switches function at the network layer (Layer 3) of the OSI model. Both devices learn, record, and maintain awareness of different networks. They decide the best path to these networks and maintain the following information in a routing table:

- Protocol-specific network addresses. If you run more than one protocol, each one has a network address.

- The interface the router uses to route a packet to a different network.

- A metric, which is the distance to a remote network or the weight of the bandwidth, load, delay, and path's reliability to the remote network.

NOTE

Remember that routers create broadcast domains. One interface on a router creates a single broadcast domain and collision domain. However, an interface on a switch creates only a single collision domain.

Question 6 Answer

Routers perform these tasks:

- By default, they do not forward broadcasts or multicasts.

- Routers can perform bridging, encapsulation, and routing functions.

- If a router has multiple paths to a destination, it can determine the best path to the destination.

- Routers forward traffic based on Layer 3 destination addresses.

- Routers can connect virtual LANs (VLANs) by routing traffic between them.

- Routers can provide quality of service for specified types of network traffic.

- Routers provide security, packet filtering, and address translation.

Question 7

What are broadcast domains?

Network Devices
and Topologies

Question 8

What devices are used to break up broadcast domains?

Network Devices
and Topologies

Question 7 Answer

A broadcast domain defines a group of devices that receive each others' broadcast messages. As with collisions, the more broadcasts that occur on the network, the slower the network will be. This is because every device that receives a broadcast must process it to see if the broadcast is intended for it.

NOTE

Although many broadcasts slow down your network, they are useful and are used by many protocols for communications. Segmenting your network with routers limits the size of your broadcast domain.

Question 8 Answer

Routers are used to break up broadcast domains. They create more broadcast domains and smaller broadcast areas.

NOTE

VLANs created on switches also create broadcast domains.

Question 9

Describe the difference between a physical network topology and a logical network topology.

Network Devices and Topologies

Question 10

What are the five types of physical topologies implemented in today's networks?

Network Devices and Topologies

Question 9 Answer

All of today's networks have physical and logical topologies. Physical topologies refer to the physical layout of devices and network media. Logical topologies refer to the logical paths in which data accesses the medium and transmits packets across it.

Question 10 Answer

The five most common physical network topologies implemented today are

- Bus
- Ring
- Star
- Extended star
- Mesh

NOTE

See the study sheets at the back of this book for diagrams of each of these physical topologies.

Question 11

What physical network topology connects all devices to one cable?

Question 12

Describe a star and extended star physical topology.

Question 11 Answer

A bus topology connects all devices to a single cable. This cable connects from one computer to another. In a logical bus topology, only one packet can be transmitted at a time.

Question 12 Answer

A star or extended star physical topology is made up of a central connection point, such as a hub or switch, where all cable segments connect. A star topology resembles spokes in a wheel. It is the network topology of choice in Ethernet networks.

When a star network is expanded to include additional network devices that connect to a main center network device, it is called an extended star topology.

Question 13

Describe a ring topology.

Question 14

What physical network topology connects all devices to each other?

Question 13 Answer

In a ring topology, all hosts and devices are connected in a ring or circle. There are two types of ring networks:

- **Single-ring**—In a single-ring network, all devices share a single cable, and data travels in one direction. Each device waits its turn to send data over the network.

- **Dual-ring**—A dual-ring network has a second ring to add redundancy and allows data to be sent in both directions.

Question 14 Answer

A mesh network connects all devices to each other for fault tolerance and redundancy.

Chapter 3

Local-Area Networks and Wide-Area Networks

This chapter quizzes you on the knowledge required for the INTRO exam regarding LANs and WANs. You will be quizzed on Ethernet and its standards. You will also be quizzed on WANs, their terminology, and some of the standards used in today's WANs. This chapter provides a high-level view of LAN and WAN concepts. More-detailed views are included in later chapters.

Question 1
What are LANs?

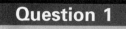

Question 2
What are LAN standards?

Question 1 Answer

LANs are high-speed, low-error data networks that cover a small geographic area. LANs are usually located in a building or campus and do not cover a large distance. They are relatively inexpensive to develop and maintain. LANs connect computers, printers, terminals, and other devices in a single building or a limited area.

Question 2 Answer

LAN standards define the physical medium and connectors used to connect to the medium at the physical layer. They also define how devices communicate at the data link layer. LAN standards encompass Layers 1 and 2 of the OSI model. Examples of LAN standards are Ethernet and IEEE 802.3.

Question 3

What do the Ethernet and IEEE 802.3 standards define?

Local-Area Networks and Wide-Area Networks

Question 4

Define the Fast Ethernet standard.

Local-Area Networks and Wide-Area Networks

Question 3 Answer

The Ethernet and IEEE 802.3 standards define a bus topology LAN that operates at a baseband signaling rate of 10 Mbps, referred to as 10BASE. Within the Ethernet standards are protocol specifications that define the transmission medium and access. There are three protocol specifications:

- **10BASE2**—Known as thin Ethernet. Uses thin coaxial cable as its medium. Provides access for multiple stations on the same segment.

- **10BASE5**—Called thick Ethernet. Uses a thick coaxial cable as its medium. The maximum segment length of 10BASE5 is more than twice that of 10BASE2.

- **10BASE-T**—Provides access for a single station only, so all stations connect to a switch or hub. The physical topology of 10BASE-T is that of a star network. It uses unshielded twisted-pair (UTP) Category 3, 4, 5, and 5e as its network medium.

Question 4 Answer

The Ethernet standard that defines Fast Ethernet is IEEE 802.3u. This standard raises the speed of the Ethernet standard of 10 Mbps to 100 Mbps with only minimal changes to the existing cable structure. The Fast Ethernet standard defines different protocol specifications depending on the physical medium used. The following are the four different Fast Ethernet specifications:

- **100BASE-FX**—Uses two strands of multimode fiber-optic cable as its medium. Its maximum segment length is 400 meters.

- **100BASE-T**—Defines UTP as its medium. Its maximum segment length is 100 meters.

- **100BASE-T4**—Uses four pairs of Category 3 to 5 UTP as its medium. Its maximum segment length is 100 meters.

- **100BASE-TX**—Specifies two pairs of UTP or shielded twisted-pair (STP) as its medium. It has a maximum segment distance of 100 meters.

Question 5

What does BASE mean in 10BASE-T and 100BASE-T?

Local-Area Networks and Wide-Area Networks

Question 6

What is Gigabit Ethernet?

Local-Area Networks and Wide-Area Networks

Question 5 Answer

BASE in 10BASE-T and 100BASE-T refers to the baseband signaling method. Baseband is a network technology in which only one carrier frequency is used. This means that when a device transmits, it uses the entire bandwidth on the wire and doesn't share it. Ethernet defined baseband technology.

Question 6 Answer

Gigabit Ethernet is an extension of the IEEE 802.3 Ethernet standard. It increases the speed of the Ethernet protocol to 1000 Mbps or 1 Gbps. IEEE 802.3z specifies Gigabit over fiber, and IEEE 802.3ab specifies Gigabit over twisted-pair cable.

Question 7

What is carrier sense multiple access collision detect (CSMA/CD)?

Local-Area Networks and Wide-Area Networks

Question 8

WANs operate at what three layers of the OSI model?

Local-Area Networks and Wide-Area Networks

Question 7 Answer

CSMA/CD describes the Ethernet access method. In CSMA/CD, many stations can transmit on the same cable, and no station has priority over any other. Before a station transmits, it listens on the wire (carrier sense) to make sure that no other station is transmitting. If no other station is transmitting, the station transmits across the wire. If a collision occurs, the transmitting stations detect the collision and run a backoff algorithm. The backoff algorithm is a random amount of time that each station waits before retransmitting.

Question 8 Answer

WANs operate at the physical, data link, and network layers of the OSI model.

A WAN interconnects LANs that are separated by a large geographic distance that is not supported by typical LAN media.

Question 9

What are the four available WAN connection types?

Question 10

List four devices used to connect to a WAN or used on a WAN.

Question 9 Answer

The four available WAN connection types are

- Dedicated connections (leased lines)
- Circuit-switched connections
- Packet-switched connections
- Cell-switched connections

NOTE

For a detailed explanation of each connection, see Chapter 5 in Part II, "Establishing Serial Point-to-Point Connections."

Question 10 Answer

Four devices used to connect to a WAN or used on a WAN are

- **Routers**—Connects the LAN to the WAN. Routers provide network layer services and route data from one network to another.
- **WAN switches**—Used in the WAN network, switches are multiport devices that switch Frame Relay, X.25, and ATM traffic. They operate at the data link layer of the OSI model.
- **Modems**—Interpret analog and digital signals. Modems modulate and demodulate a signal, allowing data to be transmitted over telephone lines.
- **CSUs/DSUs**—Convert from one digital format to another. CSUs/DSUs are a digital interface (sometimes two separate interfaces) that connects the physical interface of a data terminal equipment (DTE) device to the interface of a data communications equipment (DCE) device. An example of a DTE device is a terminal, and an example of a DCE device is a switch. Most routers today offer an integrated CSU/DSU interface.

Question 11

Define customer premises equipment (CPE), and give an example.

Local-Area Networks and Wide-Area Networks

Question 12

What is the demarcation point (demarc)?

Local-Area Networks and Wide-Area Networks

Question 11 Answer

CPE is equipment that is located on the customer's (or subscriber's) premises. It is equipment owned by the customer or equipment leased by the service provider to the customer. An example is your router.

Question 12 Answer

The demarc is a point where the CPE ends and the local loop begins. It is the point between the wiring that comes in from the local service provider (telephone company) and the wiring installed to connect the customer's CPE to the service provider. It is the last responsibility of the service provider and is usually a network interface device (NID) located in the customer's telephone wiring closet. Think of the demarc as the boundary between the customer's wiring and the service provider's wiring.

Question 13
What is the local loop?

Question 14
What is the central office (CO)?

Question 13 Answer

The local loop is the physical cable that extends from the demarc to the central office.

Question 14 Answer

The CO is the WAN service provider's office where the local loop terminates and where circuit switching occurs.

Question 15
What is WAN signaling?

Local-Area Networks and Wide-Area Networks

Question 16
What are WAN data link layer protocols?

Local-Area Networks and Wide-Area Networks

Question 15 Answer

WAN signaling is the process of sending a transmission signal over a physical medium for communication. WAN transmission facilities feature standardized signaling schemes that define transmission rates and media types. For example, the signaling standard for a T1 line in North America is DS1 with a transmission rate of 1.544 Mbps.

Question 16 Answer

Designed to operate over dedicated lines, multipoint, and multiaccess switched services such as Frame Relay, data link layer protocols provide the data link layer encapsulations associated with synchronous serial lines. Examples include HDLC, PPP, SLIP, LAPD, and LAPF.

NOTE

For a detailed explanation of the most common data link layer protocols used on WANs today, see Chapter 5 in Part II.

Question 17
Describe Wireless signals.

Question 18
What is the radio spectrum?

Question 17 Answer

Wireless signals are electromagnetic waves that travel through air or space. They do not require a network medium such as copper or fiber, but use air as its medium. Because wireless signals are not bound by physical cable, they are very versatile and can be implemented in a variety of ways.

Question 18 Answer

The part of the electromagnetic spectrum that transmits voice, video, and data is referred to as the radio spectrum.

Question 19

What is the frequency range the radio spectrum uses?

Local-Area Networks and Wide-Area Networks

Question 20

What are the most common types of wireless data communication used today?

Local-Area Networks and Wide-Area Networks

Question 19 Answer

The radio spectrum uses frequencies from 3 kilohertz (kHz) to 300 gigahertz (GHz).

Question 20 Answer

The most common types of wireless data communication used today are:

- **Infrared (IR)**—Provides very high data rates at a low cost, but at a very short distance. Must be line of sight.

- **Narrowband**—Provides low data rates at a medium cost. A license is required and covers a limited distance.

- **Spread spectrum**—Has a medium cost but very high data rates. It is limited to campus coverage. Cisco Aironet products are an example of spread spectrum wireless devices.

- **Broadband personal communications service (PCS)**—Mainly used for cellular networks, PCS provides low data rates and broad coverage.

- **Circuit and packet data (cellular and cellular digital packet data [CDPD])**—Provides low data rates, high packet fees, and national coverage.

- **Satellite**—Provides worldwide coverage and has low data rates at a high cost.

Question 21

What is modulation?

Question 22

What is the wireless standard used in most of today's wireless LANs?

Question 21 Answer

Modulation is the process by which amplitude, frequency, or phase of an RF or light wave is change to transmit data. The most common methods of modulation are:

- Amplitude modulation (AM)
- Frequency modulation (FM)

Question 22 Answer

802.11b is the most common wireless standard used in today's LANs. 802.11a is new and upcoming wireless standard that improves upon 802.11b.

Question 23

Name two security protocols used in today's 802.11b networks.

Question 23 Answer

Two security protocols used in today's 802.11b networks are:

- **WEP**—40-bit or 128-bit encryption over an 802.11b network. Uses the RC4 stream cipher for encryption. Can be hacked into very easily.

- **802.1/EAP**—Provides centralized authentication and dynamic key distribution for encryption. EAP allows wireless clients that support different authentication types to communicate with different back-end servers.

Chapter 4

Network Media

This chapter covers the different types of network media used in today's LANs and WANs. Suppose that you are setting up your first Cisco router or that you have not configured one in some time. The company you are installing the router for wants the Ethernet interface to connect to a server that will act as the firewall. You cannot remember if you should use a straight-through Category 5 cable or a crossover cable. This scenario is more common than you think. Fortunately, this section covers the rules of cabling Cisco devices. You'll learn when to use a crossover Ethernet cable and a straight-through Ethernet cable and what devices they connect to so that you will not find yourself in this predicament. In addition, you'll learn the proper way to set up a console connection to a Cisco device, the difference between broadband and baseband, and about timeslots. This chapter covers topics required for the INTRO and CCNA exams.

Question 1

Describe twisted-pair cable.

Network
Media

Question 2

What is UTP cable?

Network
Media

Question 1 Answer

Twisted-pair cable is a transmission medium that consists of pairs of cables twisted together to provide protection against crosstalk. When electrical current flows through a wire, it creates a small, circular magnetic field around the wire. When two wires are placed close together, their magnetic fields cancel each other out and cancel out other magnetic interference.

Twisted-pair cable is the cabling used in telephone communications and in most Ethernet networks. Two types of twisted-pair cable exist: unshielded twisted-pair (UTP) and shielded twisted pair (STP).

Question 2 Answer

UTP cable is a type of twisted-pair cable that relies solely on the cancellation effects produced by the twisted wire pairs to limit electromagnetic interference (EMI) and radio frequency interference (RFI). UTP cable is often installed using an RJ-45 connector. UTP cabling must follow precise specifications dictating how many twists are required per meter of cable. Advantages of UTP are ease of installation and cost. A disadvantage of UTP is that it is more prone to EMI than other media.

Question 3

What are the differences between STP and UTP cable?

Network Media

Question 4

What is the maximum cable length for STP?

Network Media

Question 3 Answer

STP cable combines the twisting techniques of UTP, but each pair of wires is wrapped in a metallic foil. The four pairs of wires then are wrapped in a metallic braid or foil. STP reduces electrical noise and EMI. STP is installed with an STP data connector but can also use an RJ-45 connector. An advantage of STP is that it prevents outside interference. Two disadvantages are that it is more expensive than UTP and is difficult to install.

NOTE

STP is rarely used in Ethernet networks and is mainly used in Europe. Do not confuse Shield Twisted Pair (STP) cable for Spanning Tree Protocol (STP).

Question 4 Answer

The maximum cable length for STP is 100 meters or 328 feet.

Question 5

What type of network medium is used in thinnet?

Question 6

What are the two types of fiber-optic cable? Describe the characteristics of each type.

Question 5 Answer

Thinnet and thicknet use coaxial cable as their network medium. The difference between the two is the thickness of the coaxial cable used. Coaxial cable can be cabled over a longer distance than UTP, but it is more costly than UTP.

Question 6 Answer

The two types of fiber-optic cable are

- Single-mode
- Multimode

Single-mode fiber allows only one mode (or wavelength) of light through the fiber. It is capable of greater distances and higher bandwidth than multimode fiber and often is used for campus backbones. Single-mode fiber uses lasers as the light-generating method. Its maximum cable length is more than 10 km.

Just as the name implies, multimode fiber allows multiple modes of light to propagate through the fiber. It uses LEDs as a light-generating device. Its maximum cable length is 2 km.

Question 7

What is a straight-through Ethernet cable, and when would you use it?

Network Media

Question 8

What is a crossover Ethernet cable, and when would you use it?

Network Media

Question 7 Answer

A straight-through Ethernet cable is the same at both ends. A straight-through cable uses pins 1, 2, 3, and 6. The send and receive wires are not crossed. You should use a straight-through Ethernet cable when connecting dissimilar devices (a DTE to a DCE). Examples include connecting PCs (DTE) to switches or hubs (DCE) or connecting a router (DTE) to a switch or hub (DCE).

NOTE

An exception to this rule is that you must use a crossover cable when connecting a router to a PC.

Question 8 Answer

A crossover Ethernet cable has the send and receive wires crossed at one of the ends. On a Category 5 cable, the 1 and 3 wires are switched, and the 2 and 6 wires are switched on one of the cable's ends. You should use a crossover cable when connecting similar devices (DCE to DCE), such as when you connect a router to a router, a switch to a switch or hub, a hub to a hub, or a PC to a PC.

Question 9

What is the maximum cable length for each of the following?

10BASE2

10BASE5

10BASE-T

10BASE-FL

100BASE-T

Question 10

What is the difference between baseband and broadband?

Question 9 Answer

The maximum cable lengths are as follows:

- **10BASE2 (thinnet)**—185 meters
- **10BASE5 (thicknet)**—500 meters
- **10BASE-T**—100 meters
- **10BASE-FL**—On multimode fiber:
  - 400 m (1312 ft) for any repeater-to-DTE fiber segment
  - 500 m (1640 ft) with four repeaters and five segments
  - 1000 m (3280 ft) for any interrepeater fiber segment
  - 2km (6561 ft) without a repeater
- **100BASE-T**—100 meters

Question 10 Answer

Baseband is a network technology in which only one carrier frequency is used (such as Ethernet). Broadband is a network technology in which several independent channels are multiplexed into one cable (for example, a T1 line).

Question 11
What is serial transmission?

Network
Media

Question 12
In WAN communications, what is clocking?

Network
Media

Question 11 Answer

Serial transmission is a method of data transmission in which bits of data are transmitted sequentially over a single channel. WANs use serial transmission.

Question 12 Answer

Clocking is the method used to synchronize data transmission between devices on a WAN. The CSU/DSU (DCE device) controls the clocking of the transmitted data.

NOTE

If you connect two serial interfaces back-to-back in a lab, one interface must provide clocking.

Question 13

How many channels (timeslots) are in a full point-to-point or Frame Relay T1 line?

Question 14

How do you set up a console session to a Cisco device?

Question 13 Answer

A T1 line has 24 channels or timeslots. Each channel is 64 Kb.

This information is useful, because not all companies buy a full T1 line. ISPs offer fractional T1 lines that are half the cost of a T1; this might be an option for branch offices that do not require a full T1. When configuring a router for a fractional T1, you need to configure the proper timeslots on the CSU/DSU. If the CSU/DSU is internal to the router (a WIC), you configure the timeslots in the router's serial interface. If the CSU/DSU is external, you configure the external device. The default configuration on a Cisco interface is a full T1 (all 24 channels).

Question 14 Answer

To set up a console session to a Cisco device, you connect a rollover cable to the console port on the Cisco device. You then connect the other end to a DB-9 adaptor and connect the DB-9 adaptor to the serial port on your PC. You then configure a terminal emulation application to the following com settings: 9600 bps, 8 data bits, no parity, 1 stop bit, and no flow control.

NOTE

A rollover cable is a thin cable that has RJ-45 connectors at each end. The wiring on one end is the opposite on the other. Wire 1 on one end is wire 8 on the other end. This cable is provided with every Cisco product you purchase.

Chapter 5

Switching Fundamentals

During the past five years, switching has become one of the cornerstones of today's LANs. By replacing a hub with a switch, you can effectively double or triple your LAN's speed and alleviate common network problems such as collisions.

Note that some of these topics go slightly beyond the strict scope of what you will need to know for the INTRO exam, so spend only a small portion of your study time reviewing these topics. This chapter introduces the types of LAN switching (including Layer 3 and 4 switching), spanning tree, and VLANs.

If you are looking for an in-depth quiz on spanning tree and other advanced switching functions, see Chapter 1, "Configuring Catalyst Switch Operations," and Chapter 2, "Extending Switched Networks with VLANs," in Part II.

Question 1

What are the three ways in which LAN traffic is transmitted?

Question 2

What happens when you segment the network with hubs/repeaters?

Question 1 Answer

LAN traffic is transmitted in these three ways:

- **Unicast**—The most common type of LAN traffic. A unicast frame is intended for only one host.

- **Broadcast**—Frames intended for everyone. Stations view broadcast frames as public service announcements. All stations receive and process broadcast frames.

- **Multicast**—Traffic in which one transmitter tries to reach only a subset, or group, of the entire segment.

Question 2 Answer

Because hubs and repeaters operate at the physical layer of the OSI model, segmenting a network with these devices appears as an extension to the physical cable. Hubs and repeaters are transparent to devices. They are unintelligent devices. All devices that connect to a hub/repeater share the same bandwidth. Hubs/repeaters create a single broadcast and collision domain.

Question 3

What is the advantage of segmenting a network with bridges/switches?

Question 4

List four advantages that Layer 2 switches have over bridges.

Question 3 Answer

Bridges/switches operate at Layer 2 of the OSI model and filter by MAC address. Each port on a bridge/switch provides full dedicated bandwidth and creates a single collision domain. Because bridges/switches operate at Layer 2 of the OSI model, they cannot filter broadcasts, and they create a single broadcast domain.

Question 4 Answer

Four advantages that Layer 2 switches have over bridges are

- A high-speed backplane that lets multiple simultaneous conversations occur.

- Data-buffering capabilities are used to store and forward packets to the correct ports or port.

- Higher port densities versus bridges.

- Lower latency than bridges. Layer 2 switches are implemented in hardware, allowing millions of bits per second to be transmitted at the same time.

Question 5

What is a broadcast storm?

Question 6

A fundamental concept behind LAN switching is that it provides microsegmentation. What is microsegmentation?

Question 5 Answer

Broadcast storms occur when many broadcasts are sent simultaneously across all network segments. They are usually caused by a bad NIC, faulty network device, or virus. All devices on a network process broadcast packets, so an excess of broadcasts on a network causes all devices to slow down.

Question 6 Answer

Microsegmentation is a network design (functionality) in which each workstation or device on a network gets its own dedicated segment (collision domain) to the switch. Each network device gets the segment's full bandwidth and does not have to share the segment with other devices. Microsegmentation reduces collisions, because each segment is its own collision domain.

Question 7

What three major functions do Layer 2 switches provide?

Question 8

Describe full-duplex transmission.

Question 7 Answer

The three major functions that Layer 2 switches provide are

- Address learning
- Packet forwarding/filtering
- Loop avoidance by spanning tree

Question 8 Answer

Full-duplex transmission is achieved by microsegmentation, in which each network device has its own dedicated segment to the switch. Because the network device has its own dedicated segment, it does not have to worry about sharing the segment with other devices. With full-duplex transmission, the device can send and receive at the same time, effectively doubling the amount of bandwidth between nodes.

Question 9

What are the three switching methods (frame transmission modes) in Cisco Catalyst switches?

Switching Fundamentals

Question 10

What is the Cisco Catalyst store-and-forward switching method?

Switching Fundamentals

Question 9 Answer

The three frame operating modes that handle frame switching are

- Store-and-forward
- Cut-through
- Fragment-free

NOTE

Remember that these switching methods are modes that determine how the entire switch handles frame switching. They are not operating modes for individual ports.

Question 10 Answer

In the store-and-forward switching method, the switch's incoming interface receives the entire frame before forwarding it. The switch computes the cyclic redundancy check (CRC) to make sure that the frame is not bad. If the frame is good, the switch forwards it. If the CRC is bad, the switch drops it. If the frame is a runt (less than 64 bytes, including the CRC) or a giant (more than 1518 bytes, including the CRC), the switch discards it. Because the switch stores the frame before forwarding it, latency is introduced in the switch. Latency through the switch varies with the frame's size.

Question 11

What is the Cisco Catalyst cut-through switching method?

Switching Fundamentals

Question 12

What is the Cisco Catalyst fragment-free switching method?

Switching Fundamentals

Question 11 Answer

In cut-through switching mode, the switch checks only the frame's destination address and immediately begins forwarding the frame out the appropriate port. Because the switch checks the destination address in only the header and not the entire frame, the switch forwards a collision frame or a frame that has a bad CRC. This results in a fixed latency switch. Cut-through can be used only between same-speed interfaces.

Question 12 Answer

Also known as modified cut-through, fragment-free switching checks the first 64 bytes before forwarding the frame. If the frame is less than 64 bytes, the switch discards it. Ethernet specifications state that collisions should be detected during the first 64 bytes of the frame. By reading the first 64 bytes of the frame, the switch can filter most collisions, although late collisions are still possible.

Question 13

What is Spanning-Tree Protocol (STP)?

Switching
Fundamentals

Question 14

How does STP maintain a loop-free network?

Switching
Fundamentals

Question 13 Answer

STP is a loop-prevention bridge-to-bridge protocol. Its main purpose is to dynamically maintain a loop-free network. It does this by sending out bridge protocol data units (BPDUs), discovering any loops in the topology, and blocking one or more redundant links.

Question 14 Answer

STP maintains a loop-free network by

- Electing a root bridge
- Electing a root port on each nonroot bridge
- Electing designated ports on each segment
- Putting in the blocking state any redundant port that is not a root port or designated port

Question 15

What are the five spanning tree port states?

Question 16

What is a Layer 3 switching device?

Question 15 Answer

The five spanning tree port states are

- Blocking
- Listening
- Learning
- Forwarding
- Disabled

NOTE

Remember that root and designated ports forward traffic and that nondesignated ports block traffic but still listen for BPDUs.

Question 16 Answer

A Layer 3 switching device is a switch that has routing (Layer 3) functionality. It is a cross between a router and a switch. Each port on the switch is a separate LAN port, but the forwarding engine can store and forward packets based on Layer 3 information. In basic terms, a Layer 3 switch performs hardware-based routing.

Question 17

What are Layer 4 switching devices?

Switching
Fundamentals

Question 18

What are VLANs?

Switching
Fundamentals

Question 17 Answer

Layer 4 switching devices perform hardware-based Layer 3 routing that accounts for Layer 4 control information. A Layer 4 switch can make forwarding decisions based not just on MAC addresses or source/destination IP addresses but on Layer 4 information such as port numbers. With a Layer 4 switch, the network administrator can program the switch to perform quality of service (QoS) or to control network traffic flow.

Question 18 Answer

VLANs are broadcast domains in a Layer 2 network. Each broadcast domain is like a distinct virtual bridge within the switch. Each virtual bridge you create in a switch defines a broadcast domain. By default, traffic from one VLAN cannot pass to another VLAN without crossing a Layer 3 boundary such as a router or routed port. Each of the users in a VLAN is also in the same IP subnet. Each switch port can belong to only one VLAN.

Question 19

For VLANs to communicate with each other, what network component is needed?

Question 20

What is VLAN membership?

Question 19 Answer

A router is needed for inter-VLAN communication. It is important to think of a VLAN as a distinct virtual bridge in a switch that is its own IP subnet and broadcast domain. A network device cannot communicate from one IP subnet to another without a router. The same is true of a VLAN. You cannot communicate from one VLAN to another without a router.

Question 20 Answer

VLAN membership describes how a port on a switch is assigned to a VLAN.

Question 21

What are the three most common ways that VLAN membership is established?

Question 22

What are the two ways in which inter-VLAN communication can be established?

Question 21 Answer

The three most common ways of establishing VLAN membership are

- Port-driven membership
- MAC address membership
- Layer 3-based membership

The administrator statically determines port-driven membership by manually assigning each port to a particular VLAN.

MAC address and Layer 3-based memberships occur dynamically. MAC address membership is determined by a database that contains all the MAC addresses in the network and the VLAN they belong to. When the switch sees a MAC address, it performs a lookup in the database to determine what VLAN the MAC address belongs to. Layer 3-based membership occurs by looking at the Layer 3 information in the packet to determine what VLAN the packet belongs to. Because the switch has to look at the Layer 3 information, the switch must be a Layer 3 switch, and the lookup is more time-consuming than looking at the MAC address.

Question 22 Answer

The two ways in which inter-VLAN communication can be established are

- Logically
- Physically

Logical connectivity involves a single connection, called a trunk link, from the switch to a router. The trunk link uses a VLAN protocol to differentiate between VLANs. This configuration is called a "router on a stick."

Physical connectivity involves a separate physical connection for each VLAN.

Question 23

What are trunk links?

Switching
Fundamentals

Question 24

What are the two most common trunking protocols supported by Cisco switches?

Switching
Fundamentals

Question 23 Answer

By default, each port on a switch can belong to only one VLAN. For devices that are in VLANs (that span multiple switches) to talk to other devices in the same VLAN, you must use trunking or have a dedicated port per VLAN. Trunk links allow the switch to carry multiple VLANs across a single link.

Question 24 Answer

The two most common trunking protocols supported by Cisco are

- Inter-Switch Link (ISL)
- IEEE 802.1Q

Question 25
What is Inter-Switch Link (ISL)?

Switching
Fundamentals

Question 26
Describe 802.1Q tagging.

Switching
Fundamentals

Question 25 Answer

ISL is a Cisco-proprietary protocol used to interconnect switches that have multiple VLANs. It maintains VLAN information as traffic goes between switches, allowing the traffic to enter the correct VLAN. ISL operates in a point-to-point environment.

Question 26 Answer

802.1Q tagging provides a standard method for identifying frames that belong to a particular VLAN. It does this by using an internal process that modifies the existing Ethernet frame with the VLAN identification. Because 802.1Q modifies the existing frame, the identification process can work on both access links and trunk links. This is because the frame appears as a regular Ethernet packet.

NOTE

An access link has only one VLAN assigned to it.

Chapter 6

Interconnecting Networks with TCP/IP

Created by the Department of Defense (DoD) as the protocol for the Internet, TCP/IP is the most widely used protocol in the world today. It is the protocol used on the Internet and most network operating systems (NOSs). Because TCP/IP is the protocol that you're likely to encounter the most as a network engineer, it is critical that you thoroughly understand this protocol and how it works. TCP/IP is based on a four-layer model, not a seven-layer model like the OSI model. This is because the TCP/IP model was created before the OSI model.

This chapter covers the most essential topics required for the INTRO and CCNA exams, including the TCP/IP layered model, sockets, the three-way handshake, and subnetting. Subnetting is an integral part of both exams and is required for you to be a successful engineer. Unfortunately, there is no easy way to become a subnetting expert. It requires a lot of work and effort. The best way to become really good at subnetting is to continually practice it until you can easily find the number of hosts, gateways, and broadcast addresses in a network.

Question 1

What is a protocol?

Interconnecting
Networks with
TCP/IP

Question 2

What are the four layers of the TCP/IP model?

Interconnecting
Networks with
TCP/IP

Question 1 Answer

A protocol is a standard set of rules that determine how network devices communicate with each other. A protocol describes the format that the message must take and how network devices must exchange a message.

Question 2 Answer

The four layers of the TCP/IP model are

- Application (process)
- Host-to-host (transport)
- Internet
- Network interface (physical and data link)

Question 3

What two protocols function at the transport (host-to-host) layer of the TCP/IP model?

Question 4

What are the three mechanisms TCP uses to establish and maintain a connection-oriented connection?

Question 3 Answer

The two protocols that function at the host-to-host layer of the TCP/IP model are TCP (Transmission Control Protocol) and UDP (User Datagram Protocol). TCP is a connection-oriented, reliable protocol. UDP is a connectionless and unacknowledged protocol.

NOTE

Connection-oriented concerns the three-way handshake. Reliability deals with ACKs and NAKs. UDP is a connectionless, unreliable protocol, but this doesn't mean that it is unreliable. UDP uses best-effort delivery and on most networks today can send a packet with minimal to no packet loss without the overhead of TCP.

Question 4 Answer

The three mechanisms that TCP uses to establish and maintain a connection-oriented connection are

- Packet sequencing
- Acknowledgments, checksums, and timers
- Windowing

Question 5

What are the steps for the TCP three-way handshake?

Question 6

What are the protocol numbers for TCP and UDP?

Question 5 Answer

The steps for the TCP three-way handshake are as follows:

- The source host sends a SYN to the destination host.
- The destination host replies to the source with an ACK. At the same time, it sends a SYN to the source host.
- The source host replies with an ACK.

For the INTRO exam, remember this: Step 1, SYN; Step 2, SYN/ACK; Step 3, ACK.

Question 6 Answer

The protocol number for TCP is 6. The protocol number for UDP is 17.

NOTE

Protocol numbers are the link in the IP header to point to upper-layer protocols such as TCP and UDP.

Question 7

What are TCP and UDP port numbers?

Question 8

What is the number range for "well-known" port numbers?

Question 7 Answer

To pass information (such as e-mail) to upper layers, TCP and UDP use port numbers. These port numbers are predefined and keep track of different conversations among different hosts at the same time. Originating source port numbers are dynamically assigned by the source host, which is a number greater than 1023.

Question 8 Answer

Defined in RFC 1700, the well-known port numbers are 1 to 1023.

Question 9

What is the main advantage of UDP over TCP?

Question 10

What are some protocols that operate at the TCP/IP Internet layer?

Question 9 Answer

Although UDP has different advantages over TCP, the main advantage is its low overhead. Because UDP segments are not acknowledged, they do not carry the overhead that TCP does, thus allowing faster transmissions and greater efficiency.

Question 10 Answer

Some protocols that operate at the TCP/IP Internet layer are

- IP
- ICMP
- ARP
- RARP

NOTE IP is the main connectionless routed protocol at the Internet layer (or OSI network layer). IP has various "associated" protocols, such as ICMP, ARP, and RARP.

Question 11
What is IP?

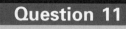

Question 12
What is Internet Control Message Protocol (ICMP)?

Question 11 Answer

IP is a connectionless protocol that provides best-effort delivery of packets.

Question 12 Answer

ICMP is a management protocol for IP. ICMP messages are carried in IP packets and are used to send error and control messages. An example of a utility that uses ICMP is echo and echo reply (ping).

Question 13

What is Address Resolution Protocol (ARP)?

Question 14

What is Reverse Address Resolution Protocol (RARP)?

Question 13 Answer

ARP is used to resolve a known IP address to a MAC address. For a host to communicate with another host, it must know the MAC address of the destination host (if they are on the same network) or the next-hop router. This is the reason for ARP.

NOTE

ARP takes the IP address and resolves it to the MAC address via a local broadcast. For a device on a remote network, the router acts as a proxy for the remote device, thus allowing the local device to communicate with the remote device. For the CCNA exam, remember that you have an IP address and you need a MAC address.

Question 14 Answer

RARP is a protocol used to find the IP address of a station that knows its MAC address. It is mainly used for diskless workstations that boot up and need an IP address. An RARP request is a broadcast packet. BOOTP is an example of RARP.

NOTE

Remember that you have a MAC address and you need an IP address.

Question 15

True or false: ICMP is implemented by all hosts configured for TCP/IP.

Question 16

What are BOOTP and DHCP?

Question 15 Answer

True. ICMP operates at the Internet layer (OSI network layer) and is used by IP for many different services. ICMP messages are carried as IP packets.

Question 16 Answer

BOOTP is a protocol used by a device to obtain an IP address at startup. A client with BOOTP enabled uses UDP to send a broadcast datagram. When the BOOTP server sees the broadcast, it responds to the client's MAC address with the IP address the client should use.

DHCP is a newer version of BOOTP and has replaced it altogether. DHCP allows a host to obtain an IP address quicker than BOOTP. All that is required for using DHCP is a defined range of IP addresses on a DHCP server.

Question 17

What is a socket?

Question 18

**What are the different classes of IP addressing
and the address ranges of each class?**

Question 17 Answer

A socket is an IP address combined with a TCP or UDP port number. When a host wants to talk to another host, it sends its IP address along with the application (port number) it wants to communicate with. For example, if host 192.168.0.3 wants to talk to host 192.168.0.2 by e-mail, host 192.168.0.3 sends its IP address and destination port number (192.168.0.3:1023) to the host 192.168.0.2 with the port number it wants to communicate with (192.168.0.2:25).

Question 18 Answer

The address ranges are as follows:

- **Class A**—1.0.0.0 to 126.0.0.0
- **Loopback**—127.0.0.0 to 127.255.255.255
- **Class B**—128.0.0.0 to 191.255.0.0
- **Class C**—192.0.0.0 to 223.255.255.0
- **Class D**—224.0.0.0 to 239.255.255.255 (multicasting)
- **Class E**—240.0.0.0 to 255.255.255.254 (reserved)

NOTE

127.0.0.0 is also a Class A network, but it is reserved.

Question 19

What does RFC 1918 define?

Question 20

What is IPv6?

Question 19 Answer

RFC 1918 defines reserved (private) networks and addresses that are not routed on the Internet. These addresses are 10.0.0.0 to 10.255.255.255, 172.16.0.0 to 172.31.255.255, and 192.168.0.0 to 192.168.255.255. They are used as internal private addresses. Private addresses are widely used today, along with proxy servers and Network Address Translation (NAT), to help "stretch" the current IP address space.

Question 20 Answer

IP version 6 (IPv6) is the new version of IP that is starting to be implemented in today's networks. The current version is IPv4. IPv6 was created to address some of the faults of IPv4, particularly the exhaustion of IPv4 addresses and the size of the Internet routing tables. IPv6 uses 128-bit binary addresses, which allows 3.4×10^{38} IP addresses.

Question 21

What is CIDR?

Question 22

How many usable subnets and hosts will you have if you subnet the network address 192.168.1.0 with the subnet mask 255.255.255.240?

Question 21 Answer

Classless Interdomain Routing (CIDR) is a new addressing scheme for the Internet that allows for more-efficient use of IP addresses than the old Class A, B, and C scheme. It is more flexible and offers route aggregation (supernetting). A CIDR address is a network address that does not use original Class A, B, and C rules. For example, a CIDR address can look like this: 192.168.2.0 255.255.255.248.

Question 22 Answer

If you subnet 192.168.1.0 with a 28-bit mask (255.255.255.240), you will have 14 networks with 14 hosts in each network. If you look at the network address and subnet mask in binary, you see that in the last octet you have 4 bits for networks and 4 bits for hosts:

- 11000000.10101000.00000000.00000000
- 11111111.11111111.11111111.11110000
- Apply these bits to the following formula:

    $2^x - 2$ = the number of subnets or hosts where x is the number of masked bits.

- $2^4 - 2 = 14$ subnets. You then apply the same equation to find the hosts, and you receive 14.

Question 23

Your Internet service provider gives you the IP network address 172.16.0.0/16. You have 18 networks, each with 1200 hosts. You want to assign one IP range per network, leaving room for future growth. What subnet mask would best achieve your goals?

Interconnecting Networks with TCP/IP

Question 24

What are the TCP port numbers to the following applications?

- HTTP
- FTP
- SMTP
- Telnet

Interconnecting Networks with TCP/IP

Question 23 Answer

255.255.248.0.

If you look at this subnet mask in binary, you see that there are 5 subnet bits for the network address:

11111111.11111111.$\boxed{11111}$000.00000000

If you use the subnet equation ($2^5 - 2 = 30$), 30 available networks are provided with the subnet mask, which fulfils the requirement for 18 networks and allows for adequate growth. This leaves you with 11 bits to be assigned to hosts, giving you 2046 ($2^{11} - 2 = 2046$) address, giving you more than enough IP addresses to be assigned to hosts. If you use a subnet mask of 255.255.240.0, you will meet the requirement of 1200 hosts ($2^{12} - 2 = 4094$ available hosts), but you won't have enough networks ($2^4 - 2 = 14$ available networks).

Question 24 Answer

The TCP port numbers are:

- HTTP: 80
- FTP: 20 and 21
- SMTP: 25
- Telnet: 23

Chapter 7

Routing

Routing is the act of finding a path to a destination and moving data across this path from source to destination. Routing is what makes the Internet work. Without routing, you wouldn't be able to send e-mail, view your favorite websites, or listen to music streams on the Internet. Routing is considered a hop-by-hop paradigm: Data is moved from router to router until it reaches the destination. Designed for the INTRO exam, this chapter covers the most basic terminology of routing and introduces you to IGPs, EGPs, and the routing protocols used today. A routing protocol is designed to dynamically find routing in an internetwork and maintain route awareness. With the dramatic growth of the Internet, routing protocols have helped reduce the administrative overhead required to maintain all routing tables on the Internet. Imagine having to statically maintain and manage more than 113,000 routes on one router!

This chapter quizzes your knowledge of the more basic terminology used in routing. For a more complete look at routing and how to configure Cisco routers with routing protocols, see Chapter 3, "Determining IP Routes," in Part II.

Question 1

Define routing.

Routing

Question 2

What are the two key functions a router performs?

Routing

Question 1 Answer

Routing is the act of finding a path to a destination and moving information across an internetwork from the source to the destination.

Question 2 Answer

The two key functions a router performs are routing and switching. The routing mechanism is responsible for learning and maintaining awareness of the network topology. The switching function is the process of moving packets from an inbound interface to an outbound interface.

Question 3

What is a routing metric?

Question 4

What are the most common routing metrics used in routing algorithms?

Question 3 Answer

A routing metric is a factor used to determine a route's desirability. A router uses the metric to determine the best or most optimal path on which network traffic should be forwarded.

Question 4 Answer

The most common routing metrics used in routing algorithms are

- **Bandwidth**—A link's data capacity.

- **Delay**—The amount of time required to move a packet from source to destination.

- **Load**—The amount of activity on the link or network resource.

- **Reliability**—A reference to the error rate on each network link.

- **Hop count**—The number of routers a packet must take to reach its destination.

- **Ticks**—The delay on a data link using IBM PC clock ticks. 1 tick is 1/18 of a second.

- **Cost**—A value assigned by the network administrator, usually based on bandwidth or monetary expense on the link.

Question 5

What is the difference between a routed protocol and a routing protocol?

Question 6

What types of information are stored in routing tables?

Question 5 Answer

A routed protocol is a protocol suite that provides the information in its network layer to allow a packet to direct traffic. It also defines the use of fields in a packet. Examples of routed protocols are IP, IPX, and DECnet.

A routing protocol is used to find routes in an internetwork, exchange routing tables, and maintain route awareness. Routing protocols determine how routed protocols are routed. RIP, EIGRP, IS-IS, OSPF, and BGP are examples of routing protocols.

Question 6 Answer

The types of information stored in routing tables are

- Destination network address
- Next-hop address
- Exiting interface
- Metric
- Administrative distance
- Routing protocol used

Question 7

How do routing protocols maintain their routing tables with each other?

Question 8

What is administrative distance?

Question 7 Answer

Routing protocols maintain their routing tables through the transmission of routing update messages. Routing update messages are exchanged between routers at periodic intervals or when there is a change in the network topology. The information contained in the routing update messages and how and when updates are sent varies from routing protocol to routing protocol.

Question 8 Answer

Administrative distance (AD) is an integer from 0 to 255 that rates the trustworthiness of the source of the IP routing information. It is important only when a router learns about a destination route from more than one source. The path with the lower AD is the one given priority.

NOTE

If a routing protocol has multiple paths within the same routing protocol to the same destination, the metric is used as the tiebreaker. The route with the lowest metric is the path taken.

Question 9

What is the AD for each of the following?

- **Directly connected interface**
- **Static route**
- **EBGP**
- **EIGRP**
- **IGRP**
- **OSPF**
- **IS-IS**
- **RIP**
- **External EIGRP**
- **IBGP**
- **Unknown**

Routing

Question 10

What is an autonomous system (AS)?

Routing

Question 9 Answer

The ADs are as follows:

- Directly connected interface—0
- Static route—1
- EBGP—20
- EIGRP—90
- IGRP—100
- OSPF—110
- IS-IS—115
- RIP—120
- External EIGRP—170
- IBGP—200

Question
- Unknown—255

An AS is a collection of networks under common administrative control sharing a common routing strategy.

NOTE

An AS consists of routers that present a consistent view of routing to the external world. They are allocated to regional registries by the Internet Assigned Numbers Authority (IANA).

Question 11

What is the difference between Interior Gateway Protocol (IGP) and Exterior Gateway Protocol (EGP)?

Question 12

How do distance vector routing protocols function?

Question 11 Answer

IGP routes data within an autonomous system. EGP routes data between autonomous systems. Examples of IGPs are RIP, EIGRP, IS-IS, and OSPF. BGP is an example of an EGP.

Question 12 Answer

Also known as Bellman-Ford algorithms, distance vector routing protocols pass complete routing tables to neighboring routers. Neighboring routers then combine the received routing table with their own routing table. Each router receives a routing table from its directly connected neighbor. RIP and IGRP are the two most common distance vector protocols used in today's internetworks.

Question 13

How do distance vector routing protocols keep track of any changes to the internetwork?

Question 14

Slow convergence of distance vector routing protocols can cause inconsistent routing tables and routing loops. What are some mechanisms that distance vector protocols implement to prevent routing loops and inconsistent routing tables?

Question 13 Answer

Distance vector routing protocols keep track of an internetwork by periodically broadcasting updates out all active interfaces. This broadcast contains the entire routing table. This method is often called "routing by rumor."

Question 14 Answer

Here are some of the ways distance vector routing protocols prevent routing loops and inconsistent routing tables:

- Maximum hop count (count to infinity)
- Split horizon
- Route poisoning
- Holddowns
- TTL

Question 15

What are link-state protocols? List two common link-state protocols.

Routing

Question 16

Which of the following is a hybrid routing protocol?

RIPv2

IGRP

DECnet

EIGRP

Routing

Question 15 Answer

Designed to overcome the limitations of distance vector protocols, link-state protocols respond quickly to network changes and send triggered and periodic updates. Link-state protocols create a picture of the internetwork by determining the status of each interface (link) in the internetwork. When the interface goes down, link-state protocols send updates out to all the other interfaces, informing other routers of the downed link. OSPF and IS-IS are the most common link-state protocols.

Question 16 Answer

EIGRP is the only hybrid routing protocol listed. EIGRP was developed by Cisco and is considered a hybrid routing protocol because it combines the aspects of distance vector and link-state routing protocols.

Question 17

If a router with RIP enabled has two paths to the same destination, one path being four routers away and the other path ten routers away, which path does the router choose?

Routing

Question 18

If a router running RIP has a path to a network that is 16 hops away, what does the router do to any packets destined for that network?

Routing

Question 17 Answer

The router chooses the path that is four routers away from the destination. RIP bases its metric on the number of hops (routers) to a destination. The route with the smallest number of hops is considered the best path and is the one used.

NOTE

If a router running RIP has two equal paths (paths with the same number of hops) to a destination, RIP automatically load-balances between the two paths.

Question 18 Answer

The router drops all packets. RIP has a hop count limit of 15, so any routes with a hop count of 16 and greater are considered unreachable, and the packet is dropped. RIP has this limitation to prevent a packet from looping infinitely.

Question 19

What version of RIP supports variable-length subnet masks?

Routing

Question 20

What is Interior Gateway Routing Protocol (IGRP)?

Routing

Question 19 Answer

RIP version 2 (RIPv2) supports variable-length subnet masks. RIPv1 is considered a classful protocol because it does not include subnet information with the routing update. RIPv2 is considered a classless protocol because it includes the subnet information with the routing update.

Question 20 Answer

IGRP is a Cisco-proprietary distance vector routing protocol. IGRP has a default hop count of 100 hops, with a maximum hop count of 255. IGRP uses bandwidth and delay as its default metric, but it can also use reliability, load, and MTU.

Question 21

What four components does EIGRP include that are not included in IGRP?

Routing

Question 22

Which of the following are link-state protocols?

IS-IS

BGP

VLSM

RIP

OSPF

Routing

Question 21 Answer

EIGRP is an improvement over IGRP and is considered a hybrid protocol. The four components of EIGRP that are not included in IGRP are

- Dynamic neighbor discovery

- Reliable transport protocol guarantees delivery of EIGRP updates

- DUAL finite-state machine ensures a loop-free internetwork

- Protocol-dependent modules let EIGRP work with IP, IPX, and AppleTalk

Question 22 Answer

IS-IS and OSPF are link-state protocols. Both protocols support fast convergence and variable-length subnet masks.

Question 23

What type of protocol is BGP?

Routing

Question 24

What port number are BGP updates carried on?

Routing

Question 23 Answer

BGP is considered an exterior gateway protocol (EGP).

Question 24 Answer

BGP uses TCP port 179 to carry all its routing updates.

Chapter 8

WAN Technologies

The INTRO exam covers more topics on WANs than LANs. This is because WAN technology is much more vast than LAN technology. In addition, with today's global economy and the growth of the Internet, WANs are more of a necessity than a convenience.

This chapter quizzes you on the concepts on the INTRO exam regarding WAN technologies. You will be quizzed on connecting to a WAN, WAN services, technologies used in WANs, digital subscriber line (DSL), and modems. The technology used in WANs is so immense that Cisco has a dedicated certification just for WANs.

This chapter is your first step in the world of internetworking with WANs.

Question 1

WANs use a technology called multiplexing. What is it?

WAN
Technologies

Question 2

List at least eight ways you can connect to a WAN.

WAN
Technologies

Question 1 Answer

Multiplexing is a technology that lets multiple logical signals be transmitted simultaneously across a single physical channel and then combined into a single data channel at the source. This lets the signals appear as one, combining the speeds of all channels.

Question 2 Answer

Here are eight ways you can connect to a WAN:

- Leased line
- Frame Relay
- Dialup
- ISDN
- ATM
- Cable
- DSL
- X.25

NOTE

These are not the only eight ways to connect to a WAN. Other ways include PPP, LAPB, SMDS, S56, and SONET.

Question 3

How many DS0s are bundled to create a T1 line?

WAN Technologies

Question 4

At what layer of the OSI model does multiplexing occur?

WAN Technologies

Question 3 Answer

24 DS0s are bundled to create a T1 line. One DS0 is 64 kbps, so 24 × 64 kbps = 1.544 Mbps, the speed of a T1 line.

Question 4 Answer

Because multiplexing combines signals across a single physical channel, it occurs at the physical layer of the OSI model.

NOTE

You might notice that the transport layer of the OSI model also does multiplexing. The difference between the two is that the transport layer multiplexes sessions using port numbers, not physical channels.

Question 5

What are the four types of multiplexing?

Question 6

Describe packet-switched WAN connections.

Question 5 Answer

The four types of multiplexing are

- Time-division multiplexing (TDM)

- Frequency-division multiplexing (FDM)

- Wave-division multiplexing (WDM) and dense WDM (DWDM)

- Statistical-division multiplexing

In TDM, each data channel is allocated bandwidth based on time slots, regardless of whether data is transferred. Thus, bandwidth is wasted when there is no data to transfer.

In FDM, information of each data channel is allocated bandwidth based on the traffic's signal frequency. An example of this is FM radio.

In WDM and DWDM, each data channel is allocated bandwidth based on wavelength (the inverse of frequency).

In statistical multiplexing, bandwidth is dynamically allocated to data channels.

Question 6 Answer

Packet-switched connections use virtual circuits (VCs) to provide end-to-end connectivity. Packet-switched connections are similar to leased lines, except that the line is shared by other customers. A packet knows how to reach its destination by programming of switches. Frame Relay and X.25 are examples of a packet-switched connection.

Question 7

What are circuit-switched WAN connections?

WAN
Technologies

Question 8

What type of WAN link is a leased line?

WAN
Technologies

Question 7 Answer

Circuit-switched WAN connections are dedicated for only the duration of the call or the time required to transmit data. The telephone system and ISDN are examples of circuit-switched networks.

Question 8 Answer

A leased line is a point-to-point link that provides a single, pre-established WAN communication path from the customer to the remote network.

Question 9

Is Frame Relay a circuit-switched or packet-switched network?

Question 10

What type of data can an ATM network transfer?

Question 9 Answer

Frame Relay is a packet-switched network that creates VCs between two DTE devices on a network to enable bidirectional communication. These VCs can be either permanent (PVCs) or dynamically switched (SVCs).

Question 10 Answer

An ATM network can transfer voice, video, and data. ATM uses a cell-switched network. The cells used to transfer voice, video, and data are always a fixed size.

Question 11

What is the size of an ATM cell?

WAN
Technologies

Question 12

What type of data can ISDN transfer?

WAN
Technologies

Question 11 Answer

An ATM cell is a fixed 53 bytes. This includes a 5-byte header and 48 bytes of payload.

Question 12 Answer

ISDN can transfer voice, data, text, graphics, music, and video. ISDN was created to allow faster access over the existing telephone system.

Question 13
What is the data transfer speed for ISDN BRI?

WAN
Technologies

Question 14
What is the total rate in Mbps for ISDN PRI?

WAN
Technologies

Question 13 Answer

The data transfer rate for ISDN BRI is 128 kbps. The total transfer rate for ISDN BRI is 144 kbps. This consists of two 64-kbps (128-kbps) bearer (B) channels plus one 16-kbps delta (D) channel. The B channels can be used for data transfer and voice transmission. The D channel carries control and signaling information for fast call setup and can carry user data under certain circumstances. It operates at the first three layers of the OSI model.

Question 14 Answer

The total rate for ISDN PRI in the U.S. and Japan is 1.544 Mbps. PRI consists of 23 64-kbps B channels and one 64-kbps D channel. In Europe, PRI consists of 30 B channels and one D channel for a total rate of 2.048 Mbps.

NOTE

ISDN PRI uses a DSU/CSU for a T1 connection.

Question 15

What is Point-to-Point Protocol (PPP)?

Question 16

What protocol does PPP use to establish, configure, and test the data-link connection?

Question 15 Answer

PPP is an industry-standard protocol that provides router-to-router or router-to-host connections over synchronous and asynchronous links. It can be used to connect WAN links to other vendors' equipment. It works with several network-layer protocols, such as IP and IPX. PPP provides authentication (which is optional) through PAP, CHAP, or MS-CHAP.

Question 16 Answer

PPP uses Link Control Protocol (LCP) to establish, configure, and test the data-link connection.

NOTE

PPP is a data link layer protocol that has two sublayers to provide network layer services. The two PPP sublayers are Network Core Protocol (NCP) and LCP. NCP encapsulates and configures multiple network layer protocols. LCP establishes, configures, maintains, and terminates PPP connections.

Question 17

What is the default encapsulation type for serial interfaces on a Cisco router?

WAN
Technologies

Question 18

At what layer of the OSI model do modems operate?

WAN
Technologies

Question 17 Answer

The default encapsulation for a serial interface on a Cisco router is HDLC. HDLC was derived from Synchronous Data Link Control (SDLC). It is an ISO-standard bit-oriented data-link protocol that encapsulates data on synchronous links. HDLC is a connection-oriented protocol that has very little overhead. HDLC lacks a protocol field and therefore cannot encapsulate multiple network layer protocols across the same link. Because of this, each vendor has its own method of identifying the network-layer protocol. Cisco offers a propriety version of HDLC that uses a type field that acts as a protocol field, making it possible for multiple network layer protocols to share the same link.

Question 18 Answer

Modems operate at the physical layer of the OSI model. A modem is used for computer communication through a telephone line.

Question 19

What modem standard is a worldwide standard that provides 2400 bps at 600 baud?

WAN
Technologies

Question 20

What modem standard provides up to 56 kbps of downstream data transfer and up to 300 kbps of upstream data transfer?

WAN
Technologies

Question 19 Answer

V.22bis was the first worldwide modem standard for full-duplex modems providing data speeds of 2400 bps at 600 baud.

Question 20 Answer

V.90 is the modem standard that provides up to 56 kbps of downstream data transmission and up to 300 kbps of upstream data transmission.

Question 21

Describe DSL.

WAN
Technologies

Question 22

At what layer of the OSI model does DSL operate?

WAN
Technologies

Question 21 Answer

DSL is a modem technology that uses existing twisted-pair telephone lines to transfer high-speed data. Many types of DSL are used today; the most common are asymmetric DSL (ADSL) and symmetric DSL (SDSL). ADSL provides a higher downstream speed than upstream. SDSL provides the same speed for both upstream and downstream traffic.

Question 22 Answer

DSL operates at the physical layer (Layer 1) of the OSI model. DSL relies on upper-layer protocols to encapsulate the data at the CO. It uses ATM, Ethernet, or PPP at the data link layer and IP at the network layer.

Chapter 9

Operating and Configuring Cisco IOS Devices

This chapter covers the Cisco IOS commands used to operate and configure Cisco devices. First you will be quizzed on the different ways to connect to a Cisco device and the different EXEC modes in the IOS. Then you will be quizzed on the differences between starting a Cisco 1900 or 2950 series switch and a Cisco router. Finally, you will be quizzed on the different commands you can use to view your router configuration and configure your Cisco IOS device.

Once you have completed the INTRO exam, be sure to re-review this chapter when preparing for the ICND exam. The INTRO and CCNA exams might test your knowledge of any of these commands, so it is important that you learn each command's function. You might also be tested on what is contained in the output of many IOS commands. Study each question until you can answer it correctly. If the answer contains IOS output, familiarize yourself with the output. Doing so will help you recall the correct command to use when you are asked a question on the CCNA test or when you are in the field troubleshooting a Cisco device.

Question 1

What are the five ways to configure a Cisco device?

Operating and
Configuring Cisco
IOS Devices

Question 2

What two EXEC modes are supported in the Cisco IOS?

Operating and
Configuring Cisco
IOS Devices

Question 1 Answer

The five ways to configure a Cisco device are

- Console connection
- Auxiliary connection (through a modem)
- Telnet connection
- HTTP connection
- CiscoWorks 2000

NOTE

Upon initial installation, you need to connect to the Cisco device through a console connection, because you need to configure the router to accept the other connection types.

Question 2 Answer

The two EXEC modes are

- User EXEC mode (user mode)
- Privileged EXEC mode (enable or privileged mode)

Question 3

In the IOS, what is user EXEC mode?

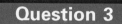

Operating and
Configuring Cisco
IOS Devices

Question 4

In the IOS, what is privileged EXEC mode?

Operating and
Configuring Cisco
IOS Devices

Question 3 Answer

User EXEC mode is the first mode you enter when you log into the IOS. This mode is limited and is mostly used to view statistics. You cannot change a router's configuration in this mode. By default, the greater-than sign (>) indicates that you are in user mode. This is how the router prompt looks in user mode:

```
Router>
```

NOTE

You can change the default user mode prompt and enable mode prompt using the prompt privileged mode command.

Question 4 Answer

In privileged EXEC mode, you can view and change the configuration in a router; you have access to all the routers commands and the powerful **debug** commands. To enter privileged mode, enter the **enable** command while in user mode. By default, the pound symbol (#) indicates that you are in privileged mode. This mode is usually protected with a password. Here is an example of how to enter privileged mode. You also see the output of the prompt:

```
Router>enable
Password:
Router#
```

Question 5

When you are in privileged EXEC mode, how do you return to user EXEC mode?

Question 6

How do you power on a Cisco 1900 or 2950 series switch?

Question 5 Answer

You can return to user EXEC mode using the **disable** IOS command. Here is an example of using the **disable** command:

```
Router#disable
Router>
```

NOTE

Other commands you can use to return to user EXEC mode are **exit** and **end**. The **exit** command changes the configuration mode, and the **end** command ends a session and returns to user EXEC mode.

Question 6 Answer

Unlike a Cisco router, a Cisco 1900 or 2950 series switch does not have a switch to turn the power on and off, so the only way to power on a Cisco switch is the plug in the power cord.

Question 7

What two types of content-sensitive help are available in the Cisco IOS for a switch and a router?

Question 8

What are the two configuration modes in the Cisco 1900 and 2950 series switches' IOS?

Question 7 Answer

Word help and command syntax help are the two types of content-sensitive help available in the IOS, whether a switch or a router. Word help uses a question mark and identifies commands that start with a character or a sequence of characters. For example, the following router output shows the use of word help for any IOS command that starts with the letters **cl**:

```
Router#cl?
clear clock
```

Command syntax help is when you use a question mark after a command to see how to complete the command:

```
Router#clock ?
  set   Set the time and date
```

Question 8 Answer

The two configuration modes in the Cisco 1900 and 2950 series switches' IOS are global configuration and interface configuration.

Global configuration is used to configure a global setting on the switch, such as an IP address or host name.

Interface configuration is used to configure an interface setting, such as port speed or duplex.

Question 9

How do you configure an IP address and subnet mask on a Catalyst 1900 switch and a Catalyst 2950 switch?

Question 10

Why would you want to assign an IP address to a Layer 2 device, such as a switch?

Question 9 Answer

To configure an IP address and subnet mask on a Catalyst 1900 switch, use the **ip address** *address mask* global configuration command:

```
Cat1900(config)#ip address 192.168.0.2 255.255.255.0
```

To configure an IP address on a Catalyst 2950 switch, you enter the VLAN1 logical interface and then assign the IP address using the **ip address** *address mask* command:

```
Cat2950(config)#interface vlan1
Cat2950(config-if)#ip address 10.1.1.2 255.0.0.0
```

Question 10 Answer

You would assign an IP address to a Layer 2 device for management and configuration. With an IP address enabled on a Cisco switch, you can Telnet into it and change the configuration. You can also enable SNMP on the device and remotely monitor the switch.

Question 11

How do you configure a default gateway on Cisco Catalyst 1900 and 2950 switches?

Question 12

What Cisco switch IOS command displays the system hardware, software version, names of configuration files, and boot images?

Question 11 Answer

The command to configure a default gateway on Cisco Catalyst 1900 and 2950 switches is the same. To configure the default gateway, use the **ip default-gateway** *ip-address* global configuration command. The following example configures the switch to use IP address 192.168.0.1 as its default gateway:

```
Cat1900(config)#ip default-gateway 192.168.0.1
```

NOTE
To remove the default gateway, use the **no ip default-gateway** command.

Question 12 Answer

The **show version switch** IOS command displays the system hardware, software version, and boot images. The following is output of the **show version** command on a Cisco 2950 switch:

```
Cat2950#sh version
Cisco Internetwork Operating System Software
IOS (tm) C2950 Software (C2950-I6Q4L2-M), Version 12.1(9)EA1d,
   RELEASE SOFTWARE
(fc1)
Copyright (c) 1986-2002 by cisco Systems, Inc.
Compiled Mon 17-Jun-02 18:55 by antonino
Image text-base: 0x80010000, data-base: 0x804E6000
<text omitted>
FCMain-Core uptime is 25 weeks, 1 day, 8 hours, 51 minutes
System returned to ROM by power-on
System image file is "flash:c2950-i6q4l2-mz.121-9.EA1d.bin"

cisco WS-C2950T-24 (RC32300) processor (revision B0) with
20821K
   bytes of memory
.
Processor board ID FAB0525P18E
Last reset from system-reset
Running Enhanced Image
24 FastEthernet/IEEE 802.3 interface(s)
2 Gigabit Ethernet/IEEE 802.3 interface(s)
<Text omitted>
```

Question 13

On a Catalyst 1900 switch, what command can you use to view the switch's IP address, subnet mask, and default gateway?

Question 14

What are global commands on a Cisco router?

Question 13 Answer

The **show ip** command displays the 1900 series switch's IP address, subnet mask, and default gateway. Here's an example:

```
Cat1900#show ip
IP Address: 192.168.0.2
Subnet Mask: 255.255.255.0
Default Gateway: 192.168.0.1
Management VLAN:   1
Domain name:
Name server 1: 0.0.0.0
Name server 2: 0.0.0.0
HTTP server : Enabled
HTTP port :   80
RIP : Enabled
Cat1900#
```

NOTE

The **show ip interfaces** command shows the IP address and subnet mask on a 2950 series switch.

Question 14 Answer

Global configuration commands are commands that affect the entire router. They can be executed only in global configuration mode.

Question 15

How do you enter global configuration mode?

Question 16

On a Cisco router, name the enhanced editing commands that are used to do the following:

Move the cursor to the beginning of the line

Move the cursor to the end of the line

Move the cursor forward one character

Move the cursor back one character

Move the cursor back one word

Delete all characters from the cursor to the beginning of the command line

Complete a word

Display a line versus a screen

Question 15 Answer

To enter global configuration mode, you enter the **config terminal** command from privileged EXEC mode. Here is an example of this command:

```
Router#config terminal
Enter configuration commands, one per line.  End with CTRL-Z.
Router(config)#
```

NOTE

Notice that the command prompt changes to (config)# in global configuration mode.

Question 16 Answer

Move the cursor to the beginning of the line—Ctrl-A

Move the cursor to the end of the line—Ctrl-E

Move the cursor forward one character—Ctrl-F

Move the cursor back one character—Ctrl-B

Move the cursor back one word—Esc-B

Delete all characters from the cursor to the beginning of the command line—Ctrl-U

Complete a word—Tab

Display a line versus a screen—Enter

NOTE

This is only a partial list of the enhanced editing commands. For the test, you should know the purpose of every command. To get a complete list, go to www.cisco.com, search for "basic command-line interface commands," and click the Editing link.

Question 17

What Cisco router command would you use to view a list of the most recently used commands?

Operating and
Configuring Cisco
IOS Devices

Question 18

Command history is enabled by default and records ten commands in its history buffer for the current session. How do you edit the number of commands that are stored in the router's history buffer?

Operating and
Configuring Cisco
IOS Devices

Question 17 Answer

The **show history** command by default displays the last ten commands used:

```
Router#show history
  en
  show running-config
  show history
  enable
  show version
  show time
  show history
Router#
```

You can also press the up arrow key (or Ctrl-P) to display the last command you entered and the down arrow key (or Ctrl-N) to display the previous commands you entered. As you use the up and down arrow keys, you are scrolling through the history buffer.

Question 18 Answer

To edit the number of command lines stored for the current session, use the **terminal history** [**size** *number-of-lines*] command in privileged EXEC mode. For example, the following changes the history size to 20 lines:

```
Router#terminal history size 20
```

NOTE

The maximum number of lines you can set for the current session is 256, but doing so wastes router memory. To turn off terminal history, use the **terminal no history** privileged mode command. If you want to set the history size larger than the current session, go to the console interface and enter the **history** [**size** *number-of-lines*] interface command as a more permanent way of changing the history buffer. This command is unavailable on a Catalyst 1900 switch.

Question 19

On a Cisco router, what does the show version command display?

Question 20

On a Cisco router, how do you display the configuration running in RAM?

Question 19 Answer

show version displays the system hardware's configuration, including RAM, Flash memory, software version, configuration register, and boot images:

```
Router#show version
Cisco Internetwork Operating System Software
IOS (tm) 2500 Software (C2500-D-L), Version 12.0(13), RELEASE
    SOFTWARE (fc1)
Copyright (c) 1986-2000 by Cisco Systems, Inc.
Compiled Wed 06-Sep-00 01:08 by linda
Image text-base: 0x030388F8, data-base: 0x00001000

--Text omitted--

Router uptime is 50 minutes
System restarted by power-on
System image file is "flash:c2500-d-l.120-13.bin"

cisco 2505 (68030) processor (revision C) with 8192K/2048K
bytes
  of memory.
Processor board ID 02073409, with hardware revision 00000000
(text omitted)32K bytes of non-volatile configuration memory.
8192K bytes of processor board System flash (Read ONLY)

Configuration register is 0x2102
```

Question 20 Answer

You display the configuration running in RAM using the **show running-config** privileged mode command:

```
Router#show running-config
Building configuration...
Current configuration:
!
version 12.0
service timestamps debug uptime
service timestamps log uptime
no service password-encryption
!
hostname Router
!
enable password cisco
!
    --More--
```

NOTE

You might know **show run** as **write terminal**, but remember **sh run** for the CCNA exam.

Question 21

On a Cisco router, how do you view the configuration stored in NVRAM?

Question 22

How do you save the active configuration to nonvolatile RAM (NVRAM)?

Question 21 Answer

You view the configuration stored in NVRAM using the **show startup-config** privileged mode command.

NOTE

You might know **show start** as **show config,** but remember **sh start** for the ICND exam.

Question 22 Answer

To save the running configuration to the startup configuration, use the **copy run start** privileged mode command.

Question 23

How do you configure a name on a Cisco router?

Question 24

How do you add a message-of-the-day (MOTD) banner on a Cisco router?

Question 23 Answer

The **hostname** *name* global configuration command is used to configure a name on a Cisco router. For example, the following command changes the router's host name to RouterA:

```
Router(config)#hostname RouterA
RouterA(config)#
```

Question 24 Answer

To add a message-of-the-day banner to a Cisco router, enter the **banner motd #** *text* **#** global configuration command. The pound signs (#) are delimiting characters. They can be any character of your choice, but they must be the same and cannot be included in your text. They signify the beginning and end of your text. The following example shows the **banner motd** command:

```
RouterA(config)#banner motd #        <ENTER>
Enter TEXT message.  End with the character '#'.
Warning only authorized users many access this Router. <ENTER>
#
RouterA(config)#
```

NOTE

The MOTD banner is displayed to anyone connecting to the router via Telnet, console port, or auxiliary port.

Question 25

Which of the following is the correct command to add the description "Link to West LA" to an interface on a Cisco router?

A. name Link to West LA

B. interface description Link to West LA

C. description Link to West LA

D. interface name Link to West LA

Question 26

On a Cisco router, how do you set a password to restrict access to privileged EXEC mode?

Question 25 Answer

C. You add a description to an interface using the **description** *interface-description* interface configuration command.

NOTE

Adding a description to an interface on a Cisco router does not have any performance effects. It just adds a description to help identify the interface.

Question 26 Answer

You set a password to restrict access to privileged EXEC mode using the **enable secret** global configuration command:

```
RouterA(config)#enable secret CCNA
```

This example sets the password to enter privileged mode to CCNA.

Question 27

On a Cisco router, how do you add a password to the console terminal?

Question 28

How do you add a password for Telnet access on a Cisco router?

Question 27 Answer

To add a password to the console terminal, use the **line console 0** global configuration command, followed by the **login** and **password** password line subcommands:

```
RouterA(config)#line console 0
RouterA(config-line)#login
RouterA(config-line)#password CCNA
```

The login subcommand forces the router to prompt for authentication. Without this command, the router will not authenticate a password. **password CCNA** sets the console password to CCNA. The password is case-sensitive.

NOTE

Sometimes, when people enter **login**, they tend to want to enter **login local**, which looks for a username/password statement in the local router configuration. If you don't have a username and password configured locally, the only way out is password recovery.

Question 28 Answer

To add a password for Telnet access, enter the **line vty 0 4** global configuration command, the **login** command, and finally the **password** line subcommand. The password is case-sensitive. In this example, the Telnet password is set to CCNA:

```
RouterA(config)#line vty 0 4
RouterA(config-line)#login
RouterA(config-line)#password CCNA
```

NOTE

Without the **login** command, the router will not let you log on via Telnet, even if a password is set.

Question 29

What command do you use to add a password to the auxiliary interface on your Cisco router?

Question 30

When you view the configuration on Cisco routers, only the enable secret password is encrypted. How do you encrypt user mode and the enable password?

Question 29 Answer

To add a password to the auxiliary interface, use the **aux** *line number* global configuration command, followed by the **login** and **password** subcommands, where *line number* is the number of the auxiliary port you want to add a password to. The password is case-sensitive. The following example sets the password for the auxiliary port to CCNA:

```
RouterA(config)#aux line 0
RouterA(config-line)#login
RouterA(config-line)#password CCNA
```

Question 30 Answer

To encrypt user mode and the enable password, use the **service password-encryption** global command:

```
RouterA(config)#service password-encryption
```

Question 31

How do you configure Cisco router interfaces?

Question 32

How do you administratively disable an interface on a Cisco router?

Question 31 Answer

To configure an interface on a Cisco router, use the **interface**
interface-type number global configuration command, where
interface-type number is the interface type and number you want
to configure. For example, if you want to configure the second
serial interface on your router, you would enter the following:

```
RouterA(config)#interface serial1
RouterA(config-if)#
```

Cisco interfaces start with 0 instead of 1, so the first interface is
0. The prompt also changes to RouterA(config-if)# to tell you
that you are in interface mode. If you have a router with a
module slot, such as the Cisco 3600, you enter interface mode by
entering the slot/port number. For example, if you have a Cisco
3600 router with two module serial interfaces, and you want to
configure the first serial interface on the second module, you
would enter **interface s1/0**.

Question 32 Answer

You administratively disable an interface on a Cisco router by
issuing the **shutdown** interface configuration command. In this
example, the serial interface is issued the shutdown command:

```
RouterA(config)#int s0
RouterA(config-if)#shutdown
00:27:14: %LINK-5-CHANGED: Interface Serial0, changed state to
   administratively down
```

NOTE

To administratively enable an interface, use the **no
shutdown** interface configuration command.

Question 33

What are some of the things the show interface *interface-type number* **command displays?**

Question 34

How do you display the status of interface S0 only?

Question 33 Answer

The **show interface** command displays the following:

- Whether the interface is administratively down
- Whether the line protocol is up or down
- An Internet address (if one is configured)
- MTU and bandwidth
- Traffic statistics on the interface
- Interface encapsulation type

Question 34 Answer

The IOS command to display the status of interface S0 only is **show interface s0**.

Question 35

On your Cisco router, you enter show interface s0 and notice that the port is administratively down. What does this mean, and how do you fix it?

Question 36

You are configuring a serial interface, and the interface says "Interface is up, line protocol is down." What does this tell you about the serial interface?

Question 35 Answer

When an interface is administratively down, it was shut down manually or was never enabled at all. To remedy this, enter the interface command **no shut**.

Question 36 Answer

If an interface says "Interface is up, line protocol is down," the interface is experiencing Layer 2 problems. This could be caused by a wrong connector or not receiving keepalives or clocking.

NOTE

If the interface says "Interface is down, line protocol is down," and it is not administratively disabled, the interface is having Layer 1 problems.

Question 37

What two commands can you use to show the clock rate on a serial interface?

Question 38

Assuming that you are using no CSU/DSU and you are using back-to-back DTE/DCE serial cables, what command would you use to set the serial interface on a router to provide clocking to another router at 64 kbps?

Question 37 Answer

To view the clock rate on a serial interface, you can use the **show running-config** privileged EXEC command and the **show controllers** privileged EXEC command.

NOTE

The **show running-config** command shows a serial interface's clock rate only if it has been configured as a DCE interface.

Question 38 Answer

The command to set the serial interface on a router to provide clocking to another router at 64 kbps is **clock rate 64000**. Setting the clock rate on an interface makes it a DCE interface.

Question 39

What Cisco IOS router command would you use to find out whether a serial interface is a DCE or DTE interface (providing clocking)?

Question 39 Answer

To see whether a serial interface is providing clocking, use the **enable** command **show controllers** *serial-interface-type serial-number.* The following example shows that serial interface 0 is providing clock rate at 56 kbps:

```
RouterA#show controllers s 0
HD unit 0, idb = 0xCCE04, driver structure at 0xD2298
buffer size 1524  HD unit 0, V.35 DCE cable, clockrate 56000
cpb = 0x81, eda = 0x4940, cda = 0x4800
RX ring with 16 entries at 0x814800
```

Part I

Chapter 10

Managing Your Network Environment

You have bought your Cisco network equipment and installed it, and your network is up and running. Then next step is to manage your network. How do you keep it up and running at optimal levels? How do you upgrade your Cisco IOS software? This chapter quizzes you on the steps to keep your network running. You will be quizzed on Cisco's proprietary management protocol, CDP, and all the commands to configure and troubleshoot this protocol. You will also be quizzed on how a Cisco router operates. Have you ever wondered where a router stores a packet after it's received, or where it keeps its routing table? This chapter covers the important physical operation of Cisco routers and reviews the many ways to manage them. Finally, you will be quizzed on backing up, restoring, and upgrading the Cisco IOS. Upgrading the IOS ensures that you are running the most secure and updated IOS. This chapter covers topics found on both the INTRO and CCNA exams.

Question 1

What is the Cisco Discovery Protocol (CDP)?

Question 2

List five types of information obtained from CDP.

Question 1 Answer

CDP is a Cisco-proprietary protocol that runs on all Cisco IOS-enabled devices. It gathers information about directly connected neighboring devices. CDP operates at Layer 2 of the OSI model and is media-independent. With CDP, you can tell the hardware type, device identifier, address list, software version, and active interfaces on neighboring Cisco devices. CDP is enabled by default on all Cisco equipment. It uses a nonroutable SNAP frame to communicate between devices.

NOTE

Because CDP is media-independent, it can operate over most media types. The only media types that CDP cannot operate over are X.25, because it doesn't support SNAP encapsulation, and Frame Relay point-to-multipoint interfaces.

Question 2 Answer

The five types of information obtained from CDP are

- Device identifiers (host name of the remote device)
- Network address list of remote devices
- Port identifiers of remote devices
- Capabilities list of remote devices
- Platform of remote devices (type of remote device)

Question 3

List four reasons to disable CDP.

Question 4

How do you disable CDP on Cisco routers?

Question 3 Answer

Four reasons to disable CDP are

- To save network bandwidth by not exchanging CDP frames.

- To conserve CPU resources on a router if CDP is not required.

- If you are connecting to non-Cisco devices.

- Security. CDP broadcasts information about the device every 60 seconds. Sniffers and other devices can view these broadcasts to discover information about your network.

Question 4 Answer

Two commands disable CDP on a Cisco router. To disable CDP on the entire device, use the **no cdp run** global command:

```
RouterB(config)#no cdp run
```

To disable CDP on an interface only, use the **no cdp enable** interface command:

```
RouterB(config)#int e0
RouterB(config-if)#no cdp enable
```

This disables CDP on Ethernet interface 0.

Question 5

What does the show cdp command display?

Managing Your Network Environment

Question 6

On a Cisco router, what does the show cdp neighbors command display?

Managing Your Network Environment

Question 5 Answer

The **show cdp** command displays global CDP information about the device. It tells you when the device will send CDP packets and the CDP holdtime:

```
RouterB#show cdp
Global CDP information:
        Sending CDP packets every 60 seconds
        Sending a holdtime value of 180 seconds
```

NOTE

Remember that the default time a device sends out CDP information is 60 seconds, and the default holdtime is 180 seconds.

Question 6 Answer

The **show cdp neighbors** command displays the following:

- Device ID (name of the device)
- The local interface (local outgoing port)
- The holdtime in seconds
- The device's capability code
- Hardware platform of the neighboring device
- Port ID of the neighboring device (remote port)

Here is some sample output from this command:

```
RouterB#show cdp neighbors
Capability Codes: R - Router, T - Trans Bridge, B - Source Route
        Bridge
                    S - Switch, H - Host, I - IGMP, r - Repeater

Device ID  Local Intrfce  Holdtme  Capability  Platform  Port ID
RouterA    Ser 0             146         R         2505     Ser 0
```

Question 7

What does the show cdp neighbors detail command display?

Managing Your Network Environment

Question 8

What does the show cdp traffic command display?

Managing Your Network Environment

Question 7 Answer

The **show cdp neighbors detail** and **show cdp entry *** commands show the same output. They both display the following:

- Device ID (host name) of the remote neighbor
- Layer 3 address of the remote device (if the device has more than one Layer 3 address on its interface, only the primary address is shown)
- Device platform and capabilities
- Local interface and outgoing port ID
- Remote device holdtime in seconds
- IOS type and version

Question 8 Answer

The **show cdp traffic** command displays information about interface traffic. This includes the number of CDP packets sent and received and CDP errors:

```
RouterB#show cdp traffic
CDP counters :

        Hdr syntax: 0, Chksum error: 0, Encaps failed:
        No memory: 0, Invalid packet: 0, Fragmented: 0
```

Question 9

What does the show cdp interface command display?

Question 10

What Cisco IOS router command can you use to see a neighbor router's IP address?

Question 9 Answer

The **show cdp interface** command displays the status of CDP on all interfaces on your device:

```
RouterB#show cdp interface
Ethernet0 is up, line protocol is down
  Encapsulation ARPA
  Sending CDP packets every 60 seconds
  Holdtime is 180 seconds
Serial0 is up, line protocol is up
  Encapsulation HDLC
  Sending CDP packets every 60 seconds
  Holdtime is 180 seconds
Serial1 is up, line protocol is up
  Encapsulation HDLC
  Sending CDP packets every 60 seconds
  Holdtime is 180 seconds
```

Question 10 Answer

To see a neighbor router's IP address, you must use the **show cdp neighbor detail** or **show cdp entry *** user mode or EXEC command.

Question 11

What IOS command shows the active outbound connections after you Telnet into multiple routers simultaneously?

Question 12

What key sequence do you use to suspend a Telnet session on a remote system and return to your local router?

Question 11 Answer

The **show sessions** command displays the active outbound Telnet sessions from that particular user on your router:

```
RouterA#show sessions
Conn Host              Address          Byte  Idle Conn Name
*  1 192.168.1.2       192.168.1.2         0     0 192.168.1.2
```

Question 12 Answer

To suspend a Telnet session, press Ctrl-Shift-6 and then press X.

Question 13

How do you reestablish a suspended Telnet session on a Cisco router?

Managing Your
Network
Environment

Question 14

How do you end a remote Telnet session on a Cisco router?

Managing Your
Network
Environment

Question 13 Answer

To reestablish a suspended Telnet session, use the **show session** command to find the session you want to resume, and then use the **resume** *session-number* command to connect to the specified session:

```
RouterA#show session
Conn Host              Address              Byte  Idle Conn Name
   1 192.168.1.2       192.168.1.2             0     0 192.168.1.2
 * 2 192.168.2.2       192.168.2.2             0     0 192.168.2.2

RouterA#resume 1
[Resuming connection 1 to 192.168.1.2 ... ]

RouterB>
```

Question 14 Answer

To end a Telnet session, use the **exit** or **logout** command while you're on the remote device:

```
RouterB>exit

[Connection to 192.168.1.2 closed by foreign host]
RouterA#
```

Question 15

Upon using the ping EXEC command, you can receive the following responses:

- .
- !
- ?
- C
- U

What does each of these responses mean?

Question 16

What is the trace EXEC command used for?

Question 15 Answer

The following table from Cisco Systems' website describes what each character means with the **ping** command.

Character	Description
.	Each period indicates that the network server timed out while waiting for a reply.
!	Each exclamation point indicates the receipt of a reply.
?	Unknown packet type.
C	A congestion experienced packet was received.
U	A destination unreachable error PDU was received.
I	The user interrupted the test.

NOTE

It is important to memorize this list.

Question 16 Answer

The **trace** EXEC command displays the path a packet used to get to a remote device:

```
RouterA#trace 192.168.2.2

Type escape sequence to abort.
Tracing the route to 192.168.2.2

  1 192.168.2.2 16 msec 16 msec *
```

NOTE

If **trace** responds with a *, this means that the probe timed out. If it responds with a ?, this means that it received an unknown packet type.

Question 17

What two Cisco IOS commands verify end-to-end connectivity?

Question 18

What are the two ways in which a Cisco router resolves host names to IP addresses?

Question 17 Answer

The two Cisco IOS commands that verify end-to-end connectivity are the **ping** and **trace** EXEC commands. The **ping** command sends an echo to the remote destination; the **trace** command shows the path from the source to the destination.

Question 18 Answer

A Cisco router resolves host names using either a DNS server or a locally configured host table on each router.

NOTE

Host name resolution is enabled by default on a Cisco router. To disable it, enter the **no ip domain-lookup** global command.

Question 19

Which router component stores the routing tables, packet buffers, and ARP cache?

Question 20

What is the function of ROM on a Cisco router?

Question 19 Answer

RAM holds the router's routing table, packet buffers, and ARP cache. The running-config is also stored in RAM. On most Cisco routers, the IOS is loaded into RAM as well.

Question 20 Answer

On a Cisco router, ROM starts and maintains the router.

Question 21

What is Flash memory used for on a Cisco router?

Question 22

What is the function of NVRAM on a Cisco router?

Question 21 Answer

Flash memory stores the Cisco IOS software image and, if there is room, multiple configuration files or multiple IOS files. On some routers (the 2500 series), it is also used to run the IOS. Flash memory is not erased when the router or switch is reloaded.

Question 22 Answer

Nonvolatile random-access memory (NVRAM) is used to hold the saved router configuration (and the switch configuration). This configuration is maintained when the device is turned off or reloaded.

Question 23

What is the main purpose of the configuration register on a Cisco router?

Question 24

What Cisco IOS command would you use to view the current configuration register value?

Question 23 Answer

The configuration register's main purpose is to control how the router boots up. It is a 16-bit software register that by default is set to load the Cisco IOS from Flash memory and to look for and load the startup-config file from NVRAM.

Question 24 Answer

The **show version** command is used to display the router's current configuration register:

```
RouterA#show version
Cisco Internetwork Operating System Software
IOS (tm) 2500 Software (C2500-D-L), Version 12.0(13),
   RELEASE SOFTWARE (fc1)
Copyright (c) 1986-2000 by cisco Systems, Inc.
Compiled Wed 06-Sep-00 01:08 by linda
Image text-base: 0x030388F8, data-base: 0x00001000
<Output omitted>
Configuration register is 0x2102
```

NOTE

You know that the **show version** command displays the system hardware, software version, names and locations of the configuration files, boot images, and the configuration register.

Question 25

How do you change the configuration register on a Cisco router?

Question 26

Where would the router boot from if the configuration register settings were changed to 0x0101?

Question 25 Answer

To change the configuration register on a Cisco router, use the **config-register** command in global configuration mode.

Question 26 Answer

The router would boot from ROM if you changed the configuration register setting to 0x0101.

NOTE

The default config register on Cisco routers is 0x2102, which tells the router to load the Cisco IOS from Flash memory and to look for and load the startup-config file from NVRAM. Most administrators use the config register for password recovery.

Question 27

What Cisco IOS command displays the contents of Flash memory?

Managing Your Network Environment

Question 28

What IOS command configures the router to boot from an alternative IOS located in Flash?

Managing Your Network Environment

Question 27 Answer

The **show flash** command displays the contents of Flash memory. This includes the images stored in Flash memory, the images' names, bytes used in Flash memory, bytes available, and the total amount of Flash memory on your router:

```
RouterA#show flash

System flash directory:
File   Length    Name/status
   1   6897716   c2500-d-l.120-13.bin
[6897780 bytes used, 1490828 available, 8388608 total]
8192K bytes of processor board System flash   (Read ONLY)
```

Question 28 Answer

The boot **system flash** *ios-file-name* global configuration command instructs the router to boot from a different IOS located in Flash memory.

Question 29

What two IOS commands would you use to back up the running configuration on a router to a TFTP server?

Managing Your Network Environment

Question 30

How do you restore your router to the factory defaults?

Managing Your Network Environment

Question 29 Answer

To back up the running configuration to a TFTP server, use the **copy running-config tftp** privileged EXEC command or the **write network** command. The following is an example of the **copy run tftp** command:

```
RouterB#copy run tftp
Address or name of remote host []? 192.168.0.2
Destination filename [routerb-confg]?
!!
780 bytes copied in 6.900 secs (130 bytes/sec)
```

Question 30 Answer

The **erase startup-config** privileged EXEC command erases your router's configuration, thus bringing it back to its factory defaults:

```
RouterB#erase startup-config
Erasing the nvram filesystem will remove all files! Continue?
 [confirm]
[OK]
Erase of nvram: complete
```

NOTE

To complete the process, you need to reload the router. An older IOS command that you can use to accomplish the same result is **write erase.**

Question 31

How do you restore a configuration file from a TFTP server into your Cisco router's RAM?

Question 32

How do you back up a Cisco router IOS?

Question 31 Answer

The **copy tftp running-config** privileged EXEC command merges the saved and running configuration into your router's RAM, so any commands not explicitly changed or removed remain in the running configuration:

```
RouterB#copy tftp running-config
Address or name of remote host []? 192.168.0.2
Source filename []? routerb-confg
Destination filename [running-config]?
Accessing tftp://192.168.0.2/routerb-confg...
Loading routerb-confg from 192.168.0.2 (via Ethernet0): !
[OK - 780/1024 bytes]
780 bytes copied in 4.12 secs (195 bytes/sec)
RouterB#
01:40:46: %SYS-5-CONFIG: Configured from tftp:
   //192.168.0.2/routerb-confg
```

Question 32 Answer

To back up the current IOS image on your router, use the **copy flash tftp** privileged EXEC mode command:

```
RouterB#copy flash tftp
Source filename [routerb-flash]? flash:c2500-d-l.120-13.bin
Address or name of remote host []? 192.168.0.2
Destination filename [c2500-d-l.120-13.bin]?
!!!!!!!!!!!!!!!!!!!!!!!!!!!!!!!!!!!!!!!!!!!!!!!!!!!!!!!!!!!!!!!!!!
!!
!!!!!!!!!!!!!!!!!!!!!!!!!!!!!!!!!!!!!!!!!!!!!!!!!!!!!!!!!!!!!!!!!!
!!
!!!!!!!!!!!!!!!!!!!!!!!!!!!!!!!!!!!!!!!!!!!!!!!!!!!!!!!!!!!!!!!!!!
!!
!!!!!!!!!!!!!!!!!!!!!!!!!!!!!!!!!!!!!!!!!!!!!!!!!!!!!!!!!!!!!!!!!!
!!
6897716 bytes copied in 90.856 secs (76641 bytes/sec)
```

Question 33

How do you upgrade or restore the Cisco router IOS?

Question 34

How do you make a Cisco router a TFTP server?

Question 33 Answer

To upgrade or restore the Cisco router IOS, use the **copy tftp flash** privileged EXEC mode command.

NOTE

To obtain a new IOS version, go to Cisco Systems' website. You need a CCO login with the appropriate access to acquire the Cisco IOS.

Question 34 Answer

To configure a Cisco router as a TFTP server, use the **tftp-server** *device file-name* global configuration command. For example, the following command configures the router to send a copy of file version-12.1, located in Flash memory, in response to a TFTP read request for that file:

```
Router#configure terminal
Enter configuration commands, one per line. End with CNTL/Z.
Router(config)#tftp-server flash version-12.1
```

Part II

ICND/CCNA

Chapter 1
Configuring Catalyst Switch Operations

Chapter 2
Extending Switched Networks with VLANs

Chapter 3
Determining IP Routes

Chapter 4
Managing IP Traffic with Access Lists and
Network Address Translation

Chapter 5
Establishing Serial Point-to-Point Connections

Chapter 6
Frame Relay

Chapter 7
ISDN

Chapter 8
Last Minute Exam Tips

Chapter 1

Configuring Catalyst Switch Operations

This chapter provides you with an overview of Ethernet LAN technologies, primarily switches and their operation. You will learn about Media Access Control (MAC) addresses, switching technologies, Spanning Tree Protocol (STP), and configuration of Cisco Catalyst switches.

The ICND and CCNA exam tests your knowledge of MAC addresses and spanning tree. You must know how many bits are in a MAC address and what the broadcast MAC address is. You must also know spanning tree inside and out. You should know how root bridges, root ports, and designated ports are chosen. This knowledge is essential not only for the ICND and CCNA tests but also for when you are out in the field. Spanning tree is important because its main purpose is to find redundant links in a Layer 2 network and block them. Network administrators might say, "Why make redundant links? Why not use a single link?" The main reason to use redundant links in a Layer 2 network is for availability and redundancy. When you're dealing with an Enterprise LAN, network availability is crucial. You do not want your network going down because one link failed. This is why many network designers incorporate redundant links in a LAN: If one link fails, the other link takes over. Because of the extra link in a network, you must understand how spanning tree handles a failed link and convergence time.

New to the ICND and CCNA exams is the Catalyst 2950 switch. The Catalyst 2950 is a line of fixed-configuration, stackable, and standalone switches that provide Fast Ethernet and Gigabit Ethernet connectivity. They can provide quality of service (QoS) and security filtering. This chapter covers configuring the Catalyst 1900 and 2950 switches.

Question 1

What is carrier sense multiple access collision detect (CSMA/CD)?

Question 2

What are MAC addresses?

Question 1 Answer

CSMA/CD describes the Ethernet access method. In CSMA/CD, many stations can transmit on the same cable, and no station has priority over any other. Before a station transmits, it listens on the wire (carrier sense) to make sure that no other station is transmitting. If no other station is transmitting, the station transmits across the wire. If a collision occurs, the transmitting stations detect the collision and run a backoff algorithm. The backoff algorithm is a random amount of time each station waits before retransmitting.

Question 2 Answer

For computers to identify each other on the data link layer, they need a MAC address (hardware address). All devices on a LAN must have a unique MAC address. A MAC address is a 48-bit (six-octet) address burned into a network interface card. The first three octets (24 bits) of the MAC address indicate the vendor that manufactured the card. This is called the Organization Unique Identifier (OUI) and is assigned to the vendor. The last three octets of the MAC address are the unique host address assigned by the vendor. An example of a MAC address is 00-80-C6-E7-9C-EF.

Question 3

What are the three types of LAN traffic?

Configuring
Catalyst Switch
Operations

Question 4

What are unicast frames?

Configuring
Catalyst Switch
Operations

Question 3 Answer

The three types of LAN traffic are

- Unicasts
- Broadcasts
- Multicasts

Question 4 Answer

Unicast frames are the most common type of LAN traffic. A unicast frame is a frame intended for only one host. In unicast frames, the only station that processes the frame is the station that has its own MAC address in the destination portion of the packet.

Question 5
What are broadcast frames?

Question 6
What is the destination address of broadcast frames?

Question 5 Answer

Broadcast frames are frames intended for everyone. Stations view broadcast frames as public service announcements. All stations receive and process broadcast frames. In large networks, broadcasts can cause serious performance degradation in network hosts.

Question 6 Answer

The destination address of broadcast frames (Layer 2 broadcast addresses) is FF-FF-FF-FF-FF-FF, or all 1s in binary.

Question 7

What are multicast frames?

Question 8

What happens when you segment the network with hubs/repeaters?

Question 7 Answer

Multicast frames address a group of devices that have a common interest. These frames allow the source to send only one copy of the frame on the network even though it is intended for several stations. Only stations that have a card that is configured by software to receive multicast frames for a particular multicast group can process a frame to that multicast address; all other stations discard multicast frames. An example of a multicast frame is 01:00:5E:01:01:01. The 01 at the beginning of the address signifies that it is an Ethernet multicast address.

Question 8 Answer

Because hubs and repeaters operate at the physical layer of the OSI model, segmenting a network with these devices appears as an extension to the physical cable. Hubs and repeaters are transparent to devices. They are unintelligent devices. All devices that connect to a hub/repeater share the same bandwidth. Hubs/repeaters create a single broadcast and collision domain.

Question 9

What is the advantage of segmenting a network with bridges/switches?

Question 10

What is the difference between bridges and switches?

Question 9 Answer

Bridges/switches operate at Layer 2 of the OSI model and filter by MAC address. Each port on a bridge/switch provides full, dedicated bandwidth and creates a single collision domain. Because bridges/switches operate at Layer 2 of the OSI model, they cannot filter broadcasts, and they create a single broadcast domain.

NOTE

Remember that switches create more collision domains and fewer collisions.

Question 10 Answer

Bridges and switches function the same way; the only difference is in how they are implemented. Bridges are implemented by software and usually have a couple of network ports. Switches are implemented in hardware by ASIC chips and have many ports.

Question 11

What are the advantages and disadvantages of segmenting a LAN with routers?

Question 12

How many bytes is the Maximum Transmission Unit (MTU) for an Ethernet frame?

Question 11 Answer

An advantage of segmenting a LAN with routers is that each interface on a router creates a single broadcast and collision domain. Routers operate at Layer 3 of the OSI model and do not propagate broadcasts. Some disadvantages are that routers are not transparent and are implemented in software, thus introducing latency in the network.

NOTE

With today's faster and more powerful routers, latency is not often an issue.

Question 12 Answer

The MTU for an Ethernet frame is 1500 bytes. You will notice that some publications state that the MTU for Ethernet is 1518 bytes. This is correct also. But what is the true answer? The MTU for Ethernet, including the header, source and destination address, data, and CRC, is 1518 bytes. The MTU for the data portion of the frame is 1500 bytes.

Question 13

What three major functions do Layer 2 switches provide?

Question 14

What are the three switching methods (frame transmission modes) in Cisco Catalyst switches?

Question 13 Answer

The three major functions that Layer 2 switches provide are

- Address learning
- Packet forwarding/filtering
- Loop avoidance by spanning tree

Question 14 Answer

The three frame operating modes to handle frame switching are

- Store-and-forward
- Cut-through
- Fragment-free

NOTE

Remember these switching methods are modes that determine how the entire switch handles frame switching. They are not operating modes for ports.

Question 15

What is the Cisco Catalyst store-and-forward switching method?

Question 16

What is the Cisco Catalyst cut-through switching method?

Question 15 Answer

In the store-and-forward switching method, the switch's incoming interface receives the entire frame before it forwards it. The switch computes the cyclic redundancy check (CRC) to make sure the frame is not bad. If the frame is good, the switch forwards it. If the CRC is bad, the switch drops it. If the frame is a runt (less than 64 bytes, including the CRC) or a giant (more than 1518 bytes, including the CRC), the switch discards it. Because the switch stores the frame before forwarding it, latency is introduced in the switch. Latency through the switch varies with the frame's size.

Question 16 Answer

In cut-through switching mode, the switch checks only the frame's destination address and immediately begins forwarding the frame out the appropriate port. Because the switch checks only the destination address in only the header and not the entire frame, the switch forwards a collision frame or a frame that has a bad CRC.

Question 17

What is the Cisco Catalyst fragment-free switching method?

Question 18

Transparent bridging (switching) provides five bridging functions to determine what to do when it receives a frame. What are these five processes?

Question 17 Answer

Also known as modified cut-through, fragment-free switching checks the first 64 bytes before forwarding the frame. If the frame is less than 64 bytes, the switch discards it. Ethernet specifications state that collisions should be detected during the first 64 bytes of the frame. By reading the first 64 bytes of the frame, the switch can filter most collisions, although late collisions are still possible.

Question 18 Answer

The five processes are

- Learning
- Flooding
- Filtering
- Forwarding
- Aging

Question 19

In transparent bridging, what is the learning process?

Question 20

In transparent bridging, what is the flooding process?

Question 19 Answer

The first process a bridge goes through when it is powered on is the learning process. The MAC address table on the bridge contains no entries, and the bridge goes through the learning process to record all workstations on every interface. In the learning process, the bridge records the source MAC address and source port number in the MAC address table every time it sees a frame. The switch is always in the learning process because it always learns source MAC addresses and updates the aging timers in its CAM table.

Question 20 Answer

When a bridge is first turned on, it has no MAC address in its table. When a switch receives a unicast frame, it knows the source address and port from which the unicast frame came, but no entry exists in its table for the destination address. This is called an unknown unicast frame. When a switch receives an unknown unicast frame, it sends the frame out all forwarding interfaces on the bridge except the interface that received the frame. This process is the flooding process.

Question 21

Describe the filtering process in transparent bridges.

Question 22

In transparent bridging, what is the forwarding process?

Question 21 Answer

The filtering process occurs when the source and destination addresses reside on the same interface on the bridge. Because the bridge does not need to forward a frame in which the destination and source addresses reside on the same interface, it filters the frame and discards it.

Question 22 Answer

The forwarding process occurs when a switch receives a unicast frame and has an entry of the destination address in its MAC table. The switch then forwards the frame to the interface where that destination address resides.

Question 23

What is the default aging timer in transparent bridges?

Question 24

What is the Spanning Tree Protocol (STP)?

Question 23 Answer

The default aging timer is 300 seconds (5 minutes).

Every time a bridge learns a source address, it time-stamps the entry. When the bridge sees a frame from this source, it updates the time stamp. If the bridge does not hear from the source for a specific amount of time (called the aging timer), the bridge deletes the entry from its MAC address table. This process is the aging process.

Question 24 Answer

STP is a loop-prevention bridge-to-bridge protocol. Its main purpose is to dynamically maintain a loop-free network. It does this by sending out Bridge Protocol Data Units (BPDUs), discovering any loops in the topology, and blocking one or more redundant links.

Question 25

How does STP maintain a loop-free network?

Question 26

What two key concepts does STP calculation use to create a loop-free topology?

Question 25 Answer

STP maintains a loop-free network by

- Electing a root bridge
- Electing a root port on each nonroot bridge
- Electing designated ports on each segment
- Putting in the blocking state any redundant port that is not a root port or designated port

Question 26 Answer

The two key concepts that STP uses to calculate a loop-free topology are

- Bridge ID (BID)
- Path cost

Question 27

In spanning tree, what is a Bridge ID (BID)?

Question 28

What is the default bridge priority in a Bridge ID for all Cisco switches?

Question 27 Answer

A BID is an 8-byte field that is composed of the bridge's 6-byte MAC address and a 2-byte bridge priority.

Question 28 Answer

32,768

Question 29

In spanning tree, what is path cost?

Question 30

What is the spanning tree path cost for each of the following?

10 Mbps
100 Mbps
1 Gbps

Question 29 Answer

Path cost is a calculation based on the link's bandwidth. It is a value assigned to each port that is based on the port's speed.

Question 30 Answer

The path costs are as follows:

10 Mbps	100
100 Mbps	19
1 Gbps	4

Question 31

When calculating a loop-free environment, spanning tree uses a four-step decision sequence to determine which switch will be the root bridge and which ports will be in the forwarding or blocking state. What are these four steps?

Question 32

How do bridges pass spanning tree information between themselves?

Question 31 Answer

The four-step decision sequence that spanning tree uses to determine the root bridge and which port will forward is as follows:

Step 1   The lowest root BID

Step 2   The lowest path cost to the root bridge

Step 3   The lowest sender BID

Step 4   The lowest port ID

Question 32 Answer

Bridges pass STP information using special frames called Bridge Protocol Data Units (BPDUs). Every time a bridge receives a BPDU, it compares it with all received BPDUs as well as with the BPDU that would be sent on that port. The bridge checks the BPDU against the four-step sequence described in Question 31 to see if it has a lower value than the existing BPDU saved for that port.

Question 33

How often do bridges send BPDUs out active ports?

Question 34

In STP, how is a root bridge elected?

Question 33 Answer

The default time that bridges send BPDUs out active ports is every 2 seconds.

NOTE

All ports on a switch listen for BPDUs in case there is a topology change.

Question 34 Answer

In STP, the bridge with the lowest BID is elected the root bridge. All ports on the root bridge are placed in the forwarding state and are called designated ports.

The BID is 8 bytes and is composed two fields: the default priority of 32,768 (2 bytes) and a MAC address (6 bytes). Because all Cisco switches use the default priority, the switch with the lowest MAC address is elected the root bridge. As a rule of thumb, lower always wins in spanning tree.

Question 35

After bridges elect the root bridge, what is the next step in the spanning tree process?

Question 36

How do nonroot bridges decide which port they will elect as a root port?

Question 35 Answer

After electing the root bridge, switches elect root ports. A root port is the port on nonroot bridges that has the lowest cost to the root bridge. Every nonroot bridge must select one root port.

Question 36 Answer

Nonroot bridges use root path cost to determine which port will be the root port. Root path cost is the cumulative cost of all links to the root bridge. The port with the lowest root path cost is elected the bridge's root port and is placed in the forwarding state.

Question 37

What is the difference between path cost and root path cost?

Configuring Catalyst Switch Operations

Question 38

If a nonroot bridge has two redundant ports with the same root path cost, how does the bridge choose which port will be the root port?

Configuring Catalyst Switch Operations

Question 37 Answer

Path cost is the value assigned to each port. It is added to BPDUs received on that port to calculate the root path cost.

Root path cost is defined as the cumulative cost to the root bridge. In a BPDU, this is the value transmitted in the cost field. In a bridge, this value is calculated by adding the receiving port's path cost to the value contained in the BPDU.

NOTE

This answer was taken from *Cisco LAN Switching* (published by Cisco Press).

Question 38 Answer

If a nonroot bridge has redundant ports with the same root path cost, the deciding factor is the port with the lower port ID (port number). For example, port number 5 is preferred over port number 7.

Question 39

After the root bridge and root ports are selected, the last step in spanning tree is to elect designated ports. How do bridges elect designated ports?

Question 40

If a bridge is faced with a tie in electing designated ports, how does it decide which port will be the designated port?

Question 39 Answer

In spanning tree, each segment in a bridged network has one designated port. This port is a single port that both sends and receives traffic to and from that segment and the root bridge. All other ports are placed in a blocking state. This ensures that only one port on any segment can send and receive traffic to and from the root bridge, ensuring a loop-free topology. The bridge containing the designated port for a segment is called the designated bridge for that segment. Designated ports are chosen based on cumulative root path cost to the root bridge.

NOTE

Every active port on the root bridge becomes a designated port.

Question 40 Answer

In the event of a tie, STP uses the four-step decision process discussed in Question 31. It first looks for the BPDU with the lowest BID; this is always the root bridge. If the switch is not the root bridge, it moves to the next step: the BPDU with the lowest path cost to the root bridge. If both paths are equal, STP looks for the BPDU with the lowest sender BID. If these are equal, STP uses the link with the lowest port ID as the final tiebreaker.

Question 41

What are the five spanning tree port states?

Question 42

What is STP blocking state?

Question 41 Answer

The five spanning tree port states are

- Blocking

- Listening

- Learning

- Forwarding

- Disabled

NOTE

Remember that root and designated ports forward traffic and that nondesignated ports block traffic but still listen for BPDUs.

Question 42 Answer

When a switch starts, all ports are in blocking state. This is to prevent any loops in the network. If there is a better path to the root bridge, the port remains in blocking state. Ports in blocking state cannot send or receive traffic, but they can receive BPDUs.

Question 43
What is STP listening state?

Question 44
What is STP learning state?

Question 43 Answer

Ports transition from a blocking state to a listening state. In this state, no user data is passed. The port only listens for BPDUs. After listening for 15 seconds (if the bridge does not find a better path), the port moves to the next state, learning state.

Question 44 Answer

In STP learning state, no user data is passed. The port quietly builds its bridging table. The default time in learning state is 15 seconds.

Question 45
What is STP forwarding state?

Question 46
What is STP forward delay?

Question 45 Answer

After the default time in learning state is up, the port moves to forwarding state. In forwarding state, the port sends and receives data.

Question 46 Answer

The forward delay is the time it takes a port to move from listening state to learning state or from learning state to forwarding state. The default time is 30 seconds.

Question 47

What is the hello time in STP timers?

Question 48

What is the Max Age timer?

Question 47 Answer

The hello time is the time interval between the sending of BPDUs. The default time is 2 seconds.

Question 48 Answer

The Max Age timer is how long a bridge stores a BPDU before discarding it. The default time is 20 seconds (ten missed hello intervals).

Question 49

What is the default amount of time a port takes to transition from blocking state to forwarding state?

Question 50

What does STP do when it detects a topology change in the network because of a bridge or link failure?

Question 49 Answer

The default amount of time a port takes to transition from blocking state to forwarding state is 50 seconds: 20 seconds for Max Age, 15 seconds for listening, and 15 seconds for learning.

Question 50 Answer

If spanning tree detects a change in the network because of a bridge or link failure, at least one bridge interface changes from blocking state to forwarding state, or vice versa.

Question 51

What are the five port roles in Rapid Spanning Tree Protocol (RSTP)?

Question 52

On Cisco Catalyst 1900 series and 2950 series switches, what are the default duplex settings for 10BASE-T/100BASE-T ports, default switching mode, and default protocols?

Question 51 Answer

The five port roles in RSTP are

- **Root**— A forwarding port elected for the STP topology.

- **Designated**—A forwarding port elected for every switched LAN segment.

- **Alternate**—A secondary (alternate) path to the root bridge.

- **Backup**—A backup for the designated port. Backup ports exist only where two ports are connected in a loopback by a point-to-point link or bridge with two or more connections to a shared LAN segment.

- **Disabled**—A port that is not active in the operation of spanning tree.

Question 52 Answer

The factory default settings for Catalyst 1900 series and 2950 series switches are as follows:

- IP address—0.0.0.0

- CDP enabled

- Switching mode—Fragment-free

- 10BASE-T ports—Half-duplex

- 100BASE-T ports—Autonegotiate

- Spanning tree enabled

- No console password

Question 53

What are the two configuration modes in a Catalyst 1900/2950 switch?

Question 54

How do you configure an IP address and subnet mask on Catalyst 1900 and 2950 series switches?

Question 53 Answer

Configuring a Catalyst 1900/2950 series switch is similar to configuring a router. The two configuration modes available are global configuration mode and interface configuration mode.

Question 54 Answer

To configure an IP address and subnet mask on Catalyst 1900 and 2950 series switches, use the **ip address** *address mask* global configuration command:

```
Cat1900(config)#ip address 192.168.0.2 255.255.255.0
```

NOTE

The 2950 switch requires you to enter the IP address in the logical VLAN 1 interface.

Question 55

How do you configure a default gateway on Cisco Catalyst 1900 and 2950 series switches?

Question 56

How do you view the IP address and default gateway on Catalyst 1900 and 2950 series switches?

Question 55 Answer

To configure a default gateway on Catalyst 1900 and 2950 series switches, use the ip **default-gateway** *ip-address* global configuration command. The following example configures the switch to use IP address 192.168.0.1 as its default gateway:

```
Cat1900(config)#ip default-gateway 192.168.0.1
```

NOTE

To remove the default gateway, use the **no ip default-gateway** command. Configuring a default gateway on a switch does not allow it to route traffic to locations. The default gateway on a switch is used for management purposes so that an administrator can connect to the device from a different subnet.

Question 56 Answer

To view the IP address and default gateway on the 1900 series switch, use the **show ip** command:

```
Cat1900#show ip
IP Address: 192.168.0.2
Subnet Mask: 255.255.255.0
Default Gateway: 192.168.0.1
Management VLAN:   1
<Text ommited>
```

To view the IP address and default gateway on the 2950 series switch, use the **show interface vlan** *vlan-number* interface command:

```
2950-Core#sh int vlan1
Vlan1 is up, line protocol is up
  Hardware is CPU Interface, address is 0006.52ba.3540
  (bia 0006.52ba.3540)
  Internet address is 10.1.1.28/8
  MTU 1500 bytes, BW 1000000 Kbit, DLY 10 usec,
    reliability 255/255, txload 1/255, rxload 1/255
  Encapsulation ARPA, loopback not set
<Text omitted>
```

Question 57

How do you change the duplex mode on Catalyst 1900 and 2950 series switches?

Question 58

How do you verify the duplex setting on Catalyst 1900 and 2950 series switches?

Question 57 Answer

To change the duplex mode on Catalyst 1900 and 2950 series switches, use the **duplex {auto | full | full-flow-control | half}** command.

The following example changes the duplex speed for Ethernet interface 1 on the switch to full duplex:

```
Cat1900(config)#interface e0/1
Cat1900(config-if)#duplex full
```

NOTE

The command to change the duplex is the same for the 1900 and 2950 series switches. The only difference is that the 2950 switch does not have the **full-flow-control** option.

The default duplex setting for Fast Ethernet 10/100/1000 is **auto**.

Question 58 Answer

To verify the duplex setting of the interfaces on Catalyst 1900 and 2950 switches, use the **show interface** *module/port* EXEC command. The following shows the duplex setting of **full** on a 2950 switch:

```
2950-Core#sh int f0/2
FastEthernet0/2 is up, line protocol is up
  Hardware is Fast Ethernet, address is 0006.52ba.3542
  (bia 0006.52ba.3542)
  MTU 1500 bytes, BW 100000 Kbit, DLY 1000 usec,
    reliability 255/255, txload 1/255, rxload 1/255
  Encapsulation ARPA, loopback not set
  Keepalive set (10 sec)
  Full-duplex, 100Mb/s
  input flow-control is off, output flow-control is off
  ARP type: ARPA, ARP Timeout 04:00:00
<Text ommited>
```

NOTE

On the 1900 series switch, the **show interface** command shows not only the duplex settings but also the spanning tree state (if the port is forwarding or disabled).

Question 59

What command can you use to check for frame check sequence (FCS) or late collision errors?

Configuring Catalyst Switch Operations

Question 60

How do you display the MAC address table on Catalyst 1900 and 2950 series switches?

Configuring Catalyst Switch Operations

Question 59 Answer

The **show interface** *type module/port* EXEC command displays FCS or
late collision errors. The following shows the interface of a Catalyst
1900 switch:

```
Cat1900#show interface e0/1
<Output omitted>
Receive Statistics                     Transmit Statistics
------------------------------         ------------------------------
---
Total good frames            0    Total frames                 0
Total octets                 0    Total octets                 0
Broadcast/multicast frames   0    Broadcast/multicast frames   0
Broadcast/multicast octets   0    Broadcast/multicast octets   0
Good frames forwarded        0    Deferrals                    0
Frames filtered              0    Single collisions            0
Errors:                           Errors:
  FCS errors                 0      Late collisions            0
  Alignment errors           0      Excessive deferrals        0
  Giant frames               0      Jabber errors              0
  Address violations         0      Other transmit errors      0
```

NOTE

If you have a half-duplex port on one end and a full-duplex
port on the other end, late collision errors and FCS errors are
caused at the full-duplex end. To avoid this, manually set both
ends to the same duplex settings.

Question 60 Answer

The **show mac-address-table** EXEC command displays the MAC
address table for the 1900 and 2950 series switches and also tells
you whether the MAC address entry is dynamic, permanent, or
static. Here's an example:

```
Cat1900#show mac-address-table
Address          Dest Interface   Type      Source Interface List
-----------------------------------------------------------------
--
0080.C6E7.9CEF   Ethernet 0/21    Dynamic   All
0030.80EF.988C   Ethernet 0/22    Dynamic   All
0040.05A2.5E92   Ethernet 0/11    Dynamic   All

2950-Core#sh mac-address-table
          Mac Address Table
-------------------------------------------------

Vlan   Mac Address      Type      Ports
----   -----------      ----      -----
   1   0002.b3b4.0e4c   DYNAMIC   Gi0/1
   1   0006.52bb.6240   DYNAMIC   Gi0/1
   1   0006.52bb.6259   DYNAMIC   Gi0/1
   1   0009.7c73.d419   DYNAMIC   Gi0/2
   1   0060.b057.8577   DYNAMIC   Fa0/11
   1   0090.27f7.0d25   DYNAMIC   Fa0/7
   1   00a0.8e1c.b47c   DYNAMIC   Fa0/1
Total Mac Addresses for this criterion: 9
```

Question 61

What are dynamic addresses on a Catalyst switch?

Question 62

What are permanent MAC addresses on a Catalyst switch?

Question 61 Answer

Dynamic addresses are addresses that the switch learns about dynamically through the learning process. If the switch does not see a MAC address for a certain amount of time, it ages the addresses out of the CAM table.

Question 62 Answer

Permanent MAC addresses are addresses that have been manually entered by an administrator and are not aged out by the switch's age timer.

Question 63

On Catalyst 1900 and 2950 series switches, how do you make a MAC address permanent?

Configuring
Catalyst Switch
Operations

Question 64

What is the maximum number of MAC addresses Catalyst 1900 and 2950 series switches can store in their MAC address tables?

Configuring
Catalyst Switch
Operations

Question 63 Answer

To make a MAC address permanent on a 1900 switch, use the **mac-address-table permanent** *mac-address type module/port* global command. The following example makes MAC address 0080.C6E7.9CEF permanent in the CAM table for port 0/21:

```
Cat1900(config)#mac-address-table permanent 0080.C6E7.9CEF
   Ethernet 0/21
```

To make a MAC address permanent for a 2950 switch, use the **mac-address-table static** *mac-address* {**vlan** *vlan-id*} **interface** *int-number* global command. The following example tells the switch to forward all traffic for MAC address 0080.C6E7.9CEF to interface F0/23 on VLAN 1:

```
2950-Core(config)#mac-address-table static 0080.c6e7.9cef
   vlan 1 int f0/23n
```

NOTE

To remove the static MAC address, issue the same command with a **no** in front of it.

Question 64 Answer

The number of MAC addresses a Catalyst switch can store varies from model to model. The 1900 switch can store 1024 MAC addresses in its CAM table, and the 2950 switch can store 8192 MAC addresses in its CAM table. When the CAM table is full, the switch floods out all new MAC addresses.

Question 65

What are static MAC addresses in Catalyst 1900 and 2950 series switches?

Question 66

How do you restrict a MAC address to a specific port on Catalyst 1900 and 2950 series switches?

Question 65 Answer

On Catalyst 1900 and 2950 series switches, static addresses allow you to restrict a MAC address to a specific port.

Question 66 Answer

To restrict a MAC address to a specific port on a 1900 switch, use the **mac-address-table restricted static** *mac-address type module/port src-if-list* global command:

```
Cat1900(config)#mac-address-table restricted static
    aaaa.aaaa.aaaa e0/1
```

This example restricts MAC address aaaa.aaaa.aaaa to Ethernet port 0/1.

To restrict a MAC address to a specific port on a 2590 switch, use the **mac-address-table secure** *mac-address* **interface [vlan** *vlan-id]* command.

```
2950-Core(config)#mac-address-table secure aaaa.aaaa.aaaa int
    f0/23 vlan 1
```

Question 67

On Catalyst 1900 and 2950 series switches, how do you configure a port to have port security?

Question 68

How do you verify whether a port has port security enabled on it?

Question 67 Answer

To enable port security, you must first enable port security on the interface by entering the **port secure** interface command and then enter the **port secure [max-mac-count** *count*] interface command. The *count* value in **max-mac-count** lets you specify the number of MAC addresses allowed on that port. The following example enables port security to allow 100 MAC addresses on a port on a 1900 switch:

```
Cat1900(config-if)#port secure
Cat1900(config-if)#port secure max-mac-count 100
```

To enable port security on a 2950 switch, you first have to enter switchport access mode by entering the **switchport mode access** interface command. You then need to enable port security on the interface by entering **switchport port-security** followed by the **switchport port-security maximum** value interface command to restrict the number of MAC addresses. For example:

```
2950-Core(config)#interface fastethernet0/1
2950-Core(config-if)#switchport mode access
2950-Core(config-if)#switchport port-security
2950-Core(config-if)#switchport port-security maximum 100
```

NOTE

The number of MAC addresses on a secure port can range from 1 to 132.

Question 68 Answer

The **show mac-address-table security** command displays the port security configurations on 1900 and 2950 switches:

```
Cat1900#show mac-address-table security
Action upon address violation : Suspend

2950-Core#show port-security interface fastethernet0/1
Port Security: Enabled
Port status: SecureUp
Violation mode: Shutdown
Maximum MAC Addresses :50
Total MAC Addresses: 11
Configured MAC Addresses: 0
Sticky MAC Addresses :11
Aging time: 20 mins
Aging type: Inactivity
SecureStatic address aging: Enabled
Security Violation count: 0
```

Question 69

How do you reset Catalyst 1900 and 2950 series switches to their factory defaults?

Question 69 Answer

To clear a switch's NVRAM, thus restoring it to factory defaults, use the following commands:

- Catalyst 1900—**delete nvram**
- Catalyst 2950—**erase startup-config**

Chapter 2

Extending Switched Networks with VLANs

In the past, network designers broke up large Layer 2 networks with routers to implement smaller broadcast domains. This was fine in the late 1980s and early 1990s, but with the introduction of multimedia applications and network-intensive services, routers could not provide the speed network designers needed. With switches becoming faster and providing routing functions (implemented in hardware), virtual LANs (VLANs) have become a popular way to break up broadcast domains. This is because switches are faster and cheaper to implement than routers. VLANs also can span multiple switches, allowing a network administrator to have a broadcast domain span different geographic locations. This is impossible to do with routers. This chapter covers VLANs, VLAN trunking, the VLAN management protocol, VTP, and the important topics needed to pass the ICND and CCNA exams.

Question 1

What are VLANs?

Question 2

**What are the four characteristics of a typical
VLAN setup?**

Question 1 Answer

VLANs are broadcast domains in a Layer 2 network. Each broadcast domain is like a distinct virtual bridge within the switch. Each virtual bridge you create in a switch defines a broadcast domain. By default, traffic from one VLAN cannot pass to another VLAN. Each user in a VLAN is also in the same IP subnet. Each switch port can belong to only one VLAN.

Question 2 Answer

Here are the four characteristics of a typical VLAN setup:

- Each logical VLAN is like a separate physical bridge.
- VLANs can span multiple switches.
- Trunks carry traffic for multiple VLANs.
- Trunk links use special encapsulation to distinguish between different VLANs.

Question 3
What are trunk links?

Question 4
What are the two methods you can use to assign a port to a VLAN?

Question 3 Answer

By default, each port on a switch can belong to only one VLAN. For devices that are in VLANs (that span multiple switches) to talk to other devices in the same VLAN, you must use trunking or have a dedicated port for each VLAN. Trunk links allow the switch to carry multiple VLANs across a single link.

NOTE

On a Catalyst 1900 switch, trunk links can be configured only on Fast Ethernet ports.

Question 4 Answer

The two methods to assign a port to a VLAN are

- Statically
- Dynamically

Statically assigning ports to a VLAN is a manual process performed by the administrator.

Assigning VLANs dynamically is done using a VLAN Membership Policy Server (VMPS). The VMPS contains a database that maps MAC addresses to VLAN membership. A dynamic port can belong to only one VLAN at a time. A Catalyst 5000 switch can be configured to be a VMPS.

Question 5

What two trunking protocols are supported by Cisco 1900 and 2950 series switches?

Extending Switched Networks with VLANs

Question 6

Describe 802.1Q tagging.

Extending Switched Networks with VLANs

Question 5 Answer

The 1900 series switch supports ISL, and the 2950 series switch supports IEEE 802.1Q.

NOTE

Both ISL and IEEE 802.1Q tagging are explicit tagging, meaning that the frame is tagged with VLAN information explicitly.

Question 6 Answer

802.1Q tagging provides a standard method of identifying frames that belong to a particular VLAN. It does this by using an internal process that modifies the existing Ethernet frame with the VLAN identification. Because 802.1Q modifies the existing frame, the identification process can work on both access links and trunk links; this is because the frame appears as a regular Ethernet packet.

NOTE

An access link has only one VLAN assigned to it.

Question 7

What is per-VLAN Spanning Tree (PVST+)?

Question 8

What is Inter-Switch Link (ISL)?

Question 7 Answer

Developed by Cisco, PVST+ runs one instance of the Spanning Tree Protocol per VLAN, allowing you to specify a different root bridge for each VLAN to enable optimal traffic flow in your network.

Question 8 Answer

ISL is a Cisco-proprietary protocol used to interconnect switches that have multiple VLANs. It maintains VLAN information as traffic goes between switches, allowing the traffic to enter the correct VLAN. ISL operates in a point-to-point environment.

Question 9

At which layer of the OSI model does ISL function?

Extending Switched Networks with VLANs

Question 10

What type of tagging method does ISL use?

Extending Switched Networks with VLANs

Question 9 Answer

ISL functions at Layer 2 of the OSI model. It encapsulates a data frame with a new ISL header and CRC. Because ISL operates at Layer 2 of the OSI model, it is protocol-independent.

Question 10 Answer

Many network professionals refer to the way ISL tags frames as an external tagging mechanism. This is because ISL encapsulates each frame and does not modify the original packet.

Question 11

How many extra bytes does ISL add to an existing Ethernet frame?

Question 12

What is VTP?

Question 11 Answer

ISL adds a 26-byte ISL header and a 4-byte CRC to each frame, extending each Ethernet frame by 30 bytes. Because ISL extends the Ethernet frame, only ISL-aware devices can interpret the frame. This is because the new frame size violates the normal Ethernet MTU of 1518 bytes. ISL tagging is implemented in ASICs, so tagging is done at wire speed.

Question 12 Answer

VLAN Trunking Protocol (VTP) is a Layer 2 messaging protocol that maintains VLAN configuration consistency throughout a common administrative domain by managing VLAN additions, deletions, and name changes across multiple switches. Without VTP, you would have to add VLAN information to each switch in the network.

Question 13

What is a VTP domain?

Question 14

What are the three VTP modes?

Question 13 Answer

A VTP domain is one or more interconnected switches that share the same VTP environment. A switch can be in only one VTP domain, and all VLAN information is propagated to all switches in the same VTP domain.

Question 14 Answer

The three VTP modes are

- Server
- Client
- Transparent

Question 15

What is VTP server mode?

Extending Switched Networks with VLANs

Question 16

What is VTP client mode?

Extending Switched Networks with VLANs

Question 15 Answer

A switch in VTP server mode can add, delete, and modify VLANs and other configuration parameters for the entire VTP domain. It is the default mode for all Catalyst switches. VLAN configurations are saved in NVRAM. When you change VLAN configuration in server mode, the change is dynamically propagated to all switches in the VTP domain.

NOTE

Cisco recommends that you have one or two switches in VTP server mode on your network.

Question 16 Answer

In VTP client mode, a switch cannot create, delete, or modify VLANs. Also, a VTP client does not save VLAN information and configuration in NVRAM. In client and server modes, VLAN information is synchronized between switches in the VTP domain.

Question 17

What is VTP transparent mode?

Question 18

How often are VTP advertisements flooded throughout the management domain?

Question 17 Answer

In transparent mode, a switch can add, modify, and delete VLANs locally. A VTP transparent switch does not advertise its VLAN configuration and does not synchronize its VLAN configuration based on received advertisements. They affect only the local switch.

NOTE

In VTP version 2, transparent switches forward VTP advertisements they receive out their trunk ports.

Question 18 Answer

VTP advertisements are flooded throughout the management domain every 5 minutes or whenever a change occurs in VLAN configuration.

NOTE

VTP advertisements are flooded only across trunk links.

Question 19

What is VTP pruning?

Question 20

What is included in VTP advertisements?

Question 19 Answer

By default, a trunk link carries traffic for all VLANs in the VTP domain. Even if a switch does not have any ports in a specific VLAN, traffic for that VLAN is carried across the trunk link. VTP pruning uses VLAN advertisements to determine when a trunk connection is needlessly flooding traffic to a switch that has no ports in the particular VLAN. VTP pruning increases available bandwidth by restricting flooded traffic to trunk lines that the traffic must use to access the appropriate network devices. By default, VTP pruning is disabled.

Question 20 Answer

VTP advertisements include the following:

- VTP revision number
- VLAN names and numbers
- Information about switches that have ports assigned to each VLAN

Question 21

What is one of the most important components of the VTP advertisement?

Extending Switched Networks with VLANs

Question 22

On Catalyst 1900 and 2950 switches, how do you reset the revision number?

Extending Switched Networks with VLANs

Question 21 Answer

The revision number is one of the most important components of the VTP advertisement. Every time a VTP server modifies its VLAN configuration, it increments the configuration number by 1. The largest configuration number in the VTP domain contains the most current information. When a client receives a revision number higher than its current number, it updates its VLAN configuration.

Question 22 Answer

To reset the configuration numbers on a Catalyst 1900 and 2950, use the **delete vtp** privileged EXEC command, and then reset the switch.

NOTE

Resetting the configuration number ensures that a newly configured switch does not delete VLAN information when added to a network.

Question 23

What VLAN number are CDP and VTP advertisements sent across?

Question 24

What must you remember before you create VLANs on a Catalyst switch?

Question 23 Answer

CDP and VTP advertisements are sent on VLAN 1, which is also known as the management VLAN.

Question 24 Answer

Before you create VLANs on a Catalyst switch, the switch must be in VTP server mode or VTP transparent mode.

Question 25

How do you configure the VTP operation mode, VTP domain, and VTP password on a Catalyst 1900 switch?

Extending Switched Networks with VLANs

Question 26

How do you configure the VTP operation mode, VTP domain, and VTP password on a Catalyst 2950 switch?

Extending Switched Networks with VLANs

Question 25 Answer

To configure the VTP operation mode on a Catalyst 1900, use the **vtp [server | transparent | client]** global configuration command. To configure the VTP domain, use the **vtp domain** *domain-name* command. To configure the VTP password, use the **vtp password** *password* global command. The following example configures the switch as a VTP server and sets the VTP domain name as cisco and the VTP password as CCNA:

```
Cat1900(config)#vtp server
Cat1900(config)#vtp domain cisco
Cat1900(config)#vtp password CCNA
```

Question 26 Answer

To configure the VTP operation mode and domain name on a 2950 switch, you first need to enter VLAN configuration mode by entering the **vlan database** privileged EXEC command. After you are in VLAN configuration mode, you can set the VLAN mode with the **vtp [server | client | transparent]** command followed by **vtp domain** *domain-name* to configure the VTP domain and **vtp password** *password* to set the VTP password:

```
2950-Core#vlan database
2950-Core(vlan)#vtp [server | client | transparent]
2950-Core(vlan)#vtp domain cisco
2950-Core(vlan)#vtp password CCNA
```

Question 27

How do you enable VTP pruning on Catalyst 1900 and 2950 switches?

Question 28

What does the show vtp privileged EXEC command display?

Question 27 Answer

To enable pruning on a 1900 switch, use the **vtp pruning enable** global command.

To enable VTP pruning on a 2950 switch, use the **vtp pruning** VLAN database configuration command.

Question 28 Answer

The **show vtp** privileged EXEC command displays the following:

- VTP version
- The number of existing VLANs on a switch and the maximum number of locally supported VLANs
- VTP domain name, password, and operating mode
- Whether VTP pruning is enabled
- The last time the VLAN configuration was modified

```
Cat1900#show vtp
VTP version: 1
    Configuration revision: 0
    Maximum VLANs supported locally: 1005
    Number of existing VLANs: 5
    VTP domain name        : cisco
    VTP password           : cisco
    VTP operating mode     : Server
    VTP pruning mode       : Disabled
    VTP traps generation   : Enabled
    Configuration last modified by:
  192.168.0.2 at 00-00-0000 00:00:00
```

Question 29

How do you set an interface for 802.1Q trunking on a Catalyst 2950 switch?

Question 30

How do you set a Fast Ethernet interface on a 1900 switch to trunk mode?

Question 29 Answer

The **switchport mode trunk** interface command enables an interface for 802.1Q trunking.

NOTE

The Catalyst 2950 supports only 802.1Q trunking, not ISL trunking. The Catalyst 1900 switch supports only ISL trunking.

Question 30 Answer

To set a Fast Ethernet interface to trunk mode for a 1900 switch, use the **trunk [on | off | desirable | auto | nonegotiate]** interface configuration command. The options for the **trunk** command are as follows:

- **on**—Configures the link in permanent trunking mode.

- **off**—Disables trunking on the interface if it is on.

- **desirable**—Tells the port to enable trunking if the opposite switch port that is connected is set to **on, desirable,** or **auto**.

- **auto**—Enables trunking on the port if the opposite switch port is set to **on** or **desirable**.

- **nonegotiate**—Configures the trunk to be in permanent ISL trunk mode with no negotiation.

Here's an example:

```
Cat1900(config)#int f0/27
Cat1900(config-if)#trunk on
```

NOTE

Remember that the Catalyst 1900 switch supports only ISL and can trunk only on Fast Ethernet interfaces.

Question 31

What command do you use to add a VLAN on Catalyst 1900 and 2950 series switches?

Question 32

After you create your VLANs on a switch, how do you add a port to a VLAN?

Question 31 Answer

To add a VLAN on a 1900 switch, use the **vlan** *vlan#* [**name** *vlan-name*] configuration command. The following example adds VLAN 10 with a name of Sales:

```
Cat1900(config)#vlan 10 name Sales
```

To add a VLAN on a 2950 switch, you first enter VLAN configuration mode and then use the **vlan** *vlan#* [**name** *vlan-name*] command. The following example adds VLAN 20 with the name of Engineering:

```
2950-Core#vlan database
2950-Core(vlan)#vlan 20 name Engineering
2950-Core(vlan)#exit
```

Question 32 Answer

To add a port to a VLAN on a Catalyst 1900 switch, use the **vlan-membership** {**static** {*vlan-number*} | **dynamic**} interface configuration command. The following example adds port 4 to VLAN 10:

```
Cat1900(config)#int e0/4
Cat1900(config-if)#vlan-membership static 10
```

To add a port to a VLAN on a Catalyst 2950 switch, use the **switchport access vlan** *vlan#* interface command. The following adds port f0/21 to VLAN 20:

```
2950-Core#int f0/21
2950-Core(config-if)#switchport access vlan 20
```

NOTE

There's no way to add multiple ports to a VLAN at the same time through the command line. You can, however, use the menu options on the Catalyst 1900 switch to assign multiple ports to a VLAN at the same time. Also, all ports belong to VLAN 1 by default.

Question 33

On a Catalyst 1900, how do you view trunk configuration?

Question 34

How do you view trunk information on a Catalyst 2950 switch?

Question 33 Answer

To view trunk configuration, use the **show trunk** [a | b] command, where **a** represents Fast Ethernet port 0/26 and **b** represents Fast Ethernet port 0/27. The following example shows that trunking is enabled on Fast Ethernet port 0/27:

```
Cat1900#show trunk b
DISL state: On, Trunking: On, Encapsulation type: ISL
```

Question 34 Answer

To view trunk information on a 2950 switch, use the **show interface** *interface* **switchport** command. This example shows the trunk information for interface fa0/23:

```
2950-Core#show interface fa0/23 switchport
Name: Fa0/23
Switchport: Enabled
Administrative mode: trunk
Operational Mode: trunk
```

Question 35

What Catalyst 1900 and 2950 command can you use to verify VLAN information?

Extending Switched Networks with VLANs

Question 36

How do you view what VLANs the ports on your switch belong to?

Extending Switched Networks with VLANs

Question 35 Answer

To verify VLAN information on a Catalyst 1900, use the **show vlan** *vlan-number* privileged EXEC command. The output in the following example shows the VLAN information for VLAN 10:

```
Cat1900#show vlan 10

VLAN Name          Status    Ports
--------------------------------
10   Sales         Enabled
--------------------------------

VLAN Type     SAID   MTU    Parent RingNo BridgeNo Stp  Trans1
     Trans2
----------------------------------------------------------------
10   Ethernet 100010 1500   0      1      1        Unkn 0      0
----------------------------------------------------------------
```

To view VLAN information on a 2950 switch, use the **show vlan id** *vlan#* command.

Question 36 Answer

To view what VLAN the ports on your switch belong to, use the **show vlan-membership** privileged EXEC command on a 1900 switch:

```
Cat1900#show vlan-membership
  Port  VLAN  Membership Type    Port  VLAN  Membership Type
  -----------------------------    -----------------------------
   1     1    Static             13    1     Static
   2     1    Static             14    1     Static
   3     1    Static             15    1     Static
   4    10    Static             16    1     Static
   5     1    Static             17    1     Static
   6    10    Static             18    1     Static
```

Use the **show vlan brief** command to see what VLANs the ports on your 2950 switch belong to:

```
2950-Core#sh vlan brief

VLAN Name                     Status    Ports
---- ------------------------ --------- ------------------------
1    default                  active    Fa0/1, Fa0/2, Fa0/3,
                                        Fa0/4, Fa0/5, Fa0/6,
                                        Fa0/7, Fa0/8, Fa0/9,
                                        Fa0/10, Fa0/11, Fa0/12,
                                        Fa0/13, Fa0/14, Fa0/15,
                                        Fa0/16, Fa0/17
20   Engineering              active    Fa0/18, Fa0/19, Fa0/20,
                                        Fa0/21, Fa0/22, Fa0/23,
                                        Fa0/24
```

Chapter 3

Determining IP Routes

Routers perform two main functions: switching and routing. The switching function is the process of moving packets from an inbound interface to an outbound interface. The switching function is also responsible for stripping the data link layer information from a packet it receives and encapsulating it with the data link layer information (MAC address) of the router's exiting interface. Routing is a relay function in which packets are forwarded from one location to another. The routing mechanism is responsible for learning and maintaining awareness of the network topology. A router functions as a hop-by-hop paradigm and performs best-effort packet delivery. The packet is delivered to the downstream router that the sending router feels is closest to the final destination. For a router to be an effective relay device, it must perform both routing and switching functions.

There are two ways a router learns about routes a packet must take: statically and dynamically. Static routes are entered manually by a network administrator. Dynamic routes are learned by a routing protocol. Routing protocols can be classified into two categories: interior and exterior. Interior routing protocols learn about routes and route packets within an autonomous system (AS). Exterior routing protocols learn about routes and route packets between autonomous systems. Routing protocols use metrics to determine what path is best for a packet to travel. A metric is a standard measurement, such as distance, used by routing protocols to determine the optimum path to a destination. Each routing protocol uses a different algorithm to determine its metric. This chapter focuses on the interior routing protocols covered on the ICND and CCNA exams.

Distance Vector Routing Protocols

RIP and IGRP are distance vector routing protocols. The name is derived from the fact that routes are advertised as vectors of distance and direction. Routers running distance vector protocols learn routes from neighboring routers' perspectives and then advertise the routes from their own perspective. Because each router depends on its neighbors for information, distance vector routing is sometimes called "routing by rumor." Routers running distance vector protocols store the route that has the best administrative distance and metric in its routing table. RIP and IGRP are also classful routing protocols. Classful routing protocols exchange routes to subnetworks in the same major network (Class A, B, or C). In other words, all networks in the internetwork must have the same subnet mask. This is because RIP and IGRP do not send the subnet mask in their routing updates, thus assuming that all networks use the same subnet mask assigned to the exiting interface.

Link-State Routing Protocols

Also known as shortest path first (SPF) protocols, link-state routing protocols learn about every router in an AS and flood information about the state of their directly connected links to each router in the AS. A link is an interface on the router. The link's state is a description of that interface. Link-state protocols use this information to build a link-state database that gives the router a picture of the network. Link-state protocols have fast convergence because of the link-state database. On the other hand, they require more CPU power and memory. OSPF is a very scalable link-state protocol. It is the interior routing protocol of choice in large internetworks. OSPF is scalable because larger networks can be divided into areas. Generally, each router in an area is concerned with the link state of the other routers in its area; it does not store the link states of routers in different areas in its link-state database, thus conserving resources. OSPF is considered a classless routing protocol; it sends information about the interface's subnet mask in its updates. The ICND and CCNA exams cover OSPF in a single area. OSPF in multiple areas is covered on the CCNP exams.

Hybrid Routing Protocols

Enhanced IGRP (EIGRP) is a hybrid routing protocol developed by Cisco. EIGRP makes decisions based on metric information it receives from neighbors, and it employs some of the mechanisms of link-state protocols. It establishes adjacencies with neighboring routers, sends only changes in its updates, and keeps a topology database of the network. EIGRP uses Diffusing Update Algorithm (DUAL) to achieve rapid convergence, conserve bandwidth, and support multiple network protocols.

Question 1

What must a router have to correctly route a packet?

Question 2

What are the three types of routes you can use in a Cisco router?

Question 1 Answer

A router needs the network address of the destination network and a routing table with valid information about the destination to correctly route a packet.

Question 2 Answer

The three types of routes are static, dynamic, and default.

Question 3

What is the difference between static and dynamic routes?

Determining IP
Routes

Question 4

How do you configure a static route on a Cisco router?

Determining IP
Routes

Question 3 Answer

Static routes are routes that an administrator manually enters into a router. Dynamic routes are routes that a router learns automatically through a routing protocol.

Question 4 Answer

To configure a static route on a Cisco router, enter the **ip route** *destination-network* [*mask*] {*next-hop-address* | *outbound-interface*} [*distance*] [*permanent*] global command. Here's an example:

```
RouterB(config)#ip route 172.17.0.0 255.255.0.0 172.16.0.1
```

This example instructs the router to route to 172.16.0.1 any packets that have a destination of 172.17.0.0 to 172.17.255.255.

Question 5

What is a default route?

Question 6

How do you configure the default route on a Cisco router?

Question 5 Answer

Also known as the gateway of last resort, a default route is a special type of static route with an all-0s network and network mask. The default route is used to direct any packets for which a next hop is not specifically listed in the routing table. By default, if a router receives a packet to a destination network that is not in its routing table, it drops the packet. When a default route is specified, the router does not drop the packet. Instead, it forwards the packet to the IP address specified in the default route.

Question 6 Answer

To configure a default route on a Cisco router, enter the following global configuration command:

```
ip route 0.0.0.0 0.0.0.0 [ip-address-of-the-next-hop-router
| outbound-interface]
```

For example:

```
RouterB(config)#ip route 0.0.0.0 0.0.0.0 172.16.0.2
```

NOTE

All Cisco routers before Cisco IOS software Release 12.0 are classful. They expect a default subnet mask on each interface of the router. If a router receives a packet for a destination subnet not in the routing table, the router forwards the packet to the best available major Class A, B, or C network. If the router does not have specific information about the major network, it drops the packet. When you are using an IOS version before Release 12.0 and are using a default route, you must use the **ip classless** global command so that the packets go to the default route.

Question 7

What is administrative distance?

Question 8

What are the three classes of routing protocols?

Question 7 Answer

Administrative distance (AD) is an integer from 0 to 255 that rates the trustworthiness of the source of the IP routing information. It is important only when a router learns about a destination route from more than one source. The path with the lower AD is the one given priority.

NOTE

If a routing protocol has multiple paths within the same routing protocol to the same destination, the metric is used as the tiebreaker. The route with the lowest metric is the path taken.

Question 8 Answer

The three classes of routing protocols are

- Distance vector
- Link-state
- Balanced hybrid

Distance vector protocols use a vector of distance and direction to find the best path, where distance is defined in terms of a metric and direction is defined as the next-hop router. Distance vector protocols broadcast the entire routing table at periodic intervals and are slow to converge because of hold-down timers. Examples include RIP and IGRP.

Link-state protocols use a topological database that is created on each router. This database keeps track of directly attached neighbors, the entire network, and the routing table. Link-state updates are typically multicast to all neighbors. (OSPF is a link-state protocol.)

Balanced hybrid protocols combine aspects of distance vector and link-state protocols. An example is EIGRP.

Question 9

What is the AD for each of the following?
- Directly connected interface
- Static route
- EIGRP
- IGRP
- OSPF
- RIP
- External EIGRP
- Unknown

Determining IP
Routes

Question 10

Name two classful routing protocols.

Determining IP
Routes

Question 9 Answer

The ADs are as follows:

- Directly connected interface   0
- Static route   1
- EIGRP   90
- IGRP   100
- OSPF   110
- RIP   120
- External EIGRP   170
- Unknown   255

Question 10 Answer

Two classful routing protocols are RIP and IGRP. Classful routing protocols require all interfaces to have the same subnet mask. Classful routing protocols do not include the subnet mask in their routing updates. Thus, they assume that all remote networks have the subnet mask of the exiting interface.

Question 11

For different VLANs to communicate with each other, they need to be routed. To perform inter-VLAN routing, what two things must occur?

Question 12

How do you route between VLANs with ISL trunks?

Question 11 Answer

To perform inter-VLAN routing, the following must occur:

- The router must know how to reach all VLANs being interconnected.

- The router must have a separate physical connection on the router for each VLAN, or trunking must be enabled on a single physical connection.

NOTE

Remember that each VLAN is a subnet and that a router is needed to route from one subnet to another.

Question 12 Answer

To route between VLANs using ISL on a Cisco router, you must do the following:

Step 1 Create a subinterface for each VLAN to be routed.

Step 2 Enable ISL encapsulation on each subinterface being configured. (ISL trunking works only on Fast Ethernet and Gigabit Ethernet interfaces.)

Step 3 Assign an IP address to the subinterface.

Step 4 Enable ISL encapsulation for the particular VLAN with the **encapsulate isl** *vlan#* subinterface command.

Here's an example:

```
RouterB(config)#int f0/0.10
RouterB(config-subif)#encapsulate isl 10
RouterB(config-subif)#ip address 172.16.0.1 255.255.0.0
```

Question 13

What commands enable routing between VLANs with 802.1Q trunks?

Question 14

How do distance vector routing protocols function?

Question 13 Answer

The **encapsulation dot1q** *vlan-id* command enables 802.1Q on a
Cisco router.

The native VLAN in 802.1Q does not carry a tag; therefore, a trunk's
major interface has an IP address. Any other configuration information
for the native VLAN subinterfaces is configured with the dot1q
encapsulation and IP address. Remember that the major interface of a
router using ISL cannot have an IP address. The following example
enables 802.1Q encapsulation on a router:

```
RouterB(config)#int f0/0
RouterB(config-if)#ip address 192.168.10.1 255.255.255.0
RouterB(config-if)#encapsulation dot1q 10
RouterB(config-if)#int f0/0.20
RouterB(config-if)#ip address 192.168.20.1 255.255.255.0
RouterB(config-if)#encapsulation dot1q 20
```

NOTE

To enable 802.1Q on a Catalyst 1900 interface, use the
switchport trunk encapsulation dot1q command. Catalyst
2950 switches support only 802.1Q encapsulation and are
enabled with the **switchport mode trunk interface**
command.

Question 14 Answer

Also known as Bellman-Ford algorithms, distance vector routing
protocols pass complete routing tables to neighboring routers.
Neighboring routers then combine the received routing table
with their own routing table. Each router receives a routing table
from its directly connected neighbor.

Question 15

How do distance vector routing protocols keep track of any changes to the internetwork?

Question 16

Slow convergence of distance vector routing protocols can cause inconsistent routing tables and routing loops. What are some mechanisms that distance vector protocols implement to prevent these problems?

Question 15 Answer

Distance vector routing protocols keep track of an internetwork by periodically broadcasting updates out all active interfaces. This broadcast contains the entire routing table. This method is often called "routing by rumor."

Question 16 Answer

Here are some of the ways distance vector routing protocols prevent routing loops and inconsistent routing tables:

- Maximum hop count (count to infinity)
- Split horizon
- Route poisoning
- Holddowns
- TTL

Question 17

What is maximum hop count?

Question 18

What is split horizon?

Question 17 Answer

If a loop is in an internetwork, a packet loops around the internetwork until the TTL in the IP packet reaches 0 and is removed. Maximum hop counts prevent routing loops by defining the maximum number of times a packet loops around the internetwork. RIP uses a hop count of up to 15, so anything that requires 16 hops is unreachable. Anytime a packet passes through a router, it is considered one hop.

Question 18 Answer

The split-horizon rule prohibits a router from advertising a route through an interface that the router itself is using to reach the destination.

Question 19

What is convergence?

Question 20

What is route poisoning?

Question 19 Answer

Convergence is when all routers have consistent knowledge and correct routing tables.

Question 20 Answer

With route poisoning, when a distance vector routing protocol notices that a route is no longer valid, the route is advertised with an infinite metric, signifying that the route is bad. In RIP, a metric of 16 is used to signify infinity. Route poisoning is used with holddowns.

NOTE

A poison reverse is an update that a router sends to the router it received the route poison from, specifying that all routers on the segment have received the poisoned route information.

Question 21
What are hold-down timers?

Question 22
What are triggered updates?

Question 21 Answer

Hold-down timers prevent regular update messages from reinstating a route that might have gone bad. Hold-down timers also tell routers to hold for a period of time any changes that might affect routes.

Question 22 Answer

Also known as flash updates, triggered updates are routing updates sent immediately out a router's interface when it notices that a directly connected subnet has changed state.

Question 23

Which of the following are used for loop avoidance?

A. Link-state advertisements

B. Poison reverse

C. Route discovery

D. Split horizon

Question 24

How is routing information maintained with link-state routing protocols?

Question 23 Answer

B and D. Poison reverse and split horizon are used for loop avoidance. OSPF uses link-state advertisements to advertise its links. Route discovery is the process of discovering all available routes.

Question 24 Answer

Link-state routing protocols use link-state advertisements (LSAs), a database describing the entire area, and the shortest path first (SPF) algorithm to maintain routing information within an internetwork.

Question 25

What are the functions of areas and autonomous systems in link-state protocols?

Question 26

What are four advantages that link-state protocols have over distance vector protocols?

Question 25 Answer

Areas are a grouping of contiguous networks. They are logical subdivisions of an autonomous system.

NOTE

An autonomous system is a collection of networks under a common administration that share a common routing strategy. An autonomous system is sometimes called a domain. It can be logically subdivided into multiple areas to reduce routing updates.

Question 26 Answer

- Link-state protocols send routing updates only when they detect a topology change.

- Fast convergence.

- Support for classless addressing.

- Networks can be segmented into area hierarchies, limiting where routing updates are flooded to.

Question 27

List three disadvantages of link-state protocols as compared to distance vector protocols.

Question 28

What is balanced hybrid routing? Give an example of a balanced hybrid routing protocol.

Question 27 Answer

- Significant demands on resources. Because link-state protocols require a topology database of the internetwork, they require a significant amount of memory and CPU cycles to run the SPF algorithm.

- Link-state protocol networks are more complex, making them more difficult to troubleshoot than distance vector protocols.

- All areas must connect to a backbone area. Therefore, implementing a link-state network requires much planning.

Question 28 Answer

Balanced hybrid routing protocols combine aspects of distance vector and link-state protocols. Balanced hybrid routing protocols use distance vectors, which are more accurate, to determine the best path to a destination network, and they use topology changes to trigger routing updates.

EIGRP is a balanced hybrid protocol that is Cisco-proprietary.

Question 29

What is IP RIP?

Question 30

**What four timers does IP RIP use to regulate its
performance?**

Question 29 Answer

IP RIP is a true distance vector routing protocol that sends its complete routing table out all active interfaces every 30 seconds. IP RIP uses a hop count as its metric to determine the best path to a remote network. The maximum allowable hop count is 15, meaning that 16 is unreachable. RIP has two versions. Version 1 is classful, and version 2 is classless. IP RIP can load-balance over as many as six equal-cost paths.

Question 30 Answer

The four timers that IP RIP uses to regulate its performance are

- **Route update timer**—The time between router updates. The default is 30 seconds.

- **Route invalid timer**—The time that must expire before a route becomes invalid. The default is 180 seconds.

- **Route hold-down timer**—If IP RIP receives an update with a hop count higher than the metric recorded in the routing table, the router goes into holddown for 180 seconds.

- **Route flush timer**—The time from when a route becomes invalid to when it is removed from the routing table. The default is 240 seconds.

Question 31

What are the commands to enable RIP on a Cisco router?

Question 32

How do you stop RIP updates from propagating out an interface on a router?

Question 31 Answer

The commands to enable RIP on a Cisco router are

- **router rip**

- **network** *connected-network-address*

For example, the following commands enable RIP and advertise networks 192.168.1.0 and 192.168.2.0:

```
RouterB(config)#router rip
RouterB(config-router)#network 192.168.1.0
RouterB(config-router)#network 192.168.2.0
```

Question 32 Answer

Sometimes you do not want RIP updates to propagate across the WAN, wasting valuable bandwidth or giving out valuable information about your internetwork. The easiest way to stop RIP updates from propagating out an interface is to use the **passive-interface** router configuration command.

Question 33

Which Cisco IOS command displays values associated with routing timers, the administrative distance, and network information associated with the entire router?

Determining IP Routes

Question 34

What commands enable RIP on a router and advertise network 172.16.0.0?

Determining IP Routes

Question 33 Answer

The IOS command **show ip protocols** displays values associated
with routing timers, the administrative distance, and network
information associated with the entire router:

```
RouterB#show ip protocols
Routing Protocol is "rip"
  Sending updates every 30 seconds, next due in 2 seconds
  Invalid after 180 seconds, hold down 180, flushed after 240
  Outgoing update filter list for all interfaces is
  Incoming update filter list for all interfaces is
  Redistributing: rip
  Default version control: send version 1, receive any version
    Interface           Send  Recv   Key-chain
    Serial0              1     1 2
    Serial1              1     1 2
  Routing for Networks:
    192.168.1.0
    192.168.2.0
  Routing Information Sources:
    Gateway          Distance       Last Update
  Distance: (default is 120)
```

Question 34 Answer

router rip

network 172.16.0.0

Question 35

How do you display the contents of a Cisco IP routing table?

Question 36

What IOS command displays RIP routing updates as they are sent?

Question 35 Answer

show ip route displays the Cisco routing table's contents:

```
RouterA#show ip route
Codes: C - connected, S - static, I - IGRP, R - RIP, M - mobile,
   B - BGP
       D - EIGRP, EX - EIGRP external, O - OSPF, IA - OSPF inter
   area
       N1 - OSPF NSSA external type 1, N2 - OSPF NSSA external
   type 2
       E1 - OSPF external type 1, E2 - OSPF external type 2,
   E - EGP
       i - IS-IS, L1 - IS-IS level-1, L2 - IS-IS level-2, * -
   candidate default
       U - per-user static route, o - ODR

Gateway of last resort is 192.168.1.1 to network 0.0.0.0

       1.0.0.0/32 is subnetted, 1 subnets
C         1.1.1.1 is directly connected, Loopback0
R      192.168.0.0/24 [120/1] via 192.168.1.1, 00:00:21, Serial0
C      192.168.1.0/24 is directly connected, Serial0
C      192.168.2.0/24 is directly connected, Ethernet0
R*     0.0.0.0/0 [120/1] via 192.168.1.1, 00:00:21, Serial0
```

[120/1] indicates that 120 is the AD and 1 is the number of hops to the remote network.

Question 36 Answer

debug ip rip displays routing updates as they are sent and received.

NOTE

Use the **no debug all** IOS command to turn off all debugging commands.

Question 37

After enabling IP RIP debugging on your router, you see the following message: "RIP:broadcasting general request on Ethernet1". What causes this message?

Question 38

What is Interior Gateway Routing Protocol (IGRP)?

Question 37 Answer

"RIP:broadcasting general request on Ethernet1" is usually displayed upon startup or if a user manually clears the routing table.

Question 38 Answer

IGRP is a Cisco-proprietary distance vector routing protocol. It has a default hop count of 100 hops, with a maximum hop count of 255. IGRP uses bandwidth and line delay as its default metric, but it can also use reliability, load, and MTU.

Question 39

What four timers does IGRP use to regulate its performance?

Question 40

How many paths can IGRP support?

Question 39 Answer

The four timers that IGRP uses to regulate its performance are as follows:

- **Route update timer**—The time between router updates. The default is 90 seconds.

- **Route invalid timer**—The time that must expire before a route becomes invalid. The default is 270 seconds.

- **Route hold-down timer**—If a destination becomes unreachable, or if the next-hop router increases the metric recording in the routing table, the router goes into holddown for 280 seconds.

- **Route flush timer**—The time from when a route becomes invalid to when it is removed from the routing table. The default is 630 seconds.

Question 40 Answer

IGRP can support up to six multiple equal or unequal paths. (Four is the default.)

NOTE

For IGRP to support multiple paths, the following rules must apply:

- The next-hop router in any of the paths must be closer to the destination than the local router is. This ensures that no routing loops occur.

- The alternative path metric must be within the specified variance of the best local metric.

Question 41

How do you enable IGRP on a Cisco router?

Determining IP
Routes

Question 42

Router A has two unequal paths to Router B. Interface S0 is connected to Router B's S0 interface at 1544 kbps, and interface S1 is connected to Router B's S1 interface at 256 kbps. By default, IGRP uses interface S0 to send traffic to Router B because it has the better metric, leaving S1 unused. How do you enable Router A to use interfaces S0 and S1 to route traffic to Router B?

Determining IP
Routes

Question 41 Answer

The way you enable IGRP on a Cisco router is similar to the way you enable RIP, except that you specify IGRP as the protocol and add an autonomous system number:

```
RouterA(config)#router igrp 10     (10 is the AS number)
RouterA(config-router)#network 192.168.0.0
RouterA(config-router)#network 192.168.1.0
RouterA(config-router)#network 192.168.2.0
```

Question 42 Answer

To enable unequal-cost routing in Router A, you use the **variance** command. It defines a multiplier by which a metric may vary from the metric of the lowest-cost route. Any route whose metric exceeds the metric of the lowest-cost route multiplied by the variance is not used. The variance must be specified in whole numbers.

For example, suppose that Router A's metric through S0 is 8576, and its metric through S1 is 41162. 41162 / 8576 = 4.8. Thus, the S1 metric is 4.8 times larger than S0, so to enable unequal-cost routing on Router A, the variance is 5. The configuration is as follows:

```
RouterA(config)#router igrp 10
RouterA(config-router)#network 192.168.0.0
RouterA(config-router)#network 192.168.1.0
RouterA(config-router)#variance 5
```

Question 43

What are some of EIGRP's improvements over IGRP?

Question 44

By default, what does EIGRP use to calculate routes?

Question 43 Answer

Here are some of EIGRP's improvements over IGRP:

- DUAL
- Incremental updates
- Loop-free networks
- Reduced bandwidth usage
- Support for multiple network layer protocols (IP, IPX, AppleTalk)
- Support for variable-length subnet masks (VLSMs), discontiguous networks, and classless routing
- Advanced distance vector capabilities
- Automatic route summarization on major network boundaries

Question 44 Answer

EIGRP uses bandwidth and delay by default to calculate its metric. It can also be configured to use reliability, load, and MTU. EIGRP's metric is the same as IGRP's metric, except that it is multiplied by 256 for improved granularity.

Question 45

In EIGRP, what is a successor?

Question 46

In EIGRP, what is the feasible successor?

Question 45 Answer

A successor is a route selected as the primary route used to reach a destination. It is the route kept in the routing table.

Question 46 Answer

The feasible successor is the backup route. These routes are selected at the same time the successors are identified, but they are kept only in the topology table, not in the routing table. They are used for fast convergence. If the successor fails, the router can immediately route through the feasible successor. A destination can have multiple feasible successors.

Question 47

What IOS commands enable EIGRP on a Cisco router and advertise 192.168.3.0 and 192.168.4.0 as its directly connected networks?

Question 48

What command would you use to see EIGRP adjacencies?

Question 47 Answer

```
RouterA(config)#router eigrp 100    (100 is the AS number)
RouterA(config-router)#network 192.168.3.0
RouterA(config-router)#network 192.168.4.0
```

Question 48 Answer

The **show ip eigrp neighbors** command displays EIGRP adjacencies and directly connected neighbors.

Question 49

What IOS command would you use to view the EIGRP neighbor states?

Determining IP Routes

Question 50

What routing metric is OSPF based on?

Determining IP Routes

Question 49 Answer

You use the **debug eigrp neighbors** command to check the
EIGRP neighbor states. This command displays the contents of
the hello packet used in EIGRP as well as the neighbors
discovered by EIGRP.

Question 50 Answer

Bandwidth. OSPF's metric is a cost value based on bandwidth or
the speed of its connection. The default formula used to calculate
OSPF cost is

$$Cost = 100,000,000 / \text{bandwidth in bps}$$

For example, OSPF assigns the cost of 10 to a 10 MB Ethernet
line ($100,000,000 / 10,000,000 = 10$).

NOTE

This is a tricky question in some ways. For example,
with this question, you might have to choose between
cost and bandwidth. Bandwidth is the more correct
answer, because OSPF metric uses a cost based on
bandwidth.

Question 51

How do OSPF-speaking routers build adjacencies and exchange routing tables?

Question 52

What does the Hello protocol do in an OSPF network?

Question 51 Answer

OSPF-speaking routers build adjacencies by sending Hello packets out all OSPF-enabled interfaces. If the routers share a common data link and agree on certain parameters set in their Hello packets, they become neighbors. If these parameters are different, the routers do not become neighbors, and communication stops. OSPF routers form adjacencies with certain routers. These routers are determined by the data link media type. As soon as adjacencies are formed, each router sends LSAs to all adjacent routers. These LSAs describe the state of each of the router's links. Because of the varying types of link-state information, OSPF defines multiple LSA types. Finally, a route that receives an LSA from a neighbor records the LSA in a link-state database and floods a copy of the LSA to all its other neighbors. When all databases are complete, each router uses the SPF algorithm to calculate a loop-free topology and builds its routing table based on this topology.

Question 52 Answer

In OSPF, the Hello protocol ensures that communication between OSPF-speaking routers is bidirectional. It is the means by which neighbors are discovered and acts as keepalives between neighbors. It also establishes and maintains neighbor relationships and elects the designated router (DR) and backup designated router (BDR) to represent the segment on broadcast and nonbroadcast multiaccess (NBMA) networks.

Question 53

What are the five network types that OSPF defines?

Question 54

What is the IP multicast address of Hello protocols?

Question 53 Answer

The five network types that OSPF defines are

- Broadcast networks
- NBMA networks
- Point-to-point networks
- Point-to-multipoint networks
- Virtual links

Examples of broadcast networks are Ethernet and Token Ring. OSPF routers on broadcast networks elect a DR and BDR. All the routers form adjacencies with the DR and BDR. On broadcast networks, all OSPF packets are multicast to the DR and BDR.

NBMA networks are Frame Relay, X.25, and ATM. They can connect more than two routers but have no broadcast capability. NBMA networks elect a DR and BDR, and all OSPF packets are unicast.

Point-to-point networks, such as a T1, connect a single pair of routers and always become adjacent.

Point-to-multipoint networks are a special configuration of NBMA networks in which networks are treated as a collection of point-to-point links. Routers on these networks do not elect a DR or BDR, and because all links are seen as point-to-point, all OSPF packets are multicast.

Virtual links are a special configuration that the router interprets as unnumbered point-to-point networks. The administrator creates virtual links.

Question 54 Answer

Hello protocols are periodically sent out each interface using IP multicast address 224.0.0.5 (All SPF Routers). The HelloInterval each router uses to send out the Hello protocol is based on the media type. The default HelloInterval of broadcast, point-to-point, and point-to-multipoint networks is 10 seconds. On NBMA networks, the default is 30 seconds.

Question 55

If you have eight routers on an Ethernet network and you establish adjacencies with only the DR and BDR, how many circuits do you have?

Question 56

What is the OSPF router ID, and where does an OSPF router receive its router ID?

Question 55 Answer

14. The formula for figuring out the number of circuits (adjacencies or connections) needed to establish adjacencies on the DR and BDR is $2(n - 1)$, where n is the number of routers in the network. So if you have eight routers in a network, $2(8 - 1) = 14$ adjacencies.

Question 56 Answer

For OSPF to initialize, it must be able to define a router ID for the entire OSPF process. A router can receive its router ID from several sources. The most common and stable source is the IP address set on the loopback interface. The loopback interface is a logical interface that never goes down. If no loopback address is defined, an OSPF-enabled router selects the numerically highest IP address on all its interfaces as its router ID.

Question 57

An OSPF-enabled router has the following IP addresses configured on its interfaces:

Ethernet 0192.168.9.5
Serial 0172.16.3.1
Ethernet 1192.168.24.1

What is the router ID of the OSPF-enabled router?

Question 58

What are link-state advertisements?

Question 57 Answer

The router ID is 192.168.24.1 because it is the numerically highest IP address on all interfaces on the router. If the router had a loopback address configured, it would choose the loopback address as the router ID (even if the loopback IP address was numerically lower than other IP addresses configured on the router).

Question 58 Answer

Link-state advertisements (LSAs) are what OSPF-speaking routers send out all interfaces, describing the state of the router's links. LSAs are also packets that OSPF uses to advertise changes in the condition of a specific link to other OSPF routers.

Question 59

How many LSAs are there in OSPF?

Question 60

What are five reasons why you would use OSPF instead of RIP?

Question 59 Answer

Six different and distinct link-state packet formats are used in OSPF—each for a different purpose. The ICND exam will test you on only two LSA types—Type 1 and Type 2.

Type 1 LSAs are router LSAs and are generated by each router for each area to which it belongs. These LSAs describe the states of the router's links to the area and are flooded within a single area.

Type 2 LSAs are network LSAs and are generated by the DR and BDR. They describe the set of routers attached to a particular network. They are flooded within a single area.

Question 60 Answer

The reasons why you would use OSPF instead of RIP are as follows:

- Support for VLSMs
- Fast convergence
- No reachability limitations
- More efficient use of bandwidth
- Path selection is based on bandwidth rather than hops

Question 61

How do you enable OSPF on a Cisco router?

Determining IP
Routes

Question 62

What command enables a loopback interface
on a Cisco router?

Determining IP
Routes

Question 61 Answer

The **router ospf** *process-id* command enables the OSPF process, and the **network** *address wildcard-mask* **area** *area-id* command assigns networks to a specific OSPF area. Notice that you must specify the wildcard mask instead of the subnet mask. For example, the following commands enable OSPF process 10 and advertise the network 192.168.10.0/24 in area 0:

```
RouterA(config)#router ospf 10
RouterA(config-router)#network 192.168.10.0 0.0.0.255 area 0
```

NOTE

The process ID is locally significant to the router, because all OSPF routes are assumed to belong to the same OSPF domain.

Question 62 Answer

RouterA(config)#**interface loopback** *number* configures a loopback interface. The *number* option specifies the loopback interface number you are creating.

NOTE

Remember that a loopback interface is a logical interface in the router. If you have a loopback interface created on an OSPF-enabled router, the router ID is the loopback address.

Question 63

What IOS command displays the OSPF neighbor information on a per-interface basis?

Determining IP
Routes

Question 63 Answer

The **show ip ospf neighbor** command displays OSPF neighbor information on a per-interface basis.

Chapter 4

Managing IP Traffic with Access Lists and Network Address Translation

Access lists can be one of the most confusing topics on the ICND and CCNA exams. This section breaks down access lists and gives you the information you need to successfully implement them in your network. Access lists can be used to protect specific networks from certain users or other networks. You can even use them to block web traffic or any other type of IP traffic. When implementing access lists in your network, remember that they use excess router processing time. The longer the access list, the greater the burden it puts on the router processor. Before you implement any access list, make sure it will not degrade the router's performance. Also try to keep access lists short.

New to the ICND and CCNA exams are topics such as Network Address Translation (NAT) and Port Address Translation (PAT). NAT was introduced as a temporary solution to help slow down the exhaustion of IP addresses on the Internet. The idea behind NAT is that not all hosts on a network are on the Internet at the same time, so why assign a valid address to a host that will use it only part of the time? NAT works by translating a range of valid IP addresses assigned to a larger range of internal hosts. To the outside world, it looks as though the hosts are using valid IP addresses, but in reality, they are using illegal addresses that are translated into valid IP addresses. PAT is another solution to help slow down the exhaustion of IP addresses. PAT works by translating one valid address to many internal hosts. It accomplishes this by looking at the internal host's source TCP/UDP port number and changing it to a different valid external address with a different TCP/UDP port number. Because it changes the source port number, no two hosts are assigned the same port number, thus allowing multiple simultaneous connections with the same IP address. You must understand Cisco NAT terminology and how to configure NAT and PAT.

Question 1

What three types of IP access lists can be configured on a Cisco router?

Question 2

What criteria do standard IP access lists use to filter packets?

Question 1 Answer

The three types of IP access lists are standard, extended, and named.

Question 2 Answer

Standard IP access lists filter packets by the *source address*. This results in the packet's being permitted or denied for the entire protocol suite based on the source network IP address.

NOTE

Because standard IP access lists filter by source address, you should place the access list as close to the destination network as possible. Doing this helps you avoid denying unnecessary traffic and ensures that the source still has access to other, nonfiltered destinations.

Question 3

What criteria do extended IP access lists use to filter packets?

Question 4

In what two ways can IP access lists be applied to an interface?

Question 3 Answer

Extended IP access lists filter packets by source address, destination address, protocols, and port numbers.

NOTE

Extended access lists should be placed as close to the source as possible. This prevents unwanted traffic from passing through the network.

Question 4 Answer

Access lists can be applied as inbound or outbound access lists. Inbound access lists process packets as they enter a router's interface and before they are routed. Outbound access lists process packets as they exit a router's interface and after they are routed.

NOTE

Inbound access lists are more effective than outbound access lists, because they save the overhead of routing table lookups. Outbound access lists process packets going through the router, not traffic originating from the router.

Question 5

How many access lists can be applied to an interface on a Cisco router?

Question 6

How are access lists processed?

Question 5 Answer

Only one access list per protocol, per direction, per interface can be applied on a Cisco router. Multiple access lists are permitted per interface, but they must be for different protocols.

NOTE

Because different IOS versions work differently with an empty access list, you should first create an access list and then apply it to an interface.

Question 6 Answer

Access lists are processed in sequential, logical order, evaluating packets from the top down, one statement at a time. As soon as a match is made, the permit or deny option is applied, and the packet is not applied to any more access list statements. Because of this, the order of the statements within any access list is significant.

Question 7

What is at the end of each access list?

Question 8

What are the number ranges used to define standard and extended IP access lists?

Question 7 Answer

At the end of each access list, an implicit **deny** statement denies any packet not filtered in the access list.

NOTE

You can override this with a **permit ip any any** at the end of the access list.

Question 8 Answer

The number ranges used to define standard and extended IP access lists are as follows:

- **Standard IP access lists**—1 to 99 and 1300 to 1999 (expanded range)

- **Extended IP access lists**—100 to 199 and 2000 to 2699 (expanded range)

Question 9

When implementing access lists, what are wildcard masks?

Question 10

What is the IOS command syntax used to create a standard IP access list?

Question 9 Answer

Wildcard masks define the subset of the 32 bits in the IP address that must be matched. Wildcards are used with access lists to specify a host, network, or part of a network. Wildcard masks work the opposite of subnet masks. In subnet masks, 1 bits are matched to the network portion of the address, and 0s are wildcards that specify the host range. In wildcard masks, when 0s are present, the octet address must match. Mask bits with a binary value of 1 are wildcards. For example, if you have an IP address 172.16.0.0 with a wildcard mask of 0.0.255.255, the first two portions of the IP address must match 172.16, but the last two octets can be in the range 1 to 255.

NOTE

Remember that a wildcard mask bit 0 means to check the corresponding bit value and that a wildcard mask bit 1 means to ignore the corresponding bit value.

Question 10 Answer

The command syntax to create a standard IP access list is

```
access-list access-list-number {permit | deny} source-address
[wildcard-mask]
```

access-list-number is a number from 1 to 99 or 1300 to 1999.

For example:

```
RouterA(config)#access-list 10 deny 192.168.0.0 0.0.0.255
```

This creates access list number 10, which denies any IP address between 192.168.0.1 and 192.168.255.255.

Question 11

After you create a standard or extended IP access list, how do you apply it to an interface on a Cisco router?

Question 12

What are the two things you must do to activate an access list?

Question 11 Answer

To apply an access list to an interface on a Cisco router, use the **ip access-group** interface command:

```
ip access-group access-list-number {in | out}
```

For example, the following applies access list 10 to serial interface 0 as an inbound access list:

```
RouterA(config)#int s0
RouterA(config-if)#ip access-group 10 in
```

NOTE

When you use the **ip access-group** command, **out** is the default option. To remove an access list from a router, first remove it from the interface by entering the **no ip access-group** *access-list-number direction* command. Then remove the access list by entering the **no access-list** *access-list-number* global command. Remember that you cannot remove one line from an access list. If you want to edit an access list, you must remove the entire access list and then edit it.

Question 12 Answer

The two things you must do to activate an access list are

- Create the access list.
- Apply the access list as part of a group on an interface.

Question 13

Create a standard access list that permits the following networks:

192.168.200.0

192.168.216.0

192.168.232.0

192.168.248.0

Question 14

What is the Cisco IOS command syntax used to create an extended access list?

Question 13 Answer

There are two ways to do this. First, you can create one access list that contains an entry for each network:

```
access-list 10 permit 192.168.200.0 0.0.0.255
access-list 10 permit 192.168.216.0 0.0.0.255
access-list 10 permit 192.168.232.0 0.0.0.255
access-list 10 permit 192.168.248.0 0.0.0.255
```

A second way to do this is to create a single entry with wildcard masks:

```
access-list 10 permit 192.168.200.0 0.0.48.255
```

To see how this one statement denies all the networks, you must look at it in binary:

- .200 = 11001000
- .216 = 11011000
- .232 = 11101000
- .248 = 11111000

All the bits match except the third and fourth bits. With wildcard masks, these are the bits you want to match. Therefore, your wildcard mask would be 00110000 in binary, which is 48.

Question 14 Answer

Here is the Cisco IOS command syntax to create an extended access list:

```
access-list access-list-number {permit | deny} protocol
    source-address source-wildcard [operator port]
    destination-address destination-wildcard [operator port]
```

protocol examples include IP, TCP, UDP, ICMP, GRE, and IGRP.

operator port can be **lt** (less than), **gt** (greater than), **eq** (equal to), or **neq** (not equal to) and a protocol port number.

Question 15

Create an extended access list denying web traffic to network 192.168.10.0.

Question 16

What is true of the following access list?

```
access-list 110 deny ip host 172.16.0.2 any
access-list 110 permit ip any any
```

Question 15 Answer

The following commands deny web traffic to network
192.168.10.0:

```
access-list 101 deny tcp any 192.168.10.0 0.0.0.255 eq www
access-list 101 permit ip any any
```

NOTE

This denies any web traffic to network 192.168.10.0
and permits any other IP traffic. Because access lists are
processed in sequential order, the first statement denies
Web traffic, and the last statement permits all other IP
traffic. If the last statement were not included, all IP
traffic would be denied because of the implicit **deny any**
at the end of each access list. Access lists should always
have one **permit** statement.

Question 16 Answer

The access list denies any traffic from the host 172.16.0.2 and
permits all other traffic.

Question 17

Create an access list the permits only Telnet traffic from network 192.168.10.0 255.255.255.0 to connect to the Cisco router.

Managing
IP Traffic...

Question 18

What IOS command can you use to see whether an IP access list is applied to an interface?

Managing
IP Traffic...

Question 17 Answer

```
RouterA(config)#access list 10 permit ip 192.168.10.0
  0.0.0.255
RouterA(config)#line vty 0 4
RouterA(config-if)#access-class 10 in
```

Question 18 Answer

The IOS command to see whether an IP access list is applied to an interface is

```
show ip interface interface-type interface-number
```

For example:

```
RouterA#show ip interface s0
Serial0 is up, line protocol is up
  Internet address is 192.168.1.2/24
  Broadcast address is 255.255.255.255
  Address determined by non-volatile memory
  MTU is 1500 bytes
  Helper address is not set
  Directed broadcast forwarding is enabled
  Multicast reserved groups joined: 224.0.0.9
  Outgoing access list is not set
  Inbound  access list is 10
  Proxy ARP is enabled
  Security level is default
  Split horizon is enabled
  --Text Omitted--
```

Question 19

How can you display all access lists on a Cisco router?

Question 20

Define the following Cisco NAT terminology:

Inside local address

Inside global address

Outside local address

Outside global address

Question 19 Answer

To display all access lists on a Cisco router, use the **show running-config** or **show access-list** command:

```
RouterA#show access-list
Standard IP access list 10
    deny   192.168.0.0, wildcard bits 0.0.0.255
Extended IP access list 101
    permit tcp any any eq www
    permit udp any any eq domain
    permit udp any eq domain any
    permit icmp any any
    deny tcp 192.168.10.0 0.0.0.255 any eq www
RouterA#
```

Question 20 Answer

Inside local address—The IP address assigned to a host on the inside, private network. This usually is a private IP address.

Inside global address—A legal routable IP address that represents one or more inside local IP addresses to the outside world.

Outside local address—The IP address of an outside host as it appears to the inside, private network. This usually is a private IP address.

Outside global address—The IP address assigned to a host on the outside network by the host's owner. This usually is a routable IP address.

Question 21

What is overload NAT?

Question 22

What are three benefits of NAT?

Question 21 Answer

Overload NAT is another term for Port Address Translation (PAT). It has a many-to-one mapping.

NOTE

Other types of NAT are static NAT and dynamic NAT. Static NAT provides a one-to-one translation and is useful when an inside host needs to be accessed from the outside. Dynamic NAT maps a private IP address to a routable IP address from a pool of routable IP addresses dynamically.

Question 22 Answer

Here are three benefits of NAT:

- It eliminates readdressing overhead of hosts that require external access.

- It conserves IP addresses through application port-level multiplexing.

- It hides the internal network, providing a small level of network security.

Question 23

How many internal hosts can be translated into one routable IP address through PAT?

Question 24

Configure internal host 192.168.10.5/24 to be statically translated to the external IP address 216.1.1.3/24.

Question 23 Answer

Theoretically, PAT can translate 65,536 internal hosts using one routable IP address.

Question 24 Answer

To configure static NAT, you must first create the static mapping table and then define which interfaces on your router connect to the inside network and the outside network. The following example creates the static mapping and defines interface s0 as connecting to the outside network and interface e0 as connecting to the inside network:

```
RouterB(config)#ip nat inside source static 192.168.10.5
    216.1.1.3
RouterB(config)#int s0
RouterB(config-if)#ip nat outside
RouterB(config-if)#int e0
RouterB(config-if)#ip nat inside
```

Question 25

Configure the internal host range of 192.168.10.0 255.255.255.0 to be translated using NAT to the external range of IP addresses 216.1.1.0 255.255.255.240.

Question 26

How do you configure PAT?

Question 25 Answer

Create a NAT pool called cisco:

```
RouterB(config)#ip nat pool cisco 216.1.1.1 216.1.1.14 netmask
255.255.255.240
```

Define the IP addresses that will be translated:

```
RouterB(config)#access-list 10 permit 192.168.10.0 0.0.0.255
```

Establish dynamic translation of access list 10 with the NAT pool named cisco:

```
RouterB(config)#ip nat inside source list 10 pool cisco
```

To configure dynamic NAT, you first have to create a NAT pool of external IP addresses that internal hosts can draw from. Then create an access list that defines the internal hosts to be translated. Finally, enable the translation. As with static NAT, you have to define which interface is internal and which is external.

NOTE

It is a good idea to create a PAT statement at the end of a dynamic NAT pool to ensure that you do not run out of addresses.

Question 26 Answer

To configure PAT, you first define an access list permitting the internal hosts to be translated. You then use the **ip nat inside source list** *access-list-number* **interface** *interface-type* **overload** global command. The following example enables PAT for internal host 192.168.10.0/24 using the external IP address on interface S0:

```
RouterB(config)#access-list 20 permit 192.168.10.0 0.0.0.255
RouterB(config)#ip nat inside source list 20 interface s0
overload
```

Question 27

What Cisco command clears all the NAT mappings in the NAT table?

Question 28

How do you view the active NAT translations in the NAT table?

Question 27 Answer

clear ip nat translation * clears all the NAT translations in the NAT table. This command is useful for troubleshooting NAT.

NOTE

The NAT table is stored in memory and is cleared when the router is rebooted.

Question 28 Answer

To view the active NAT translations in the NAT table, use the **show ip nat translations** command.

Question 29

What Cisco IOS command displays every packet the router translates?

Managing
IP Traffic

Question 29 Answer

To troubleshoot NAT and view every packet the router translates, use the debug ip nat command.

Chapter 5

Establishing Serial Point-to-Point Connections

Part II

This chapter provides an overview of the different types of WAN connections, WAN terminology, and encapsulation. You will be introduced to two common types of WAN encapsulation, HDLC and PPP, used on serial point-to-point connections or ISDN lines. (Frame Relay, which is another type of WAN encapsulation, is covered in the next chapter.) Serial point-to-point connections are dedicated WAN lines that provide a single preestablished path from the customer's router to the ISP's router or remote network. Serial point-to-point connections are not shared among other customers (as with Frame Relay), thus guaranteeing you the full link speed.

The terminology for WAN technologies is so vast that many people get confused and do not truly understand the technology. The industry refers to WAN links by their speed—more specifically, by their Layer 1 (physical) technology. These links are called T1, T3, T4, or OC-3 links, and we assume that this describes Layer 2 technology (Frame Relay or point-to-point). A T1 or T3 link is simply the WAN link's Layer 1 technology. T-carrier lines use multiplexers to allow several channels on one line, and a T1 line is the basic T-carrier service.

Ethernet uses MAC addresses to communicate with hosts on the network. MAC addresses are a Layer 2 technology that is unique to each host. If a host wants to communicate with another host, it uses the MAC address to locate and initiate the communication with the remote host. Just as Ethernet requires a Layer 2 technology to locate and communicate with hosts, WAN connections need a Layer 2 encapsulation method. This chapter primarily focuses on the Layer 2 technologies and encapsulation methods of WAN connections. For example, Frame Relay is a Layer 2 technology that typically runs on a T1 (Layer 1) link, but it can also run on a 56 kbps or T3 link. If you are not using Frame Relay as your Layer 2 technology, and you have a point-to-point link, what Layer 2 technology does the link use? By default, the Layer 2 encapsulation of a point-to-point link is HDLC. Every vendor makes its own implementation of HDLC that is proprietary to that vendor. For example, you cannot use HDLC on your Cisco router if your upstream router is another vendor, such as Nortel. In this case, you can use PPP as the Layer 2 encapsulation method. PPP was created as an open standard; because it is not proprietary, such as HDLC, it can be used to connect Cisco and non-Cisco devices. As you read this and the following chapters, remember that the ICND and CCNA exams will thoroughly test your knowledge of WAN connections and their technologies.

Question 1

The four WAN connection types available are leased lines, circuit-switched, packet-switched, and cell-switched. Define the differences between each connection type.

Question 2

Define customer premises equipment (CPE), and give an example.

Question 1 Answer

Leased lines are dedicated point-to-point lines that provide a single pre-established WAN communication path from the customer's network to the remote network. Leased lines are usually employed over synchronous connections. They are generally more expensive than circuit-switched lines and are always up.

Circuit-switched connections are dedicated for only the duration of the call. The telephone system and ISDN are examples of circuit-switched networks.

Packet-switched connections use virtual circuits (VCs) to provide end-to-end connectivity. Packet-switched connections are similar to leased lines, except that the line is shared by other customers. A packet knows how to reach its destination by programming switches. Frame Relay and X.25 are examples of packet-switched connections.

Cell-switched connections are similar to packet switching. The difference between the two is that cells are fixed in size, whereas packets are variable in size. An example of cell-switched technology is ATM.

Question 2 Answer

CPE is equipment that is located on the customer's (or subscriber's) premises. It is owned by the customer or leased by the service provider to the customer. An example is your router.

Question 3

What is the demarcation point (demarc)?

Question 4

What is the local loop?

Question 3 Answer

The point of demarcation (demarc) is where the CPE ends and the local loop begins. It is the point between the wiring that comes in from the local service provider (telephone company) and the wiring installed to connect the customer's CPE to the service provider. It is the last responsibility of the service provider and is usually a network interface device (NID) located in the customer's telephone wiring closet. Think of the demarc as the boundary between the customer's wiring and the service provider's wiring.

Question 4 Answer

The local loop is the physical cable that extends from the demarc (located on the customer premises) to the central office.

Question 5

What are synchronous links?

Establishing Serial Point-to-Point Connections

Question 6

What are asynchronous links?

Establishing Serial Point-to-Point Connections

Question 5 Answer

Synchronous links have identical frequencies and contain individual characters encapsulated in control bits, called start/stop bits, which designate the beginning and end of each character. Synchronous links try to use the same speed as the other end of a serial link. Synchronous transmission occurs on V.35 and other interfaces, where one set of wires carries data, and a separate set of wires carries clocking for that data.

Question 6 Answer

Asynchronous links send digital signals without timing. Asynchronous links agree on the same speed, but there is no check or adjustment of the rates if they are slightly different. Only 1 byte per transfer is sent. Modems are asynchronous.

Question 7

What are some typical Layer 2 encapsulation methods for WAN links?

Establishing Serial Point-to-Point Connections

Question 8

Describe HDLC.

Establishing Serial Point-to-Point Connections

Question 7 Answer

Here are some typical Layer 2 WAN encapsulation methods:

- High-Level Data Link Control (HDLC)
- Point-to-Point Protocol (PPP)
- Serial Line Internet Protocol (SLIP)
- X.25
- Link Access Procedure, Balanced (LAPB)
- Frame Relay
- Asynchronous Transfer Mode (ATM)

Question 8 Answer

HDLC was derived from Synchronous Data Link Control (SDLC). It is the default encapsulation type on point-to-point dedicated links and circuit-switched connections between Cisco routers. It is an ISO-standard bit-oriented data-link protocol that encapsulates data on synchronous links. HDLC is a connection-oriented protocol that has very little overhead. It lacks a protocol field and therefore cannot encapsulate multiple network layer protocols across the same link. Because of this, each vendor has its own method of identifying the network-layer protocol. Cisco offers a propriety version of HDLC that uses a type field that acts as a protocol field, making it possible for multiple network-layer protocols to share the same link.

Question 9

What is the default encapsulation on a Cisco serial interface?

Question 10

By default, Cisco uses HDLC as its default encapsulation method across synchronous lines (point-to-point links). If a serial line uses a different encapsulation protocol, how do you change it back to HDLC?

Question 9 Answer

HDLC is the default encapsulation on a Cisco serial interface.

Question 10 Answer

To change a serial line back to HDLC, use the following interface command on the serial interface you want to change:

```
Router(config-if)#encapsulation hdlc
```

If the serial interface was previously configured for Frame Relay, you can also use the **no encapsulation frame-relay** interface command to set the encapsulation back to HDLC.

Question 11

What is Point-to-Point Protocol (PPP)?

Question 12

What is SLIP?

Question 11 Answer

PPP is an industry-standard protocol that provides router-to-router or router-to-host connections over synchronous and asynchronous links. It can be used to connect WAN links to other vendors' equipment. It works with several network-layer protocols, such as IP and IPX. PPP provides authentication (which is optional) through PAP, CHAP, or MS-CHAP.

Question 12 Answer

SLIP stands for Serial Line Interface Protocol. It is a standard protocol that provides serial connections using TCP/IP. It has been replaced by PPP.

Question 13
Describe X.25/LAPB.

Establishing Serial Point-to-Point Connections

Question 14
What is Frame Relay?

Establishing Serial Point-to-Point Connections

Question 13 Answer

X.25/LAPB is an ITU-T standard that has a tremendous amount of overhead because of its strict timeout and windowing techniques. LAPB is the connection-oriented protocol used with X.25. It uses the ABM (Asynchronous Balance Mode) transfer mode. X.25/LAPB was used in the 1980s when WAN links were not as error-free as they are today. X.25 is a predecessor of Frame Relay. X.25 supports both switched and permanent virtual circuits.

Question 14 Answer

An industry standard, Frame Relay is a switched data link layer protocol that uses virtual circuits to identify the traffic that belongs to certain routers. It provides dynamic bandwidth allocation and congestion control.

Question 15

What two WAN encapsulations on a serial link are considered the most useful?

Question 16

How do you view the encapsulation type on a serial interface?

Question 15 Answer

HDLC and PPP are considered the most useful because they are the most common and easiest to configure on a Cisco router.

NOTE

This might seem like a tricky question, because it's hard to decide what are considered the most useful WAN encapsulations. However, you might see questions like this on the exams, and you'll have to choose the best answer even though there might be multiple correct ones.

Question 16 Answer

To view the encapsulation type on a serial interface, use the **show interface serial** *interface-number* command:

```
RouterB#show interface serial 0
Serial0 is up, line protocol is up
  Hardware is HD64570
  Internet address is 192.168.1.1/24
  MTU 1500 bytes, BW 1544 Kbit, DLY 20000 usec, rely 255/255,
  load 1/255
  Encapsulation HDLC, loopback not set, keepalive set (10 sec)
  Last input 00:00:00, output 00:00:03, output hang never
  Last clearing of "show interface" counters never
  Input queue: 0/75/0 (size/max/drops); Total output drops: 0
  Queueing strategy: weighted fair
  Output queue: 0/1000/64/0 (size/max total/threshold/drops)
     Conversations  0/1/256 (active/max active/max total)
     Reserved Conversations 0/0 (allocated/max allocated)
  5 minute input rate 0 bits/sec, 0 packets/sec
  5 minute output rate 0 bits/sec, 0 packets/sec
```

Question 17

What provides clocking for a serial line?

Establishing Serial Point-to-Point Connections

Question 18

What is the command to change the clock rate of a Cisco interface acting as a DCE to 56 kbps?

Establishing Serial Point-to-Point Connections

Question 17 Answer

The DCE (Data Communications Equipment) provides clocking for a serial line. Examples of DCE devices are a DSU/CSU or another serial interface on a Cisco router configured for clocking.

Question 18 Answer

The command to change the clock rate on a DCE interface is

```
Frame-Switch(config-if)#clock rate 56000
```

NOTE

Remember that the clock rate is in bits per second, not kilobytes per second, and that there is a space between **clock** and **rate**.

Question 19

What is the default bandwidth on a serial interface on a Cisco router?

Question 20

Which of the following is the correct command to change the bandwidth of a serial interface to 256 kbps?

A. bandwidth 256 k

B. bandwidth 256

C. bandwidth 256000

Question 19 Answer

1544 kbps, or T1, is the default bandwidth on a serial interface on a Cisco router. You can see this using the **show interface serial** *interface-number* command:

```
RouterA#show int s0
Serial0 is up, line protocol is up
  Hardware is HD64570
  Internet address is 192.168.1.2/24
  MTU 1500 bytes, BW 1544 Kbit, DLY 20000 usec, rely 255/255,
  load 1/255
  Encapsulation PPP, loopback not set, keepalive set (10sec)
(Text omitted)
```

Question 20 Answer

B. The command to change the bandwidth of a serial interface is the **bandwidth** *bandwidth-in-kbps* interface command. The correct command to change the bandwidth to 256 kbps is

```
RouterA(config-if)#bandwidth 256
```

Question 21

PPP can be used over what physical WAN interfaces?

Question 22

PPP is a data link layer protocol that provides network-layer services. What are the two sublayers of PPP?

Question 21 Answer

PPP can be used on the following:

- Asynchronous serial interfaces
- High-Speed Serial Interface (HSSI)
- ISDN
- Synchronous serial interfaces

Question 22 Answer

The two sublayers of PPP are the following:

- Network Core Protocol (NCP) is the component that encapsulates and configures multiple network layer protocols. Some examples of these protocols are IP Control Protocol (IPCP) and Internetwork Packet Exchange Control Protocol (IPXCP).

- Link Control Protocol (LCP) is used to establish, configure, maintain, and terminate PPP connections.

NOTE

The PPP protocol stack is specified at the physical and data link layers. For the exams, remember that PPP uses LCP to set up and configure the link and to negotiate the authentication, compression, and multilink before a connection is established. PPP uses NCP to allow communication of multiple network-layer protocols across a PPP link.

Question 23

What features does LCP offer to PPP encapsulation?

Establishing Serial Point-to-Point Connections

Question 24

What two methods of authentication can be used with PPP links?

Establishing Serial Point-to-Point Connections

Question 23 Answer

LCP offers authentication, callback, compression, error detection, and multilink to PPP encapsulation.

Question 24 Answer

The two methods of authentication on PPP links are

- Password Authentication Protocol (PAP)
- Challenge Handshake Authentication Protocol (CHAP)

PAP is the less-secure of the two methods; passwords are sent in clear text and are exchanged only upon initial link establishment. CHAP is used upon initial link establishment and periodically to make sure that the router is still communicating with the same host. CHAP passwords are exchanged as MD5 encrypted values.

Question 25

What two protocols are available for compression on PPP links?

Question 26

What three phases are used to establish a PPP session?

Question 25 Answer

The two protocols available for compression are Stacker and Predictor.

As a general rule, Predictor uses more memory than Stacker, and Stacker is more CPU-intensive than Predictor.

Question 26 Answer

The three phases used to establish a PPP session are as follows:

Step 1   **Link establishment**—Each PPP device sends LCP packets to configure and test the link (Layer 1).

Step 2   **Authentication phase (optional)**—If authentication is configured, either PAP or CHAP is used to authenticate the link. This must take place before the network layer protocol phase can begin (Layer 2).

Step 3   **Network layer protocol phase**—PPP sends NCP packets to choose and configure one or more network layer protocols to be encapsulated and sent over the PPP data link (Layer 3).

NOTE

debug ppp authentication is a great troubleshooting command to use to view the results of PPP authentication. It shows you whether the username and password were found and verified.

Question 27

What IOS command enables PPP encapsulation on a Cisco router serial interface?

Question 28

How do you enable PPP authentication using PAP or CHAP on a Cisco router?

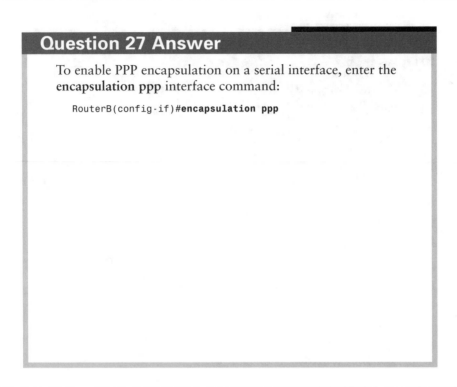

Question 27 Answer

To enable PPP encapsulation on a serial interface, enter the **encapsulation ppp** interface command:

```
RouterB(config-if)#encapsulation ppp
```

Question 28 Answer

The three steps to enable PPP authentication on a Cisco router are as follows:

Step 1 Make sure that each router has a host name assigned to it using the **hostname** command.

Step 2 On each router, define the username of the remote router and password that both routers will use with the **username** *remote-router-name* **password** *password* command.

Step 3 Configure PPP authentication with the **ppp authentication** {**chap** | **chap pap** | **pap chap** | **pap**} interface command. (If both PAP and CHAP are enabled, the first method you specify in the command is used. If the peer suggests the second method or refuses the first method, the second method is used.)

```
RouterB(config)#hostname RouterB
RouterB(config)#username RouterA password cisco
RouterB(config)#int s0
RouterB(config-if)#ppp authentication chap pap
```

Question 29

If PPP is enabled on an interface, how do you view its LCP and NCP states?

Question 29 Answer

Issue the **show interface serial** *interface-number* command to view LCP and NCP states:

```
RouterA#show int s0
Serial0 is up, line protocol is up
  Hardware is HD64570
  Internet address is 192.168.1.2/24
  MTU 1500 bytes, BW 1544 Kbit, DLY 20000 usec, rely 255/255,
  load 1/255
  Encapsulation PPP, loopback not set, keepalive set (10sec)
  LCP Open
  Open: IPCP, CDPCP
  Last input 00:00:02, output 00:00:02, output hang never
  Last clearing of "show interface" counters never
  Input queue: 0/75/0 (size/max/drops); Total output drops: 0
(text omitted)
```

Chapter 6

Frame Relay

Frame Relay is one of the most popular methods used to connect WAN links because of its speed, reliability, and cost. Frame Relay is a packet-switched technology. Packet-switched networks allow end devices to dynamically share the WAN medium and bandwidth. In a Frame Relay network, your data travels through your service provider's network along with other customers' data. The service provider programs switches to route your data in the right direction so that it does not get crossed with another customer's data. Because you are sharing the switch with other customers, you don't always get 100 percent of the WAN link. Most service providers guarantee a set speed of data transfer along the Frame Relay cloud. Sometimes you might be able to exceed this rate. For example, if you buy a T1 (1.544 Mbps) Frame Relay WAN link with a guaranteed rate of 256 kbps, you will not always operate at the full T1 speed. You are guaranteed not to go below 256 kbps, and not above it, even though at times you might. This occurs because the service provider configures multiple customers on the same circuit. If one customer isn't using the link at the time, another customer can take advantage of this unused bandwidth, thus increasing his bandwidth temporarily. This is called bursting. Because service providers can split the cost of the link over multiple customers, a Frame Relay link is considerably cheaper than a point-to-point link.

Operating at the two lower layers of the OSI model, Frame Relay is a specification for how to encapsulate your data across a WAN link. It is considered a nonbroadcast multiaccess (NBMA) technology because multiple routers can access the frame cloud but do not have broadcast ability. This chapter quizzes you on Frame Relay terminology and on how to enable Frame Relay encapsulation on a Cisco router.

Question 1

What protocol does Frame Relay rely on for error checking?

Frame Relay

Question 2

What is the difference between switched virtual circuits (SVCs) and permanent virtual circuits (PVCs)?

Frame Relay

Question 1 Answer

Frame Relay does not rely on any certain protocol for error checking. Instead, it relies on upper-layer protocols to provide error checking. For example, Frame Relay relies on TCP to provide error checking in an IP network.

NOTE

Frame Relay ensures that a packet contains an FCS to verify that the packet did not get corrupted en route to its destination. If the FCS fails, Frame Relay drops the packet.

Question 2 Answer

SVCs are virtual circuits that are dynamically established when data needs to be transferred and that are terminated when data transmission is complete. SVCs consist of four states: call setup, data transfer, idle, and call termination. PVCs are permanently established virtual circuits that operate in one of two states: idle or data transfer. When the PVC is idle, the connection between the DTE devices is still active.

Question 3

What is a Data Link Connection Identifier (DLCI)?

Question 4

What does the Frame Relay switch use to distinguish between each PVC connection?

Question 3 Answer

A DLCI is a number that identifies the logical circuit between the router and the Frame Relay switch. It is the Frame Relay Layer 2 address. The Frame Relay switch maps DLCIs between each pair of routers to create an PVC. For IP devices at the end of each virtual circuit to communicate, their IP addresses need to be mapped to DLCIs. If you are running Cisco IOS software Release 11.2 or later, mapping is done automatically using Inverse ARP. DLCIs have local significance. Think of DLCIs as the MAC address of the Frame Relay network.

Question 4 Answer

The Frame Relay switch uses DLCIs to distinguish between each PVC connection. The service provider typically assigns the DLCIs.

Question 5

What is the committed information rate (CIR)?

Frame Relay

Question 6

How does Frame Relay use Inverse ARP?

Frame Relay

Question 5 Answer

The CIR is the rate, in bits per second, at which the service provider commits to transfer data. The service provider sends any data in excess of this rate if its network has capacity at that time.

Question 6 Answer

Frame Relay uses Inverse ARP as a way to dynamically map a network layer address to a DLCI. Frame Relay uses Inverse ARP to determine the remote node's IP address by sending the Inverse ARP to the local DLCI. With Inverse ARP, the router can discover the network address of a device associated with a VC.

NOTE

Inverse ARP is automatically enabled with Cisco IOS software Release 11.2 and later. If you are running an earlier version, or if you want to disable Inverse ARP (**no frame-relay inverse-arp**), you can manually configure a static Frame Relay map in the map table.

Question 7

What is the Local Management Interface (LMI)?

Question 8

In Frame Relay, what is Forward Explicit Congestion Notification (FECN)?

Question 7 Answer

The LMI is a signaling standard between a CPE device (a router) and the Frame Relay switch that is responsible for managing and maintaining status between the devices. It is autosensed with Cisco IOS software Release 11.2 and later.

Question 8 Answer

The FECN is the bit in the Frame Relay header that signals to anything receiving the frame (switches and DTEs) that congestion is occurring in the same direction as the frame (the frame cloud). Switches and DTEs can react by slowing the rate at which data is sent in that direction.

Question 9

What is Backward Explicit Congestion Notification (BECN)?

Question 10

In the Frame Relay header, what is the discard eligibility (DE) bit?

Question 9 Answer

The BECN is the bit in the Frame Relay header that signals to switches and DTEs receiving the frame that congestion is occurring in the direction opposite the frame (backward). If switches and DTE devices detect that the BECN bit in the Frame Relay header is set to 1, they slow the rate at which data is sent in that direction.

Question 10 Answer

The DE bit is turned on for frames that are in excess of the CIR. The DE bit tells a switch which frames to discard if they must be discarded. For example, if your CIR is 256 kbps and you are using 512 kbps of bandwidth, any frame above the first 256 kbps has the DE bit turned on. If the Frame Relay switch becomes congested, it discards any frame above the first 256 kbps that has the DE turned on.

Question 11

What is the default LMI type for Cisco routers that are configured for Frame Relay?

Question 12

When a router receives LMI information, it updates its VC status to one of three states. What are these three states?

Question 11 Answer

The default LMI for Cisco routers configured for Frame Relay is Cisco. If you are running Cisco IOS software Release 11.2 or later, the Cisco router tries to autosense which LMI type the Frame Relay switch is using. If it cannot autosense the LMI type, the router uses Cisco as its LMI type. The three types of LMIs supported by Cisco routers are

- Cisco

- ANSI

- Q933a

Question 12 Answer

The three states that a VC uses to update its status are as follows:

- **Active state**—The connection is active, and routers can exchange data.

- **Inactive state**—The local connection to the Frame Relay switch is working, but the remote router's connection to the Frame Relay switch is not working.

- **Deleted state**—No LMIs are being received from the Frame Relay switch or that there is no service between the router and the Frame Relay switch.

Question 13

How do you enable Frame Relay on a Cisco router?

Frame Relay

Question 14

What command configures DLCI 16 on interface s0?

Frame Relay

Question 13 Answer

To enable Frame Relay on a Cisco router, you must first enable the serial interface for Frame Relay encapsulation with the **encapsulation frame-relay** interface command:

```
RouterB(config)#int s 0
RouterB(config-if)#ip address 192.168.1.1 255.255.255.0
RouterB(config-if)#encapsulation frame-relay
```

NOTE

When enabling Frame Relay, you might need to configure some optional parameters, such as the DLCI, **bandwidth** to define the speed of your VC, and LMI type. In its simplest form, Frame Relay is merely the process of specifying the interface's encapsulation.

Question 14 Answer

```
West-SD(config-if)#frame-relay interface-dlci 16
```

Question 15

How do you enable Frame Relay on a subinterface?

Question 16

The default encapsulation for a serial interface configured for Frame Relay is cisco. If you are connecting to a non-Cisco router, how do you change the encapsulation type?

Question 15 Answer

To enable Frame Relay on a subinterface, you must remove the IP address from the primary interface with the **no ip address** *ip-address subnet-mask* interface command, enable Frame Relay encapsulation on the serial interface, and then configure each subinterface with the IP address. For example, if you wanted to configure interface serial 0 with a subinterface, you would do the following:

```
West-SD(config-if)#no ip address 192.168.1.5 255.255.255.0
West-SD(config-if)#encap frame-relay
West-SD(config-if)#int s0.1 point-to-point
West-SD(config-if)#ip address 192.168.1.5 255.255.255.0
```

Question 16 Answer

If you are connecting to a non-Cisco router in a Frame Relay network, you need to specify **ietf** as the encapsulation type:

```
RouterB(config-if)#ip address 192.168.1.1 255.255.255.0
RouterB(config-if)#encapsulation frame-relay ietf
```

Question 17

If you are using Cisco IOS software Release 11.1 or earlier, or if you do not want to autosense the LMI type, how do you define the LMI type on a Cisco router?

Frame Relay

Question 18

If Inverse ARP is disabled on your router, how do you reenable it?

Frame Relay

Question 17 Answer

To define the LMI type on a Cisco router, use the **frame-relay lmi-type** {**ansi** | **cisco** | **q933a**} interface command:

```
RouterB(config-if)#ip address 192.168.1.1 255.255.255.0
RouterB(config-if)#encapsulation frame-relay
RouterB(config-if)#frame-relay lmi-type ansi
```

NOTE

Remember that the default LMI type is **cisco**. With Cisco IOS software Release 11.2 and later, the LMI type is autosensed by default.

Question 18 Answer

Inverse ARP is enabled by default on a Cisco router. If it is disabled, reenable it using the following command:

```
RouterB(config-if)#frame-relay inverse-arp [protocol] [dlci]
```

Supported protocols indicated by the *protocol* option include **ip**, **ipx**, **decnet**, **appletalk**, **vines**, and **xns**.

Question 19

If a remote router does not support Inverse ARP, what must you configure on the router?

Frame Relay

Question 20

If a remote router does not support Inverse ARP, you must define the address-to-DLCI table statically. How do you create these static maps?

Frame Relay

Question 19 Answer

If a remote router does not support Inverse ARP, you must configure static mapping between the local DLCI and the remote protocol address.

Question 20 Answer

To define static maps on a Cisco router, use this command:

```
RouterA(config-if)#frame-relay map protocol
  remote-protocol-address local-dlci
  [broadcast] [ietf | cisco] [payload-compress packet-by-
  packet]
```

protocol defines the supported protocol—bridging or LLC.

remote-protocol-address is the remote router's network layer address.

local-dlci defines the local router's local DLCI.

broadcast specifies whether you want to forward broadcasts over the VC, permitting dynamic routing protocols over the VC.

ietf | cisco is the encapsulation type.

For example, this command tells the router to get to IP address 192.168.1.2 using DLCI 110:

```
RouterB(config-if)#frame-relay map ip 192.168.1.2 110
  broadcast cisco
```

Question 21

How do you display the encapsulation type, DLCI number, LMI type, and whether the device is a DTE or DCE on a serial interface?

Question 22

What Cisco IOS software command displays the LMI traffic statistics and LMI type?

Question 21 Answer

To display the interface's encapsulation type, DLCI number, LMI type, and whether the device is a DTE or DCE, use the **show interface** *interface-type interface-number* command:

```
RouterA#show int s0
Serial0 is up, line protocol is up
  Hardware is HD64570
  Internet address is 192.168.1.2/24
  MTU 1500 bytes, BW 1544 Kbit, DLY 20000 usec, rely 255/255,
  load 1/255
  Encapsulation FRAME-RELAY, loopback not set, keepalive set
  (10 sec)
  LMI enq sent  3, LMI stat recvd 0, LMI upd recvd 0, DTE LMI up
  LMI enq recvd 5, LMI stat sent  0, LMI upd sent  0
  LMI DLCI 1023  LMI type is CISCO  frame relay DTE
  Broadcast queue 0/64, broadcasts sent/dropped 0/0, interface
  broadcasts 0
  Last input 00:00:05, output 00:00:07, output hang never
  Last clearing of "show interface" counters never
  Input queue: 0/75/0 (size/max/drops); Total output drops: 0
  Queueing strategy: weighted fair
<Output omitted>
```

Question 22 Answer

The **show frame-relay lmi** command displays the LMI traffic statistics and LMI type:

```
RouterA#show frame-relay lmi
LMI Statistics for interface Serial0 (Frame Relay DTE) LMI
  TYPE = CISCO
  Invalid Unnumbered info 0          Invalid Prot Disc 0
  Invalid dummy Call Ref 0           Invalid Msg Type 0
  Invalid Status Message 0           Invalid Lock Shift 0
  Invalid Information ID 0           Invalid Report IE Len 0
  Invalid Report Request 0           Invalid Keep IE Len 0
  Num Status Enq. Rcvd 1748          Num Status msgs Sent 1748
  Num Update Status Sent 0           Num St Enq. Timeouts 0
RouterA#
```

Question 23

What command displays the status of a Frame Relay virtual circuit?

Frame Relay

Question 24

How do you display the current Frame Relay map entries and information about these connections on a Cisco router?

Frame Relay

Question 23 Answer

The **show frame-relay pvc enable** command shows the status of a Frame Relay VC. It also lists all the configured PVCs and DLCI numbers and the status of each PVC.

Question 24 Answer

To view the current map entries and information about the connections, use the **show frame-relay map** command:

```
RouterA#show frame-relay map
Serial0 (up): ip 192.168.1.2 dlci 100(0x64,0x1840), dynamic,
   Broadcast, status defined, active
```

Question 25

How do you clear dynamic Frame Relay maps that were created by Inverse ARP?

Frame Relay

Question 25 Answer

Use the **clear frame-relay-inarp** privileged EXEC command to clear dynamic Frame Relay maps created by Inverse ARP.

Chapter 7

ISDN

One common use of ISDN is for backup for the primary WAN link and for low-speed connections to the Internet. ISDN is a circuit-switched technology that can support both data and voice. It uses a digital technology that is designed to run over the existing telephone network. Its speed ranges from 64 kbps to 2.048 Mbps. ISDN also has rapid call setup. The ICND exam extensively tests your knowledge of ISDN and all its protocols, terminology, and dial-on-demand routing (DDR). Because of this, it is highly recommended that you memorize all the ISDN protocols, equipment standards, and how to enable ISDN along with DDR on a Cisco router.

Question 1

In ISDN, what do E-series protocols specify?

ISDN

Question 2

What do protocols that begin with I deal with?

ISDN

Question 1 Answer

E-series protocols specify telephone network standards for
ISDN. Examples include International ISDN addressing (E.164)
and the International Telephone numbering plan (E.163).

NOTE

An easy way to remember E-series protocols is that they
specify existing standards.

Question 2 Answer

I-series protocols deal with concepts, terminology, and general
methods of ISDN (I.100), such as service aspects (I.200), user
network interfaces (I.400), and network aspects (I.300).

Question 3

What do ISDN protocols that begin with Q specify?

ISDN

Question 4

What is the data transfer speed for ISDN BRI?

ISDN

Question 3 Answer

Q-series protocols specify how switching and signaling (call setup) should operate. For example, ISDN protocol Q.921 is used for LAPD on the D channel, and protocol Q.931 is used for the ISDN network layer between the terminal and the switch.

Question 4 Answer

The data transfer rate for ISDN BRI is 128 kbps. The total transfer rate for ISDN BRI is 144 kbps. This consists of two 64 kbps (128 kbps) bearer (B) channels plus one 16 kbps delta (D) channel. The B channels can be used for data transfer and voice transmission. The D channel carries control and signaling information for fast call setup and can carry user data under certain circumstances. It operates at the first three layers of the OSI model.

NOTE

You might need to know the full kbps that BRI or PRI operates at or what speed the D channel operates at. Remember the speeds for the different channels. An easy way to remember the B channel's speed is that it is the bearer channel and "bears" all the weight of the data transfer. Thus, it is the faster channel.

Question 5

What is the total rate in Mbps for ISDN PRI?

ISDN

Question 6

In ISDN, the D channel appears to always be up and is what makes the call to the ISDN switch. What signaling protocol does the ISDN switch use to set up a path and pass the called number to the terminating ISDN switch?

ISDN

Question 5 Answer

The total rate for ISDN PRI in the U.S. and Japan is 1.544 Mbps. PRI consists of 23 64-kbps B channels and one 64-kbps D channel. In Europe, PRI consists of 30 B channels and one D channel for a total rate of 2.048 Mbps.

NOTE

ISDN PRI uses a DSU/CSU for a T1 connection.

Question 6 Answer

The ISDN local switch uses the SS7 protocol to set up a path and pass the called number to the terminating ISDN switch.

Question 7

Devices connecting to an ISDN network are known as terminal equipment (TE) and network termination (NT) equipment. What do the TE1 and TE2 equipment types refer to?

Question 8

What are ISDN NT1 and NT2 termination types?

Question 7 Answer

TE1 refers to a device that has a native ISDN interface. That is, it can plug directly into an ISDN network. TE2 refers to equipment that does not have an ISDN interface and that requires a terminal adapter (TA) to plug into an ISDN network.

Question 8 Answer

NT1 converts BRI signals into a form used by the ISDN line. It implements the physical layer specifications and connects the devices to the ISDN network. NT2 is the point where all ISDN lines are aggregated and switched using a customer-switching device.

Question 9

What is the function of the TA?

Question 10

What does the ISDN R reference point define?

Question 9 Answer

The terminal adapter converts non-ISDN signals into ISDN signals. Devices that are not native to ISDN connect to a TA to access the ISDN network.

Question 10 Answer

The R reference point defines the point between a non-ISDN-compatible device and a TA.

Question 11

What does the ISDN S point reference?

ISDN

Question 12

What does the ISDN T reference point define?

ISDN

Question 11 Answer

The S point references the points or customer equipment that connect to the NT2 or customer-switching device.

Question 12 Answer

ISDN T reference points refer to the point between NT1 and NT2 devices. T and S reference points are electronically the same and reference the outbound connection from the NT2 to the ISDN network. The S and T reference points are usually presented together as S/T.

Question 13

What is the ISDN U reference point?

ISDN

Question 14

What happens when you connect a router with a U interface into an NT1?

ISDN

Question 13 Answer

The U reference point is the point between the NT1 and the ISDN network.

NOTE

It is recommended that you memorize all the ISDN reference points. The study sheets provide an excellent diagram of the ISDN reference points that will greatly assist you in your studies.

Question 14 Answer

If you connect a router with a U interface into an NT1, you will damage the interface. This is because the U interface on a Cisco router already has a built-in NT1.

Question 15

Your Cisco router has an interface labeled BRI. Is this interface a TE1 or a TE2?

Question 16

What are SPIDs?

Question 15 Answer

If an interface on your Cisco router is labeled BRI, it is ISDN-ready and is a TE1 interface. An example of a TE2 interface is a serial interface. You need a TA to connect to the ISDN network.

Question 16 Answer

Service Profile Identifiers (SPIDs) identify your router to the switch at the central office (the ISP). They are a series of characters that look like phone numbers and are not always required.

Question 17

How do you enable ISDN BRI on a Cisco router?

ISDN

Question 18

How do you enable ISDN PRI on a Cisco router?

ISDN

Question 17 Answer

To enable ISDN BRI on a Cisco router, first you need to define the switch type that your router will connect to. The switch type is the type of switch used by your service provider. To define the ISDN switch type, enter the **isdn switch-type** *switch-type* global or interface command. Specifying the **isdn switch-type** global command specifies the ISDN switch type for the entire router. The second step is to enter the SPIDs provided by your service provider by entering the **isdn spid1** *spid-number* and **isdn spid2** *spid-number* interface commands. The following example enables ISDN on a router, specifying a Northern DMS100 switch as the switch type:

```
RouterA(config-if)#isdn switch-type basic-dms100
RouterA(config-if)#isdn spid1 123456789123
RouterA(config-if)#isdn spid2 123456789124
```

NOTE

You must contact your service provider to determine the ISDN switch type.

Question 18 Answer

To enable ISDN PRI on a Cisco router, first you define the ISDN switch type you will be connecting to, followed by the ISDN interface. Then you establish the interface port to function as PRI. The following commands accomplish this:

```
RouterA(config)#isdn switch-type isdn-switch-type
RouterA(config)#controller controller slot/port
RouterA(config-controller)#pri-group timeslots range
```

NOTE

The *range* is a range of numbers from 1 to 24. Each channel in PRI is 64 kbps, so if your PRI channel is 1.544 Mbps, your range is 1 to 24.

If you live in Europe and have an E1 ISDN line, your range is 1 to 31.

Question 19

If you have DDR enabled on your router, when does the router decide to bring up the ISDN interface and send traffic?

Question 20

How do you enable DDR on a Cisco router?

Question 19 Answer

If DDR is enabled on your router, it brings up the ISDN line when it sees interesting traffic.

NOTE

When the link is enabled, the router transmits interesting and uninteresting traffic. Only when no more interesting traffic is transmitted over the link does the idle timer start and disconnect the link.

Question 20 Answer

To enable DDR on a Cisco router, you first need to define static routes with the **ip route** command. Next, specify interesting traffic, and finally, configure the dialer information.

Question 21

How do you specify interesting traffic?

Question 22

The last step in configuring DDR on a Cisco router is to configure the dialer information. How do you do this?

Question 21 Answer

Interesting traffic can be based on protocol type or addresses for source or destination hosts using the **dialer-list** command:

```
dialer-list dialer-group protocol protocol-name
  {permit | deny | list access-list-number}
```

dialer-group is the number that identifies the dialer list. *protocol-name* can be IP, IPX, AppleTalk, DECnet, or VINES. The following **dialer-list** command creates dialer list 10, which defines as interesting all IP traffic that matches access list 100:

```
RouterA(config)#dialer-list 10 protocol ip list 100
RouterA(config)#access-list 100 permit tcy any any eq www
RouterA(config)#access-list 100 permit tcy any any eq domain
```

NOTE

The **default dialer-list** command permits all IP and IPX traffic, resulting in a huge phone bill. To avoid this, specify only the port numbers of the protocol stack you want to bring up the ISDN link. After the link is up, *all* traffic can pass through it. The only way to control the specific traffic passing through the ISDN link after the link is up is to use access lists.

Question 22 Answer

Do the following to configure the dialer information:

Step 1   Choose the interface.

Step 2   Configure an IP address on the interface.

Step 3   Configure the encapsulation type (such as PPP).

Step 4   Bind interesting traffic to the interface using the **dialer-group** *group-number* interface command:

```
RouterA(config)#int bri0
RouterA(config-if)#ip address 172.16.0.2 255.255.255.252
RouterA(config-if)#encap ppp
RouterA(config-if)#dialer-group 10
```

Question 23

How do you test connectivity on a dial-on-demand link?

ISDN

Question 24

What command can you use to view the call in progress?

ISDN

Question 23 Answer

To test connectivity on a DDR link, you must send interesting traffic.

Question 24 Answer

The **show isdn active** command shows the call in progress and the number dialed:

```
RouterA#show isdn active
Global ISDN Switchtype = basic-5ess
ISDN BRI0 interface
        dsl 0, interface ISDN Switchtype = basic-5ess
    Layer 1 Status:
        ACTIVE
    Layer 2 Status:
        TEI = 64, Ces = 1, SAPI = 0, State = MULTIPLE_FRAME
_ ESTABLISHED
    Layer 3 Status:
        0 Active Layer 3 Call(s)
    Activated dsl 0 CCBs = 0
    The Free Channel Mask:  0x80000003
    Total Allocated ISDN CCBs = 0
```

Question 25

How can you view the number of times the dial string has been successfully reached on a Cisco router?

Question 25 Answer

The **show dialer** command displays information about the interface configured for DDR, the number of times the dialer string has been successfully reached, and the fast and idle timer values for each B channel.

Chapter 8

Last-Minute Exam Tips

As your exam date approaches, you might wonder how to fully prepare for the INTRO, ICND, and CCNA exams. You have invested your time and money in this exam, and you want to pass the first time. Historically, the CCNA exam is one of the more difficult exams to pass in the networking industry; many people fail to pass the first time. Cisco takes pride in making sure that only knowledgeable people can pass the exams, so you will be tested on your knowledge of networking and using Cisco products. This chapter gives you last-minute tips to help you fully prepare for the INTRO, ICND, and CCNA exams.

30 Days Before the Exam

The INTRO, ICND, and CCNA exams cover a broad range of networking topics, from the OSI model to Frame Relay, and you can count on being tested on all these topics. At times, the information required to pass each exam might seem overwhelming. However, if you study in smaller sections, you will be more successful at retaining the information than if you tackled it all at once.

As you approach your exam date, go over all the topics on the exam. Focus on your weak areas, and use this book to help. Go over the flash cards as often as you can. Some students might want to tear the flash cards out of the book and take them everywhere they go, such as to work or to the grocery store. Make sure you understand all the information on the cards. If you are having a hard time with a certain topic, go back to your main study book and refresh yourself on the topic. The more you familiarize yourself with the flash cards and study sheets, the more successful you will be with the exam.

Use the study sheets as a quick refresher to make sure you haven't missed any topics. Look over the study sheets at night before you go to bed and whenever you have a spare moment. The practice test on the CD-ROM helps you prepare for the exam by providing over 500 review questions as well as simulation questions that mimic the simulations on the exams. Go over the practice tests and become familiar with taking the exam. For any questions you get wrong, go back and study the topic to better understand it so that you will prevail in the future.

The Day Before the Exam

The day before your scheduled exam, take a rest from studying. You have studied hard up to this point, and your mind needs a break. You want to be refreshed, alert, and ready for your big day tomorrow. Go to bed early. Get a good night's sleep so that your mind and body will be rejuvenated for the next day.

The Day of the Exam

The Cisco exams are difficult, so come prepared and without distractions on the day of your exam. If you are taking your exam on a weekday, try to take the day off from work so that your mind can be focused one hundred percent on the exam.

Arrive 30 minutes to an hour before you are scheduled for the exam. Bring with you the study sheets from this book, and go over the material before you enter the testing center. Doing this will refresh your memory.

As you enter the exam room, you will be given a small board with a marker to write on. Before you start your exam, write down as much of the information as you can remember from the study sheets. You can use this as a reference throughout the exam.

The Exam Itself

Before taking your exam, Cisco will ask you to fill out a questionnaire regarding your skills in networking and your experience with Cisco equipment. If you read the disclaimer, it says that how you answer the questions on the questionnaire determines how you are graded on the exam, although we are not sure how Cisco does this. Cisco might weigh each question differently depending on how much experience you claim to have. So answer the questionnaire wisely.

The INTRO, ICND, and CCNA exams are timed. The amount of time allotted varies according to the number of questions on the test, but you should have about 70 seconds per question. As with all Cisco exams, you cannot go back after you answer a question and change your answer, so choose your answers carefully. Read the entire question, and then read all the possible answers before choosing the correct one. Never leave any questions unanswered, because they will count against your score.

The CCNA exam is known to be tricky at times, and I'd expect that the INTRO and ICND exams might throw a curve ball or two, as well. You have to read between the lines on some of the questions. If you are prepared and have studied the flash cards and the study sheets, you will be ready for these kinds of questions. For example, you might see a question like this:

1   How does the store-and-forward switching method work?

   A. It copies the first 64 bytes of the frame and checks it for fragmentation before forwarding the frame to the destination.

   B. It looks at only the destination address in the frame and then forwards the frame.

   C. It discards frames if they are runts or giants.

   D. It copies 75% of the frame before forwarding it to its destination.

If you have memorized the flash cards, you know that flash card 15 in Part II, Chapter 1 says that the store-and-forward switching method receives the entire frame before forwarding it and that it reads the CRC to make sure the frame is good before forwarding it. If the frame is too small or too big, it discards the frame. Knowing this, you realize that options A and D are false, because the store-and-forward method looks at the entire frame. This leaves you with options B and C. B is incorrect because the store-and-forward method looks at the CRC as well as the destination address. This leaves you with the correct answer, C. On questions where you do not know the correct answer, learn to eliminate the obviously wrong options. This usually gives you two options to choose from, which gives you a greater chance of choosing the correct one.

The CCNA exam also has router simulations, in which you have to enter the correct IOS command into a box. If you receive questions of this nature, enter the full command—don't abbreviate it. For example, if you see a question that asks you to enter the command that displays the access lists enabled on interface e0, enter **show ip interface e0**. Don't enter **sh ip int e0**. Even though this is correct and you might get the question right, it is safer to enter the entire command.

As another example, you might be asked to configure an IP address on an interface. One of the most common mistakes when configuring an interface is not enabling it. By default, all Cisco router interfaces are administratively disabled, so the simulations on the ICND exam have interfaces that are administratively disabled. Be sure to enable any interface you have to configure on the ICND exam with the **no shutdown** interface command.

One of the best ways to prepare for the router simulations is to spend a little time on an actual Cisco router. Doing so helps you become more familiar with the IOS commands and gives you firsthand experience. If you do not have access to a Cisco router, you can use a router simulation. Cisco Press offers many software products that include powerful router simulators. Another option is to rent router time over the Internet. Several sites let you pay for remote router time for as little as $15 per hour. After you pay for remote time, the site's administrator contacts you and gives you the router's IP address and password. You Telnet into the router and can configure it as you like.

If you follow all of these tips, and you know your stuff, you should have no problem passing either the INTRO, ICND, or CCNA exam. Good luck.

Part III

Study Sheets

INTRO

ICND/CCNA

Component	Function
Floppy disk drive	A device for reading and writing to floppy disks.
Hard disk drive	Used to store and retrieve data from nonvolatile storage media.
Microprocessor	A silicon chip that contains a CPU.
Motherboard	The computer's main circuit board. Everything else plugs into the motherboard and is controlled by it.
Printed circuit board	A thin plate on which integrated circuits are placed.
Memory	Internal storage.
Random Access Memory (RAM)	A temporary storage place for data while programs are in use. If the computer loses power, all data in RAM that was not saved is lost.
Read-Only Memory (ROM)	Prerecorded or "startup" memory.
Erasable Programmable Read-Only Memory (EPROM)	Computer memory unavailable to the user. It usually contains very basic instructions for the computer's operation.
System unit	The computer's main "box."
Backplane	A large circuit board that has sockets for expansion cards.
Socket	A connector for expansion cards.
Interface	A device that connects to pieces of equipment (a mouse and computer, for example).
Network card	A PCB that provides network access.
Parallel port	An interface that communicates more than 1 bit of information at a time. Usually used to connect devices such as printers.
Serial port	An interface that can communicate 1 bit at a time.
Universal Serial Bus (USB)	An interface that allows other devices to be connected and disconnected without resetting the system.

Graphic Symbols

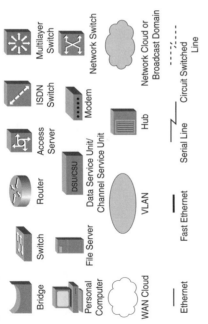

Bridge
Switch
Router
Access Server
ISDN Switch
Multilayer Switch

Personal Computer
File Server
Data Service Unit/ Channel Service Unit
DSU/CSU
Modem
Network Switch

WAN Cloud
VLAN
Hub
Network Cloud or Broadcast Domain

Ethernet
Fast Ethernet
Serial Line
Circuit Switched Line

Computing Basics

PC Components

PCs are the building blocks of networks. They have many of the same parts and systems as other network devices, such as routers and switches. You should understand the functions of the following components in case the need to troubleshoot arises.

Component	Function
Bus	Wires that connect the internal components to the CPU.
CD-ROM drive	Compact Disc Read-Only Memory.
Central Processing Unit (CPU)	The computer's "brain" where nearly all calculations are performed.
Expansion card	A printed circuit board that can be inserted for additional functionality.
Expansion slot	An opening in the computer for expansion cards.

Laptop and notebook computers are smaller, more portable versions of PCs. As chip integration techniques continue to improve, laptops are becoming every bit as functional as PCs. Laptops use PC card slots or Personal Computer Memory Card International Association (PCMCIA) card slots where credit card-size network cards, modems, or hard drives can be added.

NICs, also known as LAN adapters, provide network connectivity for PCs and laptops. NICs plug into the motherboard through an expansion slot or are presoldered to it. NICs require the following:

- **Interrupt Request Line (IRQ)**—This signal tells the CPU that an event has occurred that requires processing.
- **I/O address**—A memory location where instructional data can be stored.
- **Drivers**—Program-specific instructions.

When selecting a NIC, consider the following:

- **Network type**—Each network requires a specific type of NIC.
- **Medium type**—Twisted pair, coaxial, wireless, and so on.
- **System bus**—PCI buses are most common.

Bits, Bytes, and Measurement Terms

Although a computer can make very complicated calculations, the computer's brain uses simple instructions composed of electronic signals that represent 1s and 0s. A system with only two states is called a binary system. A single state (a single 1 or a single 0) is called a bit. A grouping of 8 bits is called a byte. The following table shows the common units.

Unit	Bytes	Bits
Bit (b)	1/8 byte	1 bit
Byte (B)	1 byte	8 bits
Kilobyte (KB)	1000 bytes	8000 bits
Megabyte (MB)	1 million bytes	8 million bits
Gigabyte (GB)	1 billion bytes	8 billion bits

It is important to pay attention to the unit of measurement. For example, many modems give their speed in kilobits per second (kbps), but many programs show download times in kilobytes per second (kBps). A modem operating at 45 kbps downloads at only 5.76 kBps (best case).

Decimal-to-Binary Conversion

Computers use a numbering system based on only 1s and 0s. This type of system is called binary or base 2. This numbering system might seem awkward at first glance, but it uses the same logic as the base 10 system we use every day. As with base 10, binary counting starts with the "ones" column until all the numbers are exhausted, and then it rolls over to the next column, which is a power of the base. For example, base 10 has ten numbers (0 through 9). When counting, you start in the "ones" column and count until you reach the highest unit. Then you move to the "tens" column. This continues with successive powers $(1, 10^1, 10^2, 10^3)$. The binary system's columns or placeholders are $2^0, 2^1, 2^2, 2^3$, and so on. The following table shows the values for the first seven places.

Base 2 Numbering System

Number of Symbols	2							
Symbols	0, 1							
Base Exponent	2^7	2^6	2^5	2^4	2^3	2^2	2^1	2^0
Place Value	128	64	32	16	8	4	2	1
Example: Convert 47 to Binary	0	0	1	0	1	1	1	1

Binary numbers are used extensively in networking. They are the basis of IP addressing. To convert between decimal and binary, it best to build a simple table like the one just shown. To convert from binary to decimal, simply add up the "place values" of the digits that are 1s. In the preceding example, the placeholders for 1, 2, 4, 8, and 32 all contain 1s. Adding those values yields 47. (101111 in binary is 47 in decimal.) To convert from decimal to binary, again build a table. Put a 1 in the highest place value (in this example, a 1 is placed in the column representing 32. (64 cannot be used, because it is greater than 47.) Now subtract the place value from the decimal number (47-32=15). The next value (16) is too large, so a 0 is placed in that column. A 1 is then placed in the 8 column, and the subtraction is performed again (15-8=7.) Repeat the process until the value of the subtraction equals 0.

Binary-to-Hexadecimal Conversion

Another common numbering system used in computing and networking is hexadecimal, or hex. Hex is a base 16 numbering system, which presents a bit of a problem, because only ten symbols exist to represent numbers. To account for the additional numbers, the letters A through F are used for the decimal values 10 to 15. Hex is also useful as shorthand for

Computing Basics Summary

- Computers use many of the same subsystems as routers, switches, and other networking gear.

- A bit is a single state (1 or 0) used in computer instructions. A byte is 8 bits and is the standard unit for computer data.

- Binary is a base 2 numbering system used extensively in computer and networking systems.

- Hex is a 16-bit numbering system and is an efficient shorthand method for very large binary numbers.

Networking Fundamentals

Networking has its own jargon and common terms. The following terms are used throughout the industry and appear many times in this study guide:

- **Network interface card (NIC)**—Pronounced "nick," this card connects a computer to a LAN.

- **Medium**—The physical transport used to carry data. Most of the time this can be just a cable (twisted pair, coaxial, fiber), but it also includes air (for wireless transmission).

- **Protocol**—A set of communication rules used by computers or network devices.

- **Cisco IOS Software**—The most widely deployed network system software. Cisco IOS services include basic connectivity, security, network management, and other advanced services. Early versions of Cisco IOS could perform only "store and forward" packet transport. The software is now a complete network solution that continues to evolve.

- **Client**—A computer or program that requests information from a server.

- **Server**—A computer or program that provides services or information to clients. Servers are often dedicated, meaning that they perform no other tasks beyond supplying information to clients.

- **Network Operating System (NOS)**—Usually refers to the operating system running on servers. This includes Windows NT, Windows 2000 Server, Novell, NetWare, and UNIX.

- **Connectivity device**—Any device that connects cable segments, connects two or more small networks into a larger one, or divides a large network into small ones.

- **Local-area network (LAN)**—A network confined to a small geographic area. This can be a room, floor, building, or campus.

---

binary. Four binary digits represent 16 numbers, which is a single hex digit. The following table shows the conversion between binary, hex, and decimal.

Decimal-to-Hexadecimal Equivalent

Binary	Hex	Decimal
0000	0	0
0001	1	1
0010	2	2
0011	3	3
0100	4	4
0101	5	5
0110	6	6
0111	7	7
1000	8	8
1001	9	9
1010	A	10
1011	B	11
1100	C	12
1101	D	13
1110	E	14
1111	F	15

Using hex, a very large binary string of 1s and 0s can be represented by just a few hex numbers. For example, 1001101100011111 in binary equals 9B1F in hex (or 39711 in decimal). To convert binary to hex, put the binary digits in groups of four, starting from the rightmost digit.

OSI MODEL

OSI MODEL		
Application	User interface.	Telnet HTTP
Presentation	Encryption and other processing.	ASCII/EBCDIC JPEG/MP3
Session	Manages multiple applications.	Operating systems Scheduling
Transport	Provides reliable or best-effort delivery and some error correction.	TCP UDP SPX
Network	Provides logical addressing used by routers and the network hierarchy.	IP IPX
Data link	Creates frames from bits of data. Uses MAC addresses to access endpoints. Provides error detection but no correction.	802.3 802.2 HDLC Frame Relay
Physical	Specifies voltage, wire speed, and cable pin-outs.	EIA/TIA V.35

Protocol Data Units (PDUs) are used to communicate between layers.

Encapsulation is the method of adding headers and trailers. As the data moves down the stack, the receiving device strips the header, which contains information for that layer (de-encapsulation).

Data Communication

For packets to travel from a source to a destination, each OSI layer of the source computer must communicate with its peer at the destination. Each part of the message is encapsulated by the layer below it, and it is unwrapped at the destination for use by the corresponding layer.

- WAN—Wide-area network. Interconnects LANs using leased carrier lines or satellite technology.
  - **Physical topology**—A network's physical shape. These shapes include linear bus, ring, star, and mesh.
  - **Logical topology**—The path that signals take from one computer to another.

Why Network Computers?

One of a network's primary functions is to increase productivity by linking computers and computer networks. Corporate networks are typically divided into user groups, which are usually based on groups of employees. Remote-access locations such as branches, home offices, and mobile workers usually connect to the corporate LAN using a WAN service.

Networking Applications

Applications are computer programs that run over networks. An entire suite of Internet applications has been developed. HTTP connects web servers with client browsers. Post Office Protocol 3 (POP3) is used in e-mail applications. FTP transfers files. Network management programs use Simple Network Management Protocol (SNMP). These applications all reside at the application layer of a standard protocol suite used throughout internetworking.

OSI Model

The OSI model is a standardized framework for network functions and schemes. It breaks otherwise-complex network interactions into simple elements, which lets developers modularize design efforts. This method allows many independent developers to work on separate network functions, which can be applied in a "plug and play" manner.

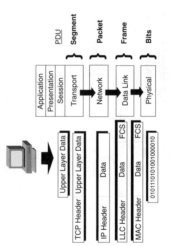

The TCP/IP Model

The TCP/IP suite of protocols is used to communicate across any set of interconnected networks. These protocols, initially developed by Defense Advanced Research Projects Agency (DARPA), are well-suited for communication across both LANs and WANs. The protocol suite includes Layer 3 and 4 specifications, as well as specifications for higher-layer applications such as e-mail and file transfer.

The TCP/IP protocol stack closely follows the OSI reference model. All standard Layer 1 and 2 protocols are supported (called the network interface layer in TCP/IP).

7	Application	
6	Presentation	
5	Session	
4	Transport	Application · 5
3	Network	Transport · 4
2	Data Link	Internet · 3
1	Physical	Data Link · 2
		Physical · 1

TCP/IP Datagrams

TCP/IP information is sent via datagrams. One message may be broken into a series of datagrams that are reassembled at the destination. Three layers are associated with the TCP/IP protocol stack:

- **Application layer**—Specifications exist for e-mail, file transfer, remote login, and other applications. Network management is also supported.

- **Transport layer**—Transport services allow multiple upper-layer applications to use the same data stream. TCP and UDP protocols exist at this layer, providing the following functions:
  —Flow control (through windowing)
  —Reliability (through sequence numbers and acknowledgments)

- **Internet layer**—Several protocols operate at the TCP/IP Internet layer:
  —IP provides connectionless, best-effort routing of datagrams.
  —ICMP provides control and messaging capabilities.
  —ARP determines the data link layer address for known IP addresses.
  —RARP determines network addresses when data link layer addresses are known.

Other Internet Layer Protocols

ICMP, ARP, and RARP are three protocols used by the Internet layer. Internet Control Message Protocol (ICMP) sends error and control messages, such as destination unreachable, time exceeded, subnet mask request, echo, and others.

Address Resolution Protocol (ARP) is used to map a known IP address to a MAC sublayer address. An ARP cache table is checked when looking for a destination address. If the address is not in the table, ARP sends a broadcast looking for the destination station.

Reverse ARP

Reverse Address Resolution Protocol (RARP) is used to map a known MAC address to an IP address. Dynamic Host Configuration Protocol (DHCP) is a modern implementation of RARP.

Networking Fundamentals Summary

- The OSI model provides a standardized method of creating and implementing network standards and schemes.

- The OSI model allows "plug and play" applications, simplified building blocks, and modularized development.

- The OSI model has seven layers. Mnemonics are useful for remembering the layers and their functions (PDNTSPA).

- Encapsulation is the process of adding layer-specific instructions and information (for the receiving device) as headers and trailers.

- De-encapsulation is the reverse of encapsulation.

- The TCP/IP model has four layers: application, transport, Internet, and network access.

Network Devices

Layer 1 devices operate at the physical layer and are only involved in transmitting signals (moving bits). The two most common Layer 1 devices are repeaters and hubs. Repeaters are necessary because a signal's quality degrades over distance, eventually becoming unreadable. Repeaters regenerate and retime (or clean up) the signal, allowing it to travel a longer distance over a given medium. Repeaters can be single-port (one in, one out) or multiport.

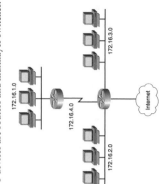

Hubs are similar to repeaters and are often called multi-port repeaters (usually having from four to 20 ports.) Hubs provide no filtering or intelligence; they simply clean up signals. Hubs also increase network reliability by isolating endpoints. Using a hub, if a single cable fails, the network continues to operate. A group of devices connected to the same physical medium is known as a collision domain. If two devices transmit a signal at the same time, a collision results. Ethernet devices use a method called carrier sense multiple access collision detect (CSMA/CD) when sending bits. When a collision occurs, both stations resend the signal after a random period. Collisions increase with the number of stations and reduce usable bandwidth.

Layer 2 devices operate at the data link layer and, in most cases, isolate endpoints, avoiding data collisions (discussed later). Devices such as bridges and switches use MAC addresses to switch data frames.

NICs are considered Layer 2 devices because they provide MAC addresses used by other Layer 2 devices.

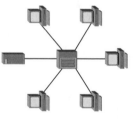

Bridge

Bridges connect LAN segments and isolate collision domains, which increases bandwidth. Bridges keep local traffic from going to other LAN segments but can filter traffic intended for other LAN segments using the MAC address of the destination endpoint. Bridges keep track of destinations in MAC address tables.

Switches (or LAN switches) are similar to bridges and have all the same functionality but are typically much faster because the switching functions are performed in hardware rather than software (which is what bridges use). Switches also support virtual LANs (VLANs, discussed later).

Layer 3 devices operate at the network layer of the OSI model, which uses a different addressing scheme than Layer 2 devices. IP addresses (discussed later) are one type of Layer 3 device. The two most common Layer 3 devices are routers and multilayer switches.

172.16.1.0

172.16.4.0

172.16.2.0

172.16.3.0

Internet

Routers pass data packets between networks based on their IP (or other Layer 3) address. Routers can make intelligent decisions about the best path a packet can take across the network. Routers also can connect different types of Layer 2 networks. Routers regulate traffic and make up the backbone of most IP networks.

Multilayer switches are the same as regular Layer 2 switches but can process and make switching decisions based on Layer 3 addresses. This advance was enabled because of high-speed software embedded in hardware ASICs. This has reduced the bottleneck that used to occur with software-based Layer 3 devices. Using Layer 3 addresses allows multilayer switches to implement quality and security policies.

Voice, DSL, and optical devices: As voice and data networks converge, several new devices have been developed. Voice gateways handle voice and data packets moving over a single network. Digital Subscriber Line Access Multiplexers (DSLAMs) serve as the handoff point between a subscriber network and a carrier network. Optical platforms are used for high-speed, long-distance transports.

Firewalls and Authentication, Authorization, and Accounting (AAA) servers work at the higher layers of the OSI model to provide security for networks. A firewall can be either a physical device or a software program. Firewalls protect systems by acting as a traffic cop for data entering a private network. Their job is to allow only valid traffic (as defined by the network admin) and block all other types of traffic. AAA servers keep unauthorized users from accessing sensitive data and monitor authorized usage to protect against theft or misuse.

Network Devices Summary

- Networking devices are used to connect networks. Hubs, switches, and routers interconnect devices within LANs, MANs, and WANs. Networking devices function at different layers of the OSI model.

- Hubs operate at Layer 1 and make no decisions. All devices connected to a hub are on a shared medium and are part of a single collision domain.

- LAN switches work at Layer 2 and decide whether to forward and flood data frames based on MAC addresses.

- Routers can make decisions regarding the best path for delivery of data on the network.

- Firewalls and AAA servers provide security to the network.

Network Topologies

A topology refers to the way in which network devices are connected. A physical topology refers to the physical layout of the endpoints and the connecting cables. A logical topology refers to how signals travel from endpoint to endpoint. The physical and logical topologies can be the same or different. An example of this is a network in which each endpoint is connected to every other endpoint (a meshed network) but the signal can flow in only sequential order (a ring network). The following sections discuss each of the topologies.

A bus or linear bus connects all devices with a single cable. The ends of the wire must be connected to a device or terminator, or signals will bounce back and cause errors. Only a single packet can be transmitted at a time on a bus, or the packets will collide and both will be destroyed (and must be resent).

In a ring topology, a frame travels in a logical order around the ring, going from one end station to the next. If an end station wants to send data, it is added to the frame. The frame continues around the ring, and the data is removed at the intended destination. The frame, however, continues. In a single ring, data travels in a single direction. In a dual ring, each ring sends data in a different direction. Two rings create redundancy, or fault tolerance, which means that if one ring fails, the system can still operate. If parts of both rings fail, a "wrap" (a connection between the two rings) can heal the fault.

Star topologies are the most commonly used physical topology in Ethernet LANs. Stars have a central connection (hub, switch, or router) where all end devices meet. Stars cost more than other topologies but are more fault-tolerant because a cable failure usually affects only one end device, or host. The disadvantage of a star is that if the central device fails, the whole system fails.

In an extended star, the central networking device connects to other networking devices, which then connect to end stations.

In a full-mesh topology, all devices are connected to all other devices. There is great redundancy on full-mesh networks, but for networks with more than a few devices, it becomes overly expensive and complicated. Partial-mesh topologies, which have at least one device with multiple connections, provide good redundancy without the expense of full meshes.

Network Topologies Summary

- A physical topology describes the plan for wiring the physical devices. A logical topology describes how information flows through a network.

- In a physical bus topology, a single cable connects all devices.

- The most commonly used architecture in Ethernet LANs is the physical star topology, in which each host is connected to a central device.

- In a ring topology, all the hosts are connected in the form of a ring or circle.

- In a full-mesh topology, all devices are connected to each other.

LANs

Ethernet is one of the most widely used LAN standards. Ethernet operates at Layer 2, the data link layer. This layer has the following functions:

- It performs physical addressing.

- It provides support for connection-oriented and connectionless services.

- It provides frame sequencing and flow control.

	Ethernet			Frame Relay
Data Link		802.2	HDLC	
		802.3		
Physical			EIA/TIA-232 v.35	

Two sublayers perform data link functions: the MAC layer and the LLC layer. Media Access Control (MAC) sublayer (802.3) is responsible for how data is sent over the wire. The MAC address is a 48-bit address expressed as 12 hex digits.

MAC defines the following:

- Physical addressing
- Network topology
- Line discipline
- Error notification
- Orderly delivery of frames
- Optional flow control

Logical Link Control (LLC) sublayer (802.2) is responsible for identifying and encapsulating different protocol types. There are two types of LLC frames: Service Access Point (SAP) and Subnetwork Access Protocol (SNAP); SNAP is used to support non-802 protocols.

The term Ethernet encompasses several LAN implementations. Physical layer implementations vary, and all support various cabling structures. There are four main categories:

- **Ethernet (DIX) and IEEE 802.3**—Operate at 10 Mbps over coaxial cable, UTP, or fiber. The standards are referred to as 10BASE2, 10BASE5, and 10BASE-T.
- **Fast Ethernet, or 100 Mbps Ethernet**—Operates over UTP or fiber.

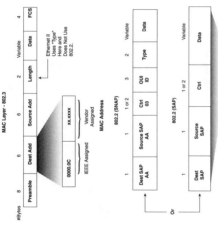

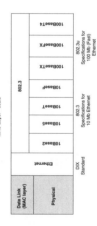

- **Gigabit Ethernet**—An 802.3 extension operates over fiber and copper at 1000 Mbps, or 1 gigabit per second (Gbps).
- **10-Gigabit Ethernet**—This is now being standardized and will offer speeds of 10 billion bits per second over fiber.

This table compares cable and connector specifications. Fast Ethernet requires unshielded twisted-pair (UTP) Category 5 (or higher) cabling.

	10BASE5	10BASET	100BASETX	100BASEFX
Media	50-ohm coax (thick	EIA/TIA Cat 3, 4, 5 UTP 2 pair	EIA/TIA Cat 5 UTP 2 pair	62.5/125 micron multimode fiber
Maximum Segment Length	500 meters	100 meters	100 meters	400 meters
Topology	Bus	Star	Star	Point-to-Point
Connector	AUI	ISO 8877 (RJ-45)	ISO 8877 (RJ-45)	Duplex media-interface connector (MIC)

A Gigabit Interface Converter (GBIC) converts electrical signals to optical signals for transmission over fiber cables (as well as the reverse process). GBICs eliminate the need to replace entire boards when optical transmission is desired.

How Ethernet Works

All stations on an Ethernet segment are connected to the same wire. Therefore, all devices receive all signals. When devices send signals at the same time, a collision occurs. A scheme is needed to detect and compensate for collisions.

- **Collision domain**—A group of devices connected to the same physical medium such that if two devices access the medium at the same time, a collision results. Ethernet devices use a method called CSMA/CD when sending bits. When a collision occurs, both stations resend the signal after a random period. Collisions increase with the number of stations.
- **Broadcast domain**—A group of devices on the network that receive one anothers' broadcast messages.

LAN Summary

- LAN standards specify cabling and signaling at the physical and data link layers of the OSI model.
- Several types of Ethernet exist: Ethernet, Fast Ethernet, Gigabit Ethernet, and 10-Gigabit Ethernet. Each type has a different transfer rate.
- Cisco GBIC cards are hot-swappable and plug into an Ethernet port.
- Ethernet uses CSMA/CD.

WANs

WANs interconnect LANs and operate at Layers 1 through 3 of the OSI model. WANs operate over large geographic areas, use carrier services, can provide full- or part-time connectivity, and use many different types of serial connections to connect networks.

Global Internet: Although any network of networks is considered an internet, the Internet is an interconnection of thousands of networks all over the world, arranged in a hierarchy. The Internet backbone carries high-speed data over carrier networks. The backbone connects many Internet service provider (ISP) networks, which in turn connect to millions of users.

WAN connections can be one of the following types:

- Dedicated connections (also called point-to-point or leased-line connections) provide a pre-established path over a carrier network between two customer networks.
- Circuit-switched connections use a dedicated physical path through a carrier network that is established and maintained only for the length of communication.
- Packet-switched connections use single point-to-point connections to exchange data over a carrier network. Frame Relay is a packet-switched technology.
- Cell switching is similar to packet switching but uses fixed cell sizes to send data (packet switching uses variable sizes).

WANs use multiple types of devices, including the following:

- Routers, which provide many services over multiple protocols
- WAN switches, which logically connect other WAN devices such as routers

A WAN service provider assigns your organization the parameters required for making the WAN link connection.

Customer Premises Equipment (CPE) is located on the subscriber's premises and includes both equipment owned by the subscriber and devices leased by the service provider.

Demarcation (demarc) marks the point where CPE ends and the local loop begins. Usually it is located in the telecommunications closet.

Local loop, or "last-mile," is the cabling from the demarc into the WAN service provider's central office.

The central office (CO) is a switching facility that provides a point of presence for WAN service.

The central office is the entry point to the WAN cloud, the exit point from the WAN for called devices, and a switching point for calls.

The toll network is a collection of trunks inside the WAN cloud.

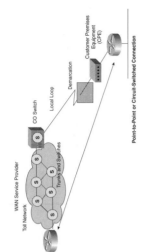

WAN Service Providers and Signaling Standards

WAN links can be ordered from service providers at various speeds using various signaling standards. The following table shows the signaling types and speeds available in the U.S.

Line Type	Signal Standard	Bit Rate Capacity
56	DS0	56 kbps
64	DS0	64 kbps
T1	DS1	1.544 Mbps
E1	ZM	2.048 Mbps
E3	M3	34.064 Mbps
J1	Y1	1.544 Mbps
T3	DS3	44.736 Mbps
OC-1	SONET	51.84 Mbps

- **Point-to-Point Protocol (PPP)**—Provides connections between devices over several types of physical interfaces such as asynchronous serial, HSSI, ISDN, and synchronous. PPP works with many network layer protocols, including IP and IPX. PPP uses PAP and CHAP for basic security.

- **X.25/Link Access Procedure, Balanced (LAPB)**—Defines connections between DTE and DCE for remote terminal access. LAPB is a data link layer protocol specified by X.25.

- **Frame Relay**—The industry-standard, switched data link layer protocol. Frame Relay (based on X.25) can handle multiple virtual circuits. **Asynchronous Transfer Mode (ATM)**: The international standard for cell relay using fixed-length (53-byte) cells for multiple service types. Fixed-length cells allow hardware processing, which greatly reduces transit delays. ATM takes advantage of high-speed transmission media such as E3, T3, and SONET.

WAN Summary

- The Internet is the interconnection of thousands of large and small networks all over the world.

- A WAN is used to interconnect LANs that are separated by a large geographic distance.

- Dedicated line, circuit switching, packet switching, and cell switching are some common WAN connection types.

- WAN devices include routers, WAN switches, modems, and access servers.

- WAN physical protocols describe how to provide electrical, mechanical, operational, and functional connection for WAN services.

- WAN data link layer protocols describe how frames are carried between systems on a single data link.

Line Type	Signal Standard	Bit Rate Capacity
OC-3	SONET	155.54 Mbps
OC-9	SONET	466.56 Mbps
OC-12	SONET	622.08 Mbps
OC-18	SONET	933.12 Mbps
OC-24	SONET	1244.16 Mbps
OC-36	SONET	1866.24 Mbps
OC-48	SONET	2488.32 Mbps

WAN Physical Layer Protocols

Physical layer protocols specify the electrical, mechanical, operational, and functional connection for WAN services. The five serial standards supported by Cisco devices are EIA/TIA-232, EIA/TIA-449, V.35, X.21, and EIA/TIA-530.

WAN Data Link Layer Protocols

Data link protocols operate over point-to-point, multipoint, and multiaccess switched services. The following are common encapsulation protocols:

- **High-Level Data Link Control (HDLC)**—The default encapsulation type on point-to-point, dedicated links, and circuit-switched connections. HDLC should be used when communicating between Cisco devices.

Leased Line   HDLC, PPP, SLIP

Packet-Switched   X.25, Frame Relay, ATM   Service Provider

Circuit-Switched   PPP, SLIP, HDLC   Telephone Company

Network Media Types

Network media refers to the physical path that signals take across a network. The most common types of media are as follows:

- Twisted-pair cable is used for telephony and most Ethernet networks. Each pair makes up a circuit that can transmit signals. The pairs are twisted to prevent interference (crosstalk). The two categories of twisted-pair cables are Unshielded Twisted-Pair (UTP) and Shielded Twisted-Pair (STP).

- UTP cables are usually connected to equipment with a Registered Jack 45 (RJ-45) connector. UTP has a small diameter that can be an advantage when space for cabling is at a minimum. It is prone to electrical noise and interference because of the lack of shielding. STP cables provide much better protection against electrical noise and interference than UTP but are thicker and more expensive. The cable speed and maximum length are the same as for UTP (speed is 10 to 100 Mbps, and maximum length is 100m).

- Coaxial cable is relatively inexpensive (but costs more than UTP) and has a much greater reach than UTP or STP (500m).

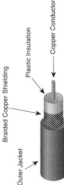

- Fiber-optic cable allows the transmission of light signals. This offers a large jump in bandwidth over other types of cables (1 Gbps or greater). The two types of optic fiber are multimode and single-mode. With multimode fiber, several modes (or wavelengths) propagate down the fiber, each taking a slightly different path. Multimode fiber is used primarily in systems with short transmission distances (less than 2 km). Single-mode fiber has only one mode in which light can propagate. Single-mode fiber is usually used for long-distance and high-bandwidth applications.

Wireless communications use radio frequencies (RFs) or infrared (IR) waves to transmit data over a LAN. Wireless adapters must be installed on a laptop (wireless NIC) to communicate with the network. Wireless gives network designers many new options, because no physical medium is required to connect end stations (which is great for installation in old buildings or offices with inadequate space for cabling).

Media Type	Maximum Length	Speed	Cost	Notes
UTP	100 m	10 to 100 Mbps	Cheap	Easy to install but prone to interference
STP	100 m	10 to 100 Mbps	More than UTP	Low crosstalk but hard to work with
Coaxial	500 m (thicknet) 185 m (thinnet)	10 to 100 Mbps	Cheap but more than UTP	Little or no interference but hard to terminate (need special equipment)
Fiber	10 km (single-mode) 2 km (multimode)	100 Mbps to 100 Gbps 100 Mbps to 9.92 Gbps	Expensive	Good security (no tapping) and good over long distances, but hard to terminate (need special equipment)

Network Media Types Summary

- Coaxial cable consists of a hollow outer cylindrical conductor that surrounds a single inner wire conductor.
- UTP cable is a four-pair wire medium used in a variety of networks.
- STP has greater protection from interference than UTP.

Cabling the LAN

LAN Specifications and Connections

The term Ethernet encompasses several LAN implementations. Physical layer implementations vary, and all support various cabling structures. There are three main categories:

- **Ethernet (DIX) and IEEE 802.3**—Operate at 10 Mbps over coaxial cable, UTP, or fiber.
- **100 Mbps Ethernet (Fast Ethernet IEEE 802.3u)**—Operates over UTP or fiber.
- **1000 Mbps Ethernet**—Gigabit Ethernet that operates over fiber and copper.

This figure compares cable and connecter specifications. Fast Ethernet requires UTP Category 5 (or higher) cabling.

An RJ-45 connector is used with UTP cabling. The two types of connections are straight-through and crossover. Straight-through cables are typically used to connect different devices, such as switch-to-router connections.

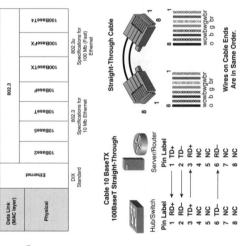

		Ethernet	802.3					802.3u	
Data Link (MAC layer)		DIX Standard	10Base2	10Base5	10BaseT	10BaseF	100BaseTX	100BaseFX	100BaseT4
Physical				802.3 Specifications for 10 Mb Ethernet				802.3u Specifications for 100 Mb (Fast) Ethernet	

Cable 10 BaseTX 100BaseT Straight-Through

Hub/Switch Pin Label		Server/Router Pin Label
1 RD+	→	1 TD+
2 RD–	→	2 TD–
3 TD+	→	3 RD+
4 NC		4 NC
5 NC		5 NC
6 TD–	→	6 RD–
7 NC		7 NC
8 NC		8 NC

Straight-Through Cable

wowbwgwbr o b g br
wowbwgwbr o b g br

Wires on Cable Ends Are in Same Order.

Crossover cables are typically used to connect similar devices, such as switch-to-switch connections. The primary exception to this rule is switch-to-hub connections, which use a crossover cable.

Some device ports are marked with an X. In general, use a straight-through cable when only one of the ports is marked.

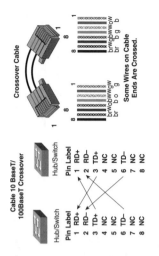

Cable 10 BaseT/ 100BaseT Crossover

Hub/Switch Pin Label	Hub/Switch Pin Label
1 RD+	1 RD+
2 RD–	2 RD–
3 TD+	3 TD+
4 NC	4 NC
5 NC	5 NC
6 TD–	6 TD–
7 NC	7 NC
8 NC	8 NC

Crossover Cable

brwbgwwowo br b o
brwgbwwowo br b g b

Some Wires on Cable Ends Are Crossed.

LAN Specifications and Connections Summary

- Ethernet has several LAN specifications, including IEEE 802.3 (10 Mbps), IEEE 802.3u (100 Mbps), and Gigabit Ethernet 802.3ae (1000 Mbps).
- UTP Category 5 or higher is required for Fast Ethernet.
- Straight-through cables are typically used to connect different device types, such as a router and a switch. The exception is a switch-to-hub connection, which requires a crossover cable.
- Crossover cables are typically used to connect similar devices, such as a switch and a switch.

Cabling the WAN

There are several ways to carry traffic across the WAN. The implementation depends on distance, speed, and the type of service required. Connection speeds typically vary from 56 Kbps to T1/E1 (1.544/2.048 Mbps, but can be as high as 10 Gbps). WANs use serial com-

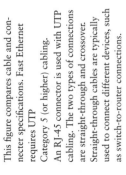

The RJ-45 Connector

Pin	Wire Pair T is Tip R is Ring
1	Pair 2 T2
2	Pair 2 R2
3	Pair 3 T3
4	Pair 1 R1
5	Pair 1 T1
6	Pair 3 R3
7	Pair 4 T4
8	Pair 4 R4

Router Connections

EIA/TI
A-232　　EIA/TI
A-449　　V.35　　X.21　　EIA-530

Network Connections at the CSU/DSU

End-User
Device　　DTE

CSU/
DSU　　DCE　　Service
Provider

Cabling Routers for Serial Connectors

When cabling routers, you need to determine if you need a data terminal equipment (DTE) connector or a data circuit-terminating equipment (DCE) connector:

- DTE is the endpoint of the user's device on the WAN link.

- DCE is the point where responsibility for delivery of data passes into the hands of the ISP.

If you connect routers back-to-back, one of the routers is a DTE, and the other is a DCE.

munication for long-distance communication. Cisco routers use a proprietary 60-pin connector, and the network end of the cable must match the service hardware.

Router Ports

Routers can have fixed or modular ports:

- With fixed ports, each port has a port type and number, such as "Ethernet 0."

- With modular ports, each port has a port type, slot number, and port number, such as "serial 1/0."

Configuring Devices

You must establish a connection via a console port to configure a Cisco device. Some devices use a rollover cable to connect a console port to a PC. To set up the connection, do the following:

Step 1　Cable the device using a rollover cable. You might need an adapter for the PC.

Step 2　Configure the terminal emulation application with the following COM port settings: 9600 bps, 8 data bits, no parity, 1 stop bit, and no flow control.

Device with
Console

RJ-45-to-RJ-45
Rollover Cable

PC

RJ-45-to-DB-9 Adapter
(Labeled Terminal)

WAN Specifications and Connections Summary

- WANs use serial transmission for long-distance communication.

- Cisco routers use a proprietary 60-pin connector on serial ports.

- A DTE/DCE is the point where the service provider assumes responsibility for the WAN. A DCE provides clocking.

- Routers have either fixed or modular ports. The syntax you use to configure each interface depends on the type of port.

- Rollover cables are used to set up a console connection.

Shared LAN Technology

Early LANs used 10BASE5 (thicknet) cables. These cables were eventually replaced by thinnet, which was cheaper and easier to work with. Some thicknet LANs were tapped into and extended using thinnet cables.

Thicknet (10BASE 5)

Relatively expensive and large in diameter

Requires repeaters every 500m

Thinnet (10BASE2) ("Cheapnet")

Less expensive and requires less space than thicknet

Requires repeaters every 185m

Thicknet (10BASE 5)	Thinnet (10BASE2) ("Cheapnet")
Limitations on the number and placement of stations	Limitations on the number and placement of stations
Difficult to pull through buildings	Difficult to pull through buildings
Adding users is relatively difficult	Adding users requires network interruption
Provides 10 Mbps shared bandwidth	Provides 10 Mbps shared bandwidth

Hubs, also called Ethernet concentrators or Ethernet repeaters, are self-contained Ethernet segments in a box. All devices connected to a hub compete for the same amount of bandwidth. Hubs let you add and remove computers without disabling the network but do not create additional collision domains. Hubs provide no filtering and forward all traffic out all ports regardless of where they are destined.

Collisions occur when two or more end stations "listen" for traffic, hear nothing, and then transmit at the same time. The simultaneous transmissions collide and all are destroyed and must be resent. Each end station resends after a random time. As the number of end stations increases, collisions increase to the point where the system is virtually unusable because collisions are constantly occurring.

There are three basic types of transmission methods:

- **Unicast transmission**—One transmitter sends to one receiver. This is the most common transmission.

- **Broadcast transmission**—One transmitter sends to all other end stations on the segment.

- **Multicast transmission**—One transmitter sends to a selected group of receivers. The receivers specifically ask for the transmission by joining a multicast group.

Bridges use the concept of segmentation to allow more end stations to be added to a LAN (called scaling). Segmentation is a method of breaking up collision domains. Bridges are more intelligent than hubs and can forward or block traffic based on the data frame's destination address (whereas hubs just send the frame to every port and end station).

Only Data Frames Intended for Segment A Are Allowed Through from Segment B.

Bridge

Collision Domain A

Collision Domain B

Layer 2 switches are really just high-speed, multiport, very smart bridges. Unlike bridges that process frames using software, switches process frames in hardware through the use of application-specific integrated circuits (ASICs). Switches also have the following features:

- **High-speed backplane**—A circuit board that allows the switch to monitor multiple conversations, which increases the network's overall speed.

- **Data buffering**—A buffer is memory storage. This function allows the switch to store frames and forward them to the correct port.

- **Higher port density**—Port density is the number of ports available on a single device. A switch can have more than 100 fast Ethernet ports.

- **Lower latency**—Latency is the measure of the time it takes an incoming frame to come back out of a switch.

All these features (particularly port density) allow microsegmentation, which means that each end station has a dedicated switch port. This eliminates collisions, because each collision domain has only a single end station. Although these features can reduce some network congestion, faster PCs can flood a network with traffic. Broadcasts and multicasts also contribute to network congestion.

Shared LAN Summary

- The earliest LAN technologies were thicknet and thinnet.

- Hubs are Layer 1 devices and are also known as Ethernet concentrators or Ethernet multiport repeaters.

- When two nodes on an Ethernet segment send data at the same time, a collision occurs.

- Three common transmission types are unicast, broadcast, and multicast.

- In a hub-based LAN, all resources are shared (in the same collision domain).

- Bridges operate at Layer 2 of the OSI model and use MAC addresses to filter traffic.

- Switches are Layer 2 devices and segment the LAN into microsegments.

- Some causes of congestion are too many users and too many network-intensive applications.

LAN Switching Basics

Ethernet switching operates at OSI Layer 2, creating dedicated network segments and interconnecting segments. Layer 2 switches have three main functions:

- **MAC address learning**—Layer 2 switches must learn the MAC addresses of devices attached to each of their ports. The addresses are stored in a MAC database.

• Forwarding and filtering—Switches determine which port a frame must be sent out to reach its destination. If the address is known, the frame is sent only on that port. If it's unknown, the frame is flooded to all ports except the one it originated from.

• Loop avoidance—When the switched network has redundant links, the switch can prevent duplicate frames from traveling over multiple paths.

Frame Transmission Modes

There are three primary frame switching modes:

• Cut-through—The switch checks the destination address and immediately begins forwarding the frame. This can decrease latency but can also transmit frames containing errors.

• Store and forward—The switch waits to receive the entire frame before forwarding. The entire frame is read, and a cyclic redundancy check (CRC) is performed. If the CRC is bad, the frame is discarded. Latency increases as a function of frame length.

• Fragment-free (modified cut-through)—The switch reads the first 64 bytes before forwarding the frame. 64 bytes is the minimum number of bytes necessary to detect and filter out collision frames. This is the default mode for the Catalyst 1900.

How Switches Learn Addresses

A switch uses its MAC address table when forwarding frames to devices. With an empty MAC address table, the switch must flood frames to all ports other than the one it arrived on. This is the least-efficient way to transmit data.

Step 1   Initially, the switch MAC address table is empty.

Step 2   Station A with the MAC address sends a frame to station C. When the switch receives this frame, it does the following:

Step 3   The switch continues to learn addresses in this manner, continually updating the table. As the MAC table becomes more complete, the switching becomes more efficient, because frames are forwarded to specific ports rather than being flooded out all ports.

MAC Address Table
E0: 0260.8c01.1111
E3: 0260.8c01.4444

A 0260.8c01.1111
B 0260.8c01.3333
C 0260.8c01.2222
D 0260.8c01.4444

E0 E1 E2 E3

• Because the MAC table is empty, the switch must flood the frame to all other ports (except E0, the frame origin).

• The switch notes the source address of the originating device and associates it with port E0 in its MAC address table entry.

Broadcast and Multicast Frames

Broadcast and multicast frames are flooded to all ports other than the originating port. Broadcast and multicast addresses never appear as a frame's source address, so the switch does not learn these addresses.

Duplexing

Duplexing is the mode of communication in which both ends can send and receive information. With full duplex, bidirectional communication can occur at the same time. Half-duplex is also bidirectional communication, but signals can flow in only one direction at a time. Simplex runs in a single direction only.

• Full duplex:
  —Can send and receive data at the same time
  —Collision-free
  —Point-to-point connection only
  —Uses a dedicated switched port with separate circuits
  —Efficiency is rated at 100 percent in both directions
  —Both ends must be configured to run in full-duplex mode

• Half duplex:
  —CSMA/CD is susceptible to collisions
  —Multipoint attachments
  —Can connect with both half- and full-duplex devices
  —Efficiency is typically rated at 50 to 60 percent
  —The duplex setting must match on devices sharing a segment

• Simplex:
  —Data is sent in one direction only and can never return to the source over the same link
  —100 percent efficiency in one direction
  —Satellite TV downlink is an example
  —Not used very often in internetworking

Redundant Topology Overview

A redundant topology has multiple connections to switches or other devices. Redundancy ensures that a single point of failure will not cause the entire switched network to fail. Layer 2 redundancy, however, can cause problems in a network, including broadcast storms, multiple copies of frames, and MAC address table instability.

Broadcast Storms

The flooding of broadcast frames can cause a broadcast storm (indefinite flooding of frames) unless there is a mechanism in place to prevent them.

An example of a broadcast storm is shown in the figure and can be described as follows:

Step 1   Host X sends a broadcast frame, which is received by Switch A.

Step 2   Switch A checks the destination and floods it to the bottom Ethernet link, Segment 2.

Step 3   Switch B receives the frame on the bottom port and transmits a copy to the top segment.

Step 4   Because the original frame arrives at Switch B via the top segment, Switch B transmits the frame a second time. The frame travels continuously in both directions.

Multiple Frame Transmissions

Most protocols cannot correctly handle duplicate transmissions. Protocols that use sequence numbering see that the sequence has been recycled. Other protocols process the duplicate frame with unpredictable results. Multiple-frame transmissions occur as follows:

Step 1   Host X sends a frame to Router Y. One copy is received over the direct Ethernet connection, Segment 1. Switch A also receives a copy.

Step 2   Switch A checks the destination address. If the switch does not find an entry in the MAC address table for Router Y, it floods the frame on all ports except the originating port.

Step 3   Switch B receives the frame on Segment 2 and forwards it on to Segment 1. Router Y has now received the same frame twice.

Database Instability

Database instability occurs when a switch receives the same frame on different ports. The following example shows how this occurs:

Step 1   Host X sends a frame to Router Y. When the frame arrives at Switches A and B, they both learn the MAC address for Host X and associate it with Port 0.

Step 2   The frame is flooded out Port 1 of each switch (assuming that Router Y's address is unknown).

Step 3   Switches A and B receive the frame on Port 1 and incorrectly associate Host X's MAC address with that port.

Step 4   This process repeats indefinitely.

Multiple Loops

Multiple loops can occur in large switched networks. When multiple loops are present, a broadcast storm clogs the network with useless traffic. Packet switching is adversely affected in such a case and might not work at all. Layer 2 cannot prevent or correct broadcast storms.

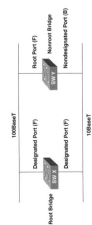

Spanning Tree Protocol

Spanning Tree Protocol prevents looping traffic in a redundant switched network by blocking traffic on the redundant links. If the main link goes down, spanning tree activates the standby path. Spanning Tree Protocol operation is transparent to end stations.

Spanning Tree Protocol was developed by DEC and was revised in the IEEE 802.1d specification. The two algorithms are incompatible. Catalyst switches use the IEEE 802.1d Spanning Tree Protocol by default.

Spanning-Tree Operation

Spanning Tree Protocol assigns roles to switches and ports so that there is only one path through the switch network at any given time. This is accomplished by assigning a single root bridge, root ports for nonroot bridges, and a single designated port for each network segment. On the root bridge, all ports are designated ports.

Link Speed	Cost (Reratify IEEE Spec)	Cost (Previous IEEE Spec)
10 Gbps	2	1
1 Gbps	4	1
100 Mbps	19	10
10 Mbps	100	100

On the root bridge, all ports are set to forwarding state. For the nonroot bridge, only the root port is set to forwarding state. The port with the lowest-cost path to the root bridge is chosen as the root port.

One designated port is assigned on each segment. The bridge with the lowest-cost path to the root bridge is the designated port.

Nondesignated ports are set to blocking state (does not forward any traffic).

Selecting the Root Bridge

Switches running Spanning Tree Protocol exchange information at regular intervals using a frame called the bridge protocol data unit (BPDU). Each bridge has a unique bridge ID. The bridge ID contains the bridge MAC address and a priority number. The midrange value of 32768 is the default priority. The bridge with the lowest bridge ID is selected as the root bridge. When switches have the same priority, the one with the lowest MAC address is the root bridge. In the figure, Switch X is the root bridge.

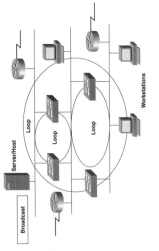

Port States

Frames take a finite amount of time to travel or propagate through the network. This delay is known as propagation delay. When a link goes down, spanning tree activates previously blocked links. This information is sent throughout the network, but not all switches receive it at the same time. To prevent temporary loops, switches wait until the entire network is updated before setting any ports to forwarding state. Each switch port in a network running Spanning Tree Protocol is in one of the following states:

Blocking → Listening → Learning → Forwarding

The forward delay is the time it takes for a port to go to a higher state. It usually takes 50 seconds for a port to go from blocking state to forwarding state, but the timers can be adjusted.

Spanning-Tree Recalculation

When a link fails, the network topology must change. Connectivity is reestablished by placing key blocked ports in forwarding state.

In the following figure, if Switch X fails, Switch Y does not receive the BPDU. If the BPDU is not received before the MAXAGE timer expires, spanning tree begins recalculating the network. In the figure, Switch Y is now the root bridge. If Switch X comes back up, spanning tree recalculates the network, and Switch X is once again the root bridge.

Time to Converge

A network is said to have converged when all ports in a switched network are in either blocking or forwarding state after a topology change.

LAN Switching Basics

- Switches can provide dedicated access to improve the shared LAN technologies.
- A switch segments a LAN into microsegments, which decreases the number of collisions and improves bandwidth.
- Full-duplex communication allows two devices to communicate with each other simultaneously and effectively doubles the throughput on a LAN.
- Switches can support multiple simultaneous conversations in a network.
- Three switching modes can be used to forward frames through a switch: store and forward, cut-through, and fragment-free.
- Spanning tree prevents the occurrence of loops in a Layer 2 network.
- When spanning tree is enabled, the ports are in one of five states: blocking, listening, learning, forwarding, or disabled.

Multilayer Switching Devices

Switching technology has advanced tremendously in recent years. There are now many options for switching traffic through the network. The options are categorized based on the OSI layer at which they operate.

Layer 2 switching devices act as multiport bridges but have much higher port density and switching speeds than typical bridges. Layer 2 switches perform switching and filtering based on Layer 2 MAC addresses and are completely transparent to higher-layer protocols and applications. Layer 2 switches allow network administrators to increase bandwidth without adding complexity to the network.

Layer 3 switching devices are a cross between a LAN switch and a router. Each switch port is still a LAN port, but the switch uses a Layer 3 (IP, IPX, or Novell NetWare) address to make decisions about packets, rather than a Layer 2 (MAC) address. Layer 3 switches can also apply security controls and other services such as quality of service (QoS), which is a method of prioritizing time-sensitive traffic. Layer 3 switches can be placed anywhere in a network and are a good cost-effective alternative to routers.

Layer 4 switching devices perform hardware-based routing. These devices can make forwarding decisions based on Layer 4 information (such as port numbers) in addition to MAC and IP addresses. Layer 4 switching is necessary if traffic must be routed based on the type of application used, rather than the traffic destination. This type of control means that you must multiply the number of network devices you have by the number of applications you are using, which can be very expensive.

Virtual LANs

Users of shared LANs are usually grouped based on where they use the network (physical rather than logical). Shared LANs have little imbedded security, because all traffic can be seen by all end stations. It is also expensive to make moves or changes in the network setup. Virtual LANs solve these problems.

The virtual LAN (VLAN) organizes physically separate users into the same broadcast domain. The use of VLANs improves performance, security, and flexibility. The use of VLANs also decreases the cost of arranging users, because no extra cabling is required.

VLAN Characteristics

VLANs allow logically defined user groups rather than user groups defined by their physical locations. For example, you can arrange user groups such as accounting, engineering, and finance, rather than everyone on the first floor, everyone on the second floor, and so on.

- VLANs define broadcast domains that can span multiple LAN segments.
- VLANs improve segmentation, flexibility, and security.
- VLAN segmentation is not bound by the physical location of users.
- Each switch port can be assigned to only one VLAN.
- Only ports assigned to a VLAN share broadcasts, improving network performance.
- A VLAN can exist on one or several switches.

This figure shows a VLAN design. Note that VLANs are defined by user functions rather than locations.

VLAN Operation

Each VLAN on a switch behaves as if it were a separate physical bridge. The switch forwards packets (including unicasts, multicasts, and broadcasts) only to ports assigned to the same VLAN from which they originated. This drastically cuts down on network traffic.

VLANs require a trunk or physical connection for each VLAN to span multiple switches. Each trunk can carry traffic for multiple VLANs.

VLAN Assignment

A port can be assigned (configured) to a given VLAN. VLAN membership can be either static or dynamic.

- **Static assignment**—The VLAN port is statically configured by an administrator.

- **Dynamic assignment**— The switch uses a VMPS (VLAN Membership Policy Server). The VMPS is a database that maps MAC addresses to VLANs. A port can belong to only one VLAN at a time. Multiple hosts can exist

SALES   HR   ENG

3rd Floor
2nd Floor
1st Floor

Switch A

Green VLAN   Green VLAN
Red VLAN   Black VLAN

Static VLAN   Dynamic VLAN
Port e0/4   Port e0/9
Trunk
VLAN5   VLAN10
VMPS
1111.1111.1111 = vlan 10
MAC = 1111.1111.1111

on a single port only if they are all assigned to the same VLAN. VLANs can also be assigned based on MAC addresses. This method offers flexibility but increases switching overhead (computer processing requirements).

VLAN membership describes how a port on a switch is assigned to a particular VLAN:

- Port-driven membership is based on the port a given work station plugs into.
- MAC address membership uses the MAC address to dynamically assign the end station to a VLAN.
- Layer 3-based membership uses information contained in the IP header to determine VLAN membership.

Trunking

The IEEE 802.1Q protocol is used to define VLAN topologies and to connect multiple switches and routers. Cisco supports 802.1Q trunking over Fast Ethernet and Gigabit Ethernet links. 802.1Q defines how to carry traffic from multiple VLANs over a single point-to-point link.

Inter-Switch Link (ISL)

ISL is a Cisco-proprietary protocol form of trunking designed to manage VLAN traffic between switches. ISL provides point-to-point links in full or duplex mode. ISL is performed with ASICs, which operate at wire speeds and enable VLANs to span the backbone.

Inter-Switch Link
Carries VLAN Identifier

VLAN Tag Added By
Incoming Port

VLAN Tag Stripped By
Forwarding Port

Inter-VLAN Routing

VLANs create Layer 2 segments. End stations in different segments (broadcast domains) cannot communicate with

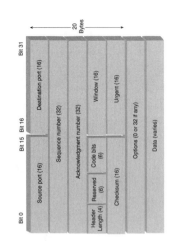

The TCP/IP protocol stack closely follows the OSI reference model. All standard Layer 1 and 2 protocols are supported (called the network interface layer in TCP/IP).

TCP

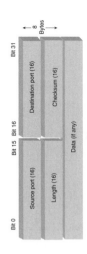

TCP is a connection-oriented, reliable protocol that is responsible for breaking messages into segments and reassembling them at the destination (resending anything not received). TCP also provides virtual circuits between applications.

UDP

UDP is a connectionless, best-effort protocol used for applications that provide their own error-recovery process. It trades reliability for speed. UDP is simple and efficient but unreliable. UDP does not check for segment delivery.

---

each other without the use of a Layer 3 device such as a router. Each VLAN must have a separate physical connection on the router, or trunking must be enabled on a single physical connection for inter-VLAN routing to work.

The figure shows a router attached to a switch. The end stations in the two VLANs communicate by sending packets to the router, which forwards them to the other VLAN. This setup is called "router on a stick."

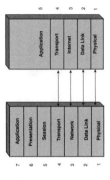

VLAN Operation Summary

- A VLAN is a logical grouping of users or devices.
- A VLAN is a broadcast domain that can span multiple physical LAN segments. VLANs improve performance, flexibility, and security by restricting broadcasts.
- VLANs forward data only to ports assigned to the same VLAN.
- VLAN ports can be assigned either statically or dynamically. Membership is based on port association, MAC address, or Layer 3 information.
- The 802.1Q trunking protocol (the most common) allows multiple VLANs to communicate over a single point-to-point link.
- ISL is a Cisco-proprietary protocol used to share and manage VLAN information across switches.
- ISL trunks encapsulate frames with an ISL header CRC.

TCP/IP Overview

The TCP/IP suite of protocols is used to communicate across any set of interconnected networks. The protocols initially developed by DARPA are well-suited for communication across both LANs and WANs.

The protocol suite includes Layer 3 and 4 specifications as well as specifications for higher-layer applications such as e-mail and file transfer.

TCP/IP Applications

- **File Transfer Protocol (FTP)**—A TCP-based protocol that supports bidirectional binary and ASCII file transfers.
- **Trivial File Transfer Protocol (TFTP)**—A UDP-based protocol that transfers outer configuration files and Cisco IOS software images between systems.
- **Network File System (NFS)**—A Sun Microsystems-based protocol for remote file access.
- **Simple Mail Transfer Protocol (SMTP)**—An e-mail delivery protocol.
- **Terminal Emulation (Telnet)**—Allows remote access to another computer.
- **Simple Network Management Protocol (SNMP)**—Provides the means to monitor and control network devices.
- **Domain Name System (DNS)**—Used to translate domain names into IP addresses.

TCP/IP Overview Summary

- The TCP/IP protocol suite includes Layer 3 and 4 specifications.
- UDP is connectionless (no acknowledgments). No software checking for segment delivery is done at this layer.
- TCP is a connection-oriented, reliable protocol. Data is divided into segments, which are reassembled at the destination. Missing segments are resent.
- Both TCP and UDP use port (or socket) numbers to pass information to the upper layers.

Transport Layer Functions

A logical connection (session) must be established to connect two devices in a network. The transport layer

- Allows end stations to multiplex multiple upper-layer segments into the same data streams.
- Provides reliable data transport between end stations (for TCP).

Establishing a TCP Connection

End stations use control bits called SYNs (for synchronize) and Initial Sequence Numbers (ISNs) to synchronize during connection establishment.

Connection-Oriented Services

A connection-oriented service establishes and maintains a connection during a transmission. The service first establishes a connection and then sends data. As soon as the data transfer is complete, the session is torn down.

Port Numbers

Both TCP and UDP can send data from multiple upper-layer applications at the same time. Port (or socket) numbers are used to keep track of different conversations crossing the network at any given time. Well-known port numbers are controlled by the Internet Assigned Numbers Authority (IANA).

For example, Telnet is always defined by port 23. Applications that do not use well-known port numbers have them randomly assigned from a specific range.

Port Number Ranges

- Numbers below 1024 are considered well-known ports.
- Numbers 1024 and above are dynamically assigned ports.
- Vendor-specific applications have reserved ports (usually greater than 1024).

Three-Way Handshake

The synchronization requires each side to send its own initial sequence number and to receive a confirmation of it in acknowledgment (ACK) from the other side.

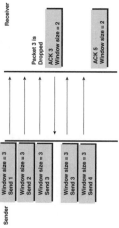

Step 1 Host A sends a SYN segment with sequence number 100.

Step 2 Host B sends an ACK and confirms the SYN it received. Host B also sends a SYN. Note that the ACK field in Host B is now expecting to hear sequence 101.

Step 3 In the next segment, Host A sends data. Note that the sequence number in this step is the same as the ACK in Step 2.

TCP Sequence and Acknowledgment Numbers

TCP uses forward reference acknowledgments. Each datagram is numbered so that at the receiving end TCP reassembles the segments into a complete message. If a segment is not acknowledged within a given time period, it is resent.

TCP Windowing

Windowing ensures that one side of a connection is not overwhelmed with data it cannot process. The window size from one end station tells the other side of the connection how much it can accept at one time. With a window size of 1, each segment must be acknowledged before another segment is sent. This is the least-efficient use of bandwidth.

Step 1 The sender sends three packets before expecting an ACK.

Step 2 The receiver can handle a window size of only 2. So it drops packet 3, specifies 3 as the next packet, and specifies a window size of 2.

Step 3 The sender sends the next two packets but still specifies its window size of 3.

Step 4 The receiver replies by requesting packet 5 and specifying a window size of 2.

A TCP/IP session can have different window sizes for each node.

TCP/IP Overview Summary

- The transport layer provides transport service from the source host to the destination host.
- The two primary protocols are TCP and UDP.
- The TCP "three-way handshake" is a synchronization process.
- Sequence numbers and acknowledgments (ACKs) are used to establish connections.
- TCP windowing is a flow-control mechanism.

TCP/IP Internet Layer Overview

TCP/IP Datagrams

TCP/IP information is sent via datagrams. One message may be broken into a series of datagrams that must be reassembled at the destination. Three layers are associated with the TCP/IP protocol stack:

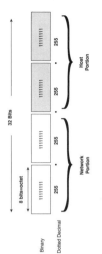

TCP/IP Internet Layer Overview Summary

- The TCP/IP protocol suite includes Layer 3 and 4 specifications.
- ICMP is implemented by all TCP/IP ports.
- ARP resolves or maps a known IP address to a MAC address. RARP is used to map a known MAC address to an IP address.
- BOOTP and DHCP are different methods used to assign IP addresses dynamically.

IP Addressing and Routing

In a TCP/IP environment, each node must have a unique 32-bit logical IP address. Each IP datagram includes the source and destination IP addresses in the header.

Host and Network Address

Each company listed on the Internet is viewed as a single network. This network must be reached before an individual host within that company can be contacted. A two-part addressing scheme allows the IP address to identify both the network and the host.

- All the endpoints within a network share a common network number.
- The remaining bits identify each host within that network.

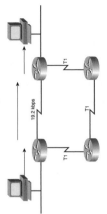

IP Address Classes

Five classes of IP exist: classes A through E. Classes A, B, and C are the most common. Class A has 8 network bits and 24 host bits. Class B has 16 network bits and 16 host bits. Class C addresses allow for many more networks, each with fewer hosts (24 network

- Application layer—Specifications exist for e-mail, file transfer, remote login, and other applications. Network management is also supported.
- Transport layer—Transport services allow multiple upper-layer applications to use the same data stream. TCP and UDP protocols exist at this layer, providing the following functions:
  - Flow control (through windowing)
  - Reliability (through sequence numbers and acknowledgments)
- Internet layer—Several protocols operate at the TCP/IP Internet layer:
  - IP provides connectionless, best-effort routing of datagrams.
  - ICMP provides control and messaging capabilities.
  - ARP determines the data link layer address for known IP addresses.
  - RARP determines network addresses when data link layer addresses are known.

Other Internet Layer Protocols

ICMP, ARP, and RARP are three protocols used by the Internet layer. Internet Control Message Protocol (ICMP) is used to send error and control messages, such as destination unreachable, time exceeded, subnet mask request, echo, and others. Address Resolution Protocol (ARP) maps a known IP address to a MAC sublayer address. An ARP cache table is checked when looking for a destination address. If the address is not in the table, ARP sends a broadcast looking for the destination station.

Reverse ARP

Reverse Address Resolution Protocol (RARP) is used to map a known MAC address to an IP address. Dynamic Host Configuration Protocol (DHCP) is a modern implementation of RARP.

bits and 8 host bits). This scheme was based on the assumption that the world would have many more small networks than large networks. Class D is used for multicast purposes, and Class E addresses are used for research. The address range for all five classes is shown in the figure.

In the next figure, networks A and B are connected by a router. Network B has a Class A address (10.0.0.0). The routing table contains entries for network addresses, not hosts within that network. In the figure, 172.16.0.0 and 10.0.0.0 refer to the wires at each end of the router.

IPv4 Versus IPv6

When the TCP/IP addressing scheme was introduced in the 1980s (resulting in the addressing scheme now used, IPv4), it was believed that there would always be available address space. However, the architect of the system could not have foreseen the advent of the Internet and the explosion of network-capable devices beyond PCs, such as cell phones and PDAs. As early as 2002, the Internet Engineering Task Force (IETF) noted two specific concerns: the exhaustion of the remaining IPv4 addresses, and the rapid increases in the size of routing tables.

Extensions to IPv4 have been developed to address these concerns, but a formal solution, IPv6, has been defined and developed. IPv6 uses a 128-bit binary value (expressed as 32 hex digits) and provides 3.4×10^{38} usable addresses (orders of magnitude that offer more addresses than IPv4).

Classless Interdomain Routing (CIDR) allows routers to summarize information about several routes and cut down on the quantity of information carried by the core routers. With ip classless configured, packets received with an unknown subnet of a directly attached network are sent to the next hop on the default route. With CIDR, several IP networks appear to networks outside the group as a single, larger entity. CIDR also allows different masks on different parts of a network.

TCP/IP Address Summary

- In a TCP/IP environment, end stations each have a 32-bit logical IP address with a network and host portion.
- The address format is known as dotted-decimal notation. The range is 0.0.0.0 to 255.255.255.255.
- There are five address classes: A, B, C, D, and E. They are suited to different types of users.
- The total number of available hosts on a network can be derived by using the formula 2^n-2, where n is the number of bits in the host portion.
- The more flexible IPv6 will replace IPv4 in the future. IPv6 has 128 bits of addressing, compared to 32 bits for IPv4.
- CIDR is a method of routing that allows more efficient allocation of IP addresses.

IP Subnetting and Calculation

Without subnets, an organization operates as a single network. These flat topologies result in short routing tables, but as the network grows, the use of bandwidth becomes very inefficient (all systems on the network receive all the broadcasts on the network). Network addressing can be made

Bits:	1	8 9	16 17	24 25	32
Class A:	0NNNNNNN	Host	Host	Host	

Range (1-126)

Bits:	1	8 9	16 17	24 25	32
Class B:	10NNNNNN	Network	Host	Host	

Range (128-191)

Bits:	1	8 9	16 17	24 25	32
Class C:	110NNNNN	Network	Network	Host	

Range (192-223)

Bits:	1	8 9	16 17	24 25	32
Class D:	1110MMMM	Multicast Group	Multicast Group	Multicast Group	

Range (224-239)

Network A

172.16.2.1
172.16.3.10
172.16.2.12

Network B

10.12.12.67
10.250.8.11
10.180.30.118

E1
10.6.24.2

E0
172.16.2.1

Routing Table
Network Interface
172.16.0.0   E0
10.0.0.0   E1

172.16	.	12	.	12
Network		Host		

10	.	180.30.118
Network		Host

172.16.0.1 172.16.0.2 172.16.0.3 172.16.255.253 172.16.255.254

172.16.0.0

more efficient by breaking the addresses into smaller segments, or subnets. Subnetting provides additional structure to an addressing scheme without altering the addresses.

In the figure, the network address 172.16.0.0 is subdivided into four subnets: 172.16.1.0, 172.16.2.0, 172.16.3.0, and 172.16.4.0. If traffic were evenly distributed to each end station, the use of subnetting would reduce the overall traffic seen by each end station by 75 percent.

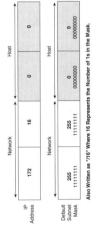 

Subnet Mask

A subnet mask is a 32-bit value written as four octets. In the subnet mask, each bit is used to determine how the corresponding bit in the IP address should be interpreted (network, subnet, or host). The subnet mask bits are coded as follows:

- Binary 1 for the network bits
- Binary 1 for the subnet bits
- Binary 0 for the host bits

Although dotted-decimal is most common, the subnet can be represented in several ways:

- **Dotted-decimal**—172.16.0.0 255.255.0.0
- **Bit count**—172.16.0.0/16
- **Hexadecimal**—172.16.0.0 0xFFFF0000

The **ip netmask-format** command can specify the format of network masks for the current session. Dotted-decimal is the default.

	Network		Host	
IP Address	172	16	0	0

	Network		Host	
Default Subnet Mask	255 11111111	255 11111111	0 00000000	0 00000000

Also Written as "/16" Where 16 Represents the Number of 1s in the Mask.

	Network	Subnet	Host
8-bit Subnet Mask	255	255	255	0

Also Written as "/24" Where 24 Represents the Number of 1s in the Mask.

Bits:	1	8	9	16	17	24	25	32
Class A:	0NNNNNNN		Host		Host		Host	
Range (1-126)								
Class B:	10NNNNNN		NNNNNNNN		Network		Host	
Range (128-191)								
Class C:	110NNNNN		Network		Network		Host	
Range (192-223)								
Class D:	1110MMMM		Multicast Group		Multicast Group		Multicast Group	
Range (224-239)								

Default Subnet Masks

Each address class has a default subnet mask. The default subnet masks only the network portion of the address, the effect of which is no subnetting. With each bit of subnetting beyond the default, you can create 2^n-2 subnets. The following figures show the effect of increasing the number of subnet bits.

Address	Subnet Address	Number of Subnets	Comments
10.5.22.5/8	255.0.0.0	0	This is the default Class A subnet address. The mask includes only the network portion of the address and provides no additional subnets.
10.5.22.5/16	255.255.0.0	254	This Class A subnet address has 16 bits of subnetting, but only the bits in the second octet (those beyond the default) contribute to the subnetting.
155.13.22.11/16	255.255.0.0	0	In this case, 16 bits are used for subnetting, but because the default for a Class B address is 16 bits, no additional subnets are created.
155.13.10.11/26	255.255.255.192	1022	This case has a total of 26 bits of subnetting, but the Class B address can use only 10 of them to create subnets. The result creates 1022 subnets ($2^{10}-2$).

How Routers Use Subnet Masks

To determine the subnet of the address, a router performs a logical AND operation with the IP address and subnet mask. Recall that the host portion of the subnet mask is all 0s. The result of this operation is that the host portion of the address is removed and the router bases its decision only on the network portion of the address.

172.16.2.160
255.255.255.192

	Network	Subnet	Host
	10101100	00010000	00000010	10100000
	11111111	11111111	11111111	11000000
	10101100	00010000	00000010	10000000

255 254 252 248 240 224 192 128
255
192 2 128

Network Number: 172 16 2 128

In the figure, the host bits are removed, and the network portion of the address is revealed. In this case, a 10-bit subnet address is used, and the network (subnet) number 172.16.2.128 is extracted.

Broadcast Addresses

Broadcast messages are sent to every host on the network. There are three kinds of broadcasts:

- Directed broadcasts can broadcast to all hosts within a subnet and to all subnets within a network. (170.34.2.255 sends a broadcast to all hosts in the 170.34.2.0 subnet.)
- Flooded broadcasts (255.255.255.255) are local broadcasts within a subnet.
- You can also broadcast messages to all hosts on all subnets within a single network. (170.34.255.255 sends a broadcast to all subnets in the 170.34.0.0 network.)

Identifying Subnet Addresses

Given an IP address and subnet mask, you can identify the subnet address, broadcast address, first usable address, and last usable address using this method:

Step 1 Write the 32-bit address, and write the subnet mask below that.
174.24.4.176
255.255.255.192

Step 2 Draw a vertical line just after the last 1 bit in the subnet mask.
174.24.4.128
174.24.4.191
174.24.4.129
174.24.4.190

174	24	4	176	
10101110	00011000	00000100	10110000	Host
11111111	11111111	11111111	11000000	Mask
10101110	00011000	00000100	10000000	Subnet
10101110	00011000	00000100	10111111	Broadcast
10101110	00011000	00000100	10000001	First
10101110	00011000	00000100	10111110	Last

Step 3 Copy the portion of the IP address to the left of the line. Place all 0s for the remaining free spaces to the right. This is the subnet number.

Step 4 Copy the portion of the IP address to the left of the line. Place all 1s for the remaining free spaces to the right. This is the broadcast address.

Step 5 Copy the portion of the IP address to the left of the line. Place all 0s in the remaining free spaces until you reach the last free space. Place a 1 in that free space. This is your first usable address.

Step 6 Copy the portion of the IP address to the left of the line. Place all 1s in the remaining free spaces until you reach the last free space. Place a 0 in that free space. This is your last usable address.

How to Implement Subnet Planning

Subnetting decisions should always be based on growth estimates rather than current needs.

To plan a subnet, follow these steps:

Step 1 Determine the number of subnets and hosts per subnet required.

Step 2 The address class you are assigned, and the number of subnets required, determine the number of subnetting bits used. For example, with a Class C address and a need for 20 subnets, you have a 29-bit mask (255.255.255.248). This allows for the Class C default 24-bit mask and 5 bits required for 20 subnets. (The formula $2n-2$ yields only 14 subnets for 4 bits, so 5 bits must be used.)

Step 3 The remaining bits in the last octet are used for the host field. In this case, each subnet has 2^3-2, or 6 hosts.

Step 4 The final host addresses are a combination of the network/subnet plus each host value. The hosts on the 192.168.5.32 subnet would be addressed as 192.168.5.33, 192.168.5.34, 192.168.5.35, and so forth.

20 Subnets
5 Hosts per Subnet
Class C Address: 192.168.5.0

192.168.5.16
192.168.5.32
192.168.5.48
Other Subnets

Implementing Subnet Planning Summary

- Breaking networks into smaller segments (or subnets) improves network efficiency.
- A 32-bit subnet mask determines the boundary between the subnet host portions of the IP address using 1s and 0s.
- A subnet defines a broadcast domain in a routed network.
- IOS supports directed, local network, and subnet broadcasts.
- Subnet planning should be based on future growth predictions rather than current needs.

Routing Basics

Routing is the process of getting packets and messages from one location to another.

Key Information a Router Needs

A router needs the following key information:

- **Destination address**—The destination (typically an IP address) of the information being sent. This includes the subnet address.
- **Sources of information**—Where the information came from (typically an IP address).
- **Possible routes**—Likely routes to get from source to destination.
- **Best route**—The best path to the intended destination.
- **Status of routes**—Known paths to destinations.

Routing Versus Routed

Network layer protocols are either routed protocols or routing protocols.

A routed protocol

- Is any network layer protocol that provides enough information within its address to allow the packet to direct user traffic.
- Defines the address format and use of fields within the packet.

Router protocols include IP, IPX, Novell NetWare, AppleTalk, and others.

Routing protocols determine how routed protocols are used by

- Providing mechanisms for sharing routing information
- Allowing routers to update each other about network changes.

RIP, EIGRP, OSPF, and BGP are examples of routing protocols.

Path Determination

Routing tables and network addresses are used to transmit packets through the network. The process of routing includes determining the optimum path through the network and then moving the packets along the path.

Routing Table

A router is constantly learning about routes in the network and storing this information in its routing table. The router uses its table to make forwarding decisions. The router learns about routes in one of two ways:

- Manually (routing information entered by the network administrator)
- Dynamically (a routing process running in the network)

Information stored in a routing table includes destination/next hop and routing metrics. Destination/next-hop tells the router whether the destination is directly connected or is available through an adjacent router.

Routing metrics are measures of path desirability. Different protocols use different metrics. Some common metrics are as follows:

- **Bandwidth**—The link's data capacity.
- **Delay**—The time required to move the packet from the current router to the destination. This is dependent on bandwidth, port delays, congestion, and distance.
- **Load**—The amount of activity on the network.
- **Reliability**—The error rate of each network link.
- **Hop count**—The number of routers the packet must travel through before reaching the destination.
- **Cost**—An arbitrary value based on bandwidth, expense, and other metrics assigned by the administrator.

Routing Overview Summary

- Routers operate at the network layer. Packets are encapsulated and de-encapsulated each time the packet passes through a router.
- Routers make a decision regarding the best path for a packet through the network.
- Routed protocols define the address format and fields within a packet.
- Routers use routing protocols to determine paths, maintain and share routing table information, and direct traffic.
- Routing algorithms use different metrics to determine the best path through the network.

Routing Protocols

Routing protocols determine the path through the network for packets. Routing protocols are divided into two classes based on how they interact with other autonomous systems: Exterior Gateway Protocols (EGPs) and Interior Gateway Protocols (IGPs).

IGP and EGP

An autonomous system refers to a group of networks under a common administrative domain. Interior Gateway Protocols (IGPs) exchange routing information within an autonomous system. Examples include Routing Information Protocol (RIP), Interior Gateway Routing Protocol (IGRP), Enhanced Interior Gateway Routing Protocol (EIGRP), Open Shortest Path First (OSPF), and Intermediate System-to-Intermediate System (IS-IS).

Exterior Gateway Protocols (EGPs) connect between autonomous systems. Border Gateway Protocol (BGP) is an example of an EGP.

Ranking Routes with Administrative Distance

Several routing protocols can be used at the same time in the same network. When there is more than a single source of routing information, the router uses an administrative distance value to rate the trustworthiness of each routing information source. The administrative distance metric is an integer from 0 to 255. In general, a route with a lower number is considered more trustworthy and is more likely to be used.

Network Protocol	Destination Network	Exit Interface
Connected	10.120.2.0	E0
Learned	172.16.1.0	S0

Routed Protocol: IP

Default Distance Values

Route Source	Default Distance
Connected interface	0
Static route address	1
EIGRP	5
BGP	20
Internal EIGRP	90
IGRP	100
IS-IS	115
RIP	120
EGP	140
ODR	160
External EIGRP	170
Internal BGP	200
Unknown	255

Routing Protocols

Routers using distance vector-based routing share routing table information with each other. This method of updating is called "routing by rumor." Each router receives updates from its direct neighbor. In the figure, Router B shares information with Routers A and C. Router C shares routing information with Routers B and D. In this case, the routing information is distance vector metrics (such as the number of hops). Each router increments the metrics as they are passed on (incrementing hop count, for example).

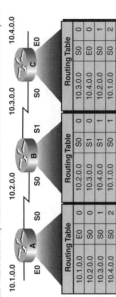

Distance—How Far?
Vector—In Which Direction?

Distance accumulation keeps track of the routing distance between any two points in the network, but the routers do not know the exact topology of an internetwork.

How Information Is Discovered with Distance Vectors

Network discovery is the process of learning about non-directly connected destinations. As the network discovery proceeds, routers accumulate metrics and learn the best paths to various destinations. In the example, each directly connected network has a distance of 0. Router A learns about other networks based on information it receives from Router B. Router A increments the distance metric for any route learned by Router B. For example, Router B knows about the networks to Router C, which is directly connected. Router B then shares this information with Router A, which increments the distance to these networks by 1.

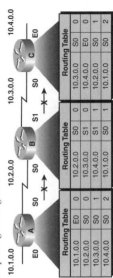

During updates, routing loops can occur if the network has inconsistent routing entries. Slow convergence on a new configuration is one cause of this phenomenon. The network is converged when all routers have consistent routing tables.

Split Horizon

Split horizon is one way to eliminate routing loops and speed up convergence. The idea behind split horizon is that it is never useful to send information about a route back in the direction from which the update came. If the router has no valid alternative path to the network, it is considered inaccessible. Split horizon also eliminates unnecessary routing updates, thus speeding convergence.

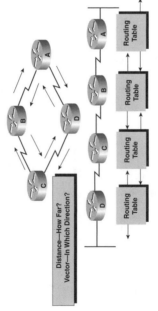

Hold-Down Timers

Hold-down timers dictate that when a route is invalid, no new route with the same or a worse metric will be accepted for the same destination for some period of time. This allows network updates to propagate throughout the network.

Route Poisoning

Route poisoning (part of split horizon) also eliminates routing loops caused by inconsistent updates. Route poisoning basically sets a route to "unreachable" and locks the table (using hold-down timers) until the network has converged.

The figure provides the following example. When network 10.4.0.0 goes down, Router C "poisons" its link to network 10.4.0.0 with an infinite cost (marked as unreachable).

Router C is no longer susceptible to incorrect updates about network 10.4.0.0 coming from neighboring routers that might claim to have a valid alternative path. After the hold-down timer expires (which is just longer than the time to convergence), Router C begins accepting updates again.

Poison Reverse

When Router B sees the metric to 10.4.0.0 jump to infinity, it sends a return message (overriding split horizon) called a poison reverse back to Router C, stating that network

10.4.0.0 is inaccessible. This message ensures that all routers on that segment have received information about the poisoned route.

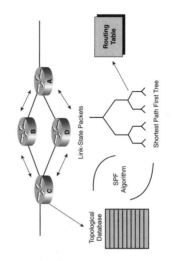

Link-State Routing

The link-state–based routing algorithm (also known as shortest path first [SPF]) maintains a database of topology information.

Unlike the distance vector algorithm, link-state routing maintains full knowledge of distant routers and how they interconnect. Network information is shared in the form of Link State Advertisements (LSAs).

Link-state routing provides better scaling than distance vector routing for the following reasons:

- Link-state sends only topology changes. Distance vector sends complete routing tables.
- Link-state updates are sent less often than distance vector updates.
- Link-state uses a two-state hierarchy (areas and autonomous systems), which limits the scope of route changes.
- Link-state supports classless addressing and summarization.
- Link-state routing converges fast and is robust against routing loops, but it requires a great deal of memory and strict network designs.

Balanced Hybrid Routing

Balanced hybrid routing combines aspects of both distance vector and link-state protocols. Balanced hybrid routing uses distance vectors with more accurate metrics, but unlike distance vector routing protocols, it updates only when there is a topology change. Balanced hybrid routing provides faster convergence while limiting the use of resources such as bandwidth, memory, and processor overhead. The Cisco Enhanced IGRP is an example of a balanced hybrid protocol.

RIPv1 and RIPv2

A classless routing protocol allows routers to summarize information about several routes to cut down on the quantity of information carried by the core routers. With ip classless configured, packets received with a unknown subnet of a directly attached network are sent to the next hop on the default route. With CIDR, several IP networks appear to networks outside the group as a single, larger entity.

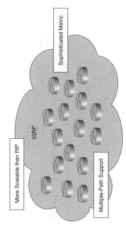

Classless routing also allows different masks on different parts of a network. Cisco devices support two versions of RIP. RIP Version 1 (RFC 1058) uses only classful routing. An enhanced version, RIP Version 2 (RFC 1723), uses classless routing.

Key RIP characteristics are as follows:

- RIP is a distance vector routing protocol.
- Hop count is used as the metric for path selection (the maximum is 15).
- Routing updates broadcast every 30 seconds (the default).
- It can load-balance over six equal-cost paths (the default is four).
- Only one network mask can be used for each classful network (RIPv1).
- RIPv2 permits variable-length subnet masks on the internetwork.
- It performs triggered updates (RIPv2 only).
- RIPv2 also supports simple route authentication.

Interior Gateway Routing Protocol (IGRP)

IGRP is a distance vector routing protocol with sophisticated metrics and improved scalability, allowing better routing in larger networks. IGRP uses delay and bandwidth as routing metrics (reliability and load are optional). IGRP has a default maximum hop count of 100 hops (RIP's maximum is 15 hops), which can be reconfigured to 255 hops.

IGRP can load-balance across six unequal paths, increasing the available bandwidth and providing route redundancy.

IGRP Metrics

IGRP achieves greater route selection accuracy than RIP with the use of a composite metric. The path that has the smallest metric value is the best route. IGRP's metric includes bandwidth, delay, reliability (based on keepalives), loading (bits per second), and MTU (maximum transmission unit). Performance can be significantly affected by adjusting IGRP metric values.

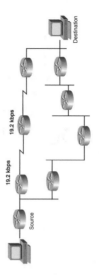

Enhanced Interior Gateway Routing Protocol (EIGRP)

EIGRP is an enhanced version of Cisco-proprietary IGRP. EIGRP scales well, converges quickly, and works with several media types.

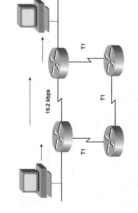

EIGRP uses four basic components to enhance its capability beyond IGRP:

- Neighbor discovery/recovery allows routers to learn about neighboring routers dynamically.
- Reliable Transport Protocol guarantees the ordered delivery of EIGRP packets to all neighbors.
- DUAL finite-state machine uses the Diffusing Update Algorithm (DUAL) to track all routes advertised by neighbors, allowing the selection of loop-free paths.
- Protocol-dependent modules enable protocol-specific requirements used to make routing decisions.

Open Shortest Path First (OSPF)

OSPF is an interior gateway protocol based on link state rather than distance vectors.

OSPF was developed in the 1980s as an answer to RIP's inability to scale well in heterogeneous internetworks. It addresses the following issues:

- **Speed to convergence**—RIP can take several minutes to converge in large networks. OSPF routing changes are immediately flooded to the rest of the network and are computed in parallel.

OSPF

- **Support for variable-length subnet masks (VLSMs)**—RIP1 does not support VLSMs. OSPF sends subnet information with routing updates (and therefore supports VLSM).
- **Network reachability**—OSPF has no reachability limitation, whereas RIP considers spans of more than 15 hops unreachable.
- **Use of bandwidth**—OSPF sends only link-state information and is less bandwidth-intensive than RIP, which sends full routing tables every 30 seconds.
- **Path-selection methods**—RIP has no concept of link cost or network delay. OSPF can make decisions based on the current state of the network as defined by a cost metric.

IS-IS

IS-IS is a dynamic link-state routing protocol developed by Digital Equipment Corporation (DEC) as part of the OSI stack. Integrated IS-IS was developed to route multiple network protocols. It provides an alternative to OSPF.

BGP

BGP is an example of an EGP. BGP exchanges information between autonomous systems and guarantees loop-free path selection. Most major companies and ISPs use BGP for route advertising on the Internet. Unlike other protocols, such as RIP, OSPF, and EIGRP, BGP does not use metrics such as hop count and bandwidth to make routing decisions. Instead, BGP uses network policies or rules using various BGP attributes.

Routing Protocols Summary

- Interior Gateway Protocols (IGPs) route data within autonomous systems. Exterior Gateway Protocols (EGPs) route data between autonomous systems.
- Distance vector protocols send all or some part of their routing table to neighbors. Distance vectors determine both the distance and direction (vector) to the destination.
- Distance vector algorithms use mechanisms such as split horizon, hold-down timers, and poison reverse updates to avoid routing loops.
- Link-state algorithms send only information about changes to the network for routing updates.
- Hybrid routing algorithms combine aspects of link-state and distance vector algorithms.
- RIP is a distance vector protocol that uses hop count as a metric.
- EIGRP is a hybrid protocol developed by Cisco. It uses a composite metric and can support multiple routed protocols.
- OSPF is a link-state protocol that uses cost as a metric.

Traditional WAN Services

WAN Connection Options

WAN services are generally leased from service providers on a subscription basis. There are three main types of WAN connections (services):

- **Leased line**—A leased line (or point-to-point dedicated connection) provides a pre-established connection through the service provider's network (WAN) to a remote network.

Synchronous Serial

- **Circuit switch**—Circuit switching provides a dedicated circuit path between sender and receiver for the duration of the call. Circuit switching is used for basic telephone service or Integrated Services Digital Network (ISDN). Circuit-switched connections are best for clients that require only sporadic WAN usage.

Asynchronous Serial
ISDN Layer 1

- **Packet switch**—With packet switching, devices transport packets using virtual circuits (VCs) that provide end-to-end connectivity. Programmed switching devices provide physical connections. Packet headers are used to identify the destination. Packet switching offers leased line-type services over shared lines, but at a much lower cost. Packet-switched networks typically use serial connections with speeds ranging from 56 kbps to T3 speeds.

Synchronous Serial

Leased Line

A leased line (or point-to-point dedicated connection) provides a pre-established connection through the service provider's network (WAN) to a remote network. Leased lines provide a reserved connection for the client, but they are costly. Leased-line connections typically are synchronous serial connections with speeds up to 45 Mbps (T3).

Multiplexing

Multiplexing is the process of combining multiple signals over a single wire, fiber, or link. With Time Division Multiplexing (TDM), lower-speed signals are brought in, assigned time slots, and placed in a higher-speed serial output. On the receiving end, the signals are reconstructed. With standard TDM, each end station essentially owns a time slot, preventing any other end station from using it, even when it is idle.

TDM Can Have
Unused Time Slots

Frame Relay

Frame Relay is a connection-oriented Layer 2 protocol that allows several data connections (virtual circuits) to be multiplexed onto a single physical link. Frame Relay relies on upper-layer protocols for error correction. Frame Relay specifies only the connection between a router and a service provider's local access switching equipment.

A connection identifier is used to map packets to outbound ports on the service provider's switch. When the switch receives a frame, a lookup table is used to map the frame to the correct outbound port. The entire path to the destination is determined before the frame is sent.

Virtual Circuits

Frame Relay connections are established using logical connections called virtual circuits. Virtual circuits can pass through several data circuit-terminating equipment (DCE) devices throughout the Frame Relay Packet-Switched Network (PSN). Several virtual circuits can be multiplexed into a single physical circuit for transmission across the network. There are two types of virtual circuits: switched virtual circuits (SVCs) and permanent virtual circuits (PVCs).

Switched Virtual Circuit (SVC)

An SVC is a temporary connection used for sporadic data transfer between DTE devices across the Frame Relay network.

SVC sessions have four distinct operational states: Call Setup, Data Transfer, Idle, and Call Termination

If the connection is idle for some predetermined amount of time, the connection is terminated. After it is terminated, a new call must be established for data to flow again.

Permanent Virtual Circuit (PVC)

A PVC is an established connection that remains up at all times. PVCs should be used when there is frequent and consistent data transfer between DTE devices.

With PVCs, no call setups or termination procedures are required. The operational states are Data Transfer and Idle.

Local Management Interface (LMI)

LMI is a signaling standard used to manage the connection between the router and the Frame Relay switch. LMIs track and manage keepalive mechanisms, multicast messages, and status. LMI can be configured, but routers can autosense LMI types by sending a status request to the Frame Relay switch. The router configures itself to match the LMI type response.

ATM and Cell Switching

Asynchronous Transfer Mode (ATM) was originally developed as a high-speed public WAN transport for voice, video, and data. ATM was later modified by the ATM Forum to include transport over private networks.

ATM networks are composed of ATM switches interconnected by point-to-point ATM links. The links connecting the switches come in two forms: User-Network Interfaces (UNIs), which connect ATM endpoints to ATM switches, and Network Node Interfaces (NNIs), which connect ATM switches.

The asynchronous part of ATM refers to the protocol's ability to use a more efficient version of time-division multiplexing (TDM). Multiplexing is a method of combining multiple data streams onto a single physical or logical connection. Time division means that each data stream has an assigned slot in a repeating sequence. With synchronous TDM, each time slot is preassigned and is held open if the station assigned to it has no data to send. Asynchronous transmission allows empty slots to be filled by stations that have data to send.

ATM Makes Efficient Use of All Time Slots

SONET

Synchronous Optical Network (SONET) supports high transmission rates (155 Mbps to 10 Gbps). ATM can run over SONET to achieve very high data transfer speeds. SONET is sometimes referred to as Synchronous Data Hierarchy (SDH) outside the U.S.

Traditional WAN Services Summary

- WAN networks offer access to internetworks and connection between geographically distant nodes.
- WAN customers pay service providers for WAN connections including dialup, leased lines, ISDN, and Frame Relay.
- WANs have a variety of protocols, all of which operate at the physical and data link layers of the OSI model.
- WAN switching methods include packet switching and circuit switching.

Dialup Access Technologies

ISDN

Integrated Services Digital Network (ISDN) is a collection of standards that define an integrated voice/data architecture over the Public Switched Telephone Network (PSTN). ISDN standards define both the hardware and call setup schemes. ISDN provides the following benefits:

- **Multiple traffic feeds**—Voice, video, telex, and packet-switched data are all available over ISDN.
- **Fast call setup**—ISDN uses out-of-band (D, or delta channel) signaling for call setup. ISDN calls can often be set up and completed in less than 1 second.
- **Fast bearer (B) channel services (64 kbps per channel)**—With multiple B channels (two B channels with BRI), ISDN offers 128 kbps. Leased lines usually provide only 56 kbps in North America.

ISDN has two types of interfaces: Basic Rate Interface (BRI) and Primary Rate Interface (PRI). Both types are broken into bearer (B) channels, which carry data, and delta channels, which carry signal and call control information. The D channel can also be used for low-rate packet data (such as alarms).

Basic Rate Interface (BRI)—BRI has two B channels (64 kbps each) and one D channel (16 kbps). BRI is sometimes written as 2B+D.

BRI (2B+D)

2 Bearer (B) Channels
64 kbps Each Used for Data

1 Data (D) Channel
16 kbps Used for Signaling

Bandwidth = 128 kbps

Primary Rate Interface (PRI)—In North America and Japan, PRI has 23 B channels and one D channel (all channels are 64 kbps). In Europe, a PRI has 30 B channels and one D channel. PRI is written as 23B+D.

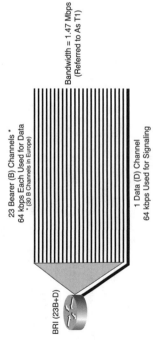

23 Bearer (B) Channels *
64 kbps Each Used for Data
* (30 B Channels in Europe)

Bandwidth = 1.47 Mbps
(Referred to As T1)

1 Data (D) Channel
64 kbps Used for Signaling

BRI (23B+D)

PPP

Point-to-Point Protocol (PPP) provides connections between devices over several types of physical interfaces, such as asynchronous serial, HSSI, ISDN, and synchronous. PPP works with several network layer protocols, including IP and IPX. PPP uses PAP and CHAP for basic security.

PPP uses a Network Control Protocol (NCP) component to encapsulate multiple protocols and the Link Control Protocol (LCP) to set up and negotiate control options on the data link.

HDLC

HDLC is a data-link protocol used on synchronous serial data links. HDLC cannot support multiple protocols on a single link because it lacks a mechanism to indicate which protocol it is carrying.

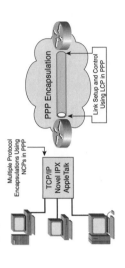

Multiple Protocol
Encapsulations Using
NCP's in PPP

TCP/IP
Novel IPX
AppleTalk

PPP Encapsulation

Link Setup and Control
Using LCP in PPP

The Cisco version of HDLC uses a proprietary field that acts as a protocol field. This field makes it possible for a single serial link to accommodate multiple network-layer protocols. Cisco's HDLC is a point-to-point protocol that can be used on leased lines between two Cisco devices. PPP should be used when communicating with non-Cisco devices.

Cisco HDLC

Flag	Address	Control	Proprietary	Data	FCS	Flag

Dialup Access Summary

* ISDN provides an integrated data, voice, and video capability that uses the public switched network.

* WAN encapsulation formats include PPP and HDLC.

* HDLC is the default encapsulation for serial lines in the Cisco IOS Software.

Analog Modems

A modem is a device used to send data over the Public Switched Telephone Network (PSTN). Modems typically send data in blocks and then perform a math function that is replicated on the receiving end. If the answers match, the data has arrived without errors. The term modem is short for modulation/demodulation, which is the process of converting analog signals into digital and back. Modems operate at Layers 1 and 2 of the OSI model. Modems can be internal to a PC or external. External modems are connected via the computer's serial or USB ports.

Several modem standards exist. The most common ones are listed in the following table.

Standard	Description
V.22	Provides 1200 bps. Was used outside the U.S.
V.22bis	First worldwide full-duplex modem standard. Operated at 2400 bps.
V.32	Standard for full duplex. Operated at 4800 or 9600 bps. This standard allowed the automatic adjustment of transmission speed based on line quality.
V.32bis	Allowed 14.4 kbps. Failed back to V.32 if phone lines were impaired.
V.34	Full duplex across phones lines at speeds up to 28.8 kbps. Backward-compatible with V.32.
V.42	Same rates as V.34, with improved error correction.
V.90	Full-duplex standard with a downstream rate of 56 kbps and an upstream rate of 330 kbps.
V.92	The latest specification. Features include quick connect, modem on hold, and PCM upstream.

Digital Subscriber Line

Basic DSL

DSL is a modem technology that uses the existing phone wires connected to virtually every home in most countries. The term xDSL refers to the different variations of DSL. DSL operates at OSI Layer 1, relying on higher-layer protocols for connection services and encapsulation.

DSL Types

The two types of DSL are asymmetric DSL (ADSL) and symmetric DSL (SDSL). ADSL's downlink speed is much greater than its uplink speed (thus the asymmetry). This was done because most users download much more from the Internet than they upload. SDSL is more useful for those running web servers, because it gives equal bandwidth to the uplink and downlink.

DSL Equipment

The twisted-pair wires that provide phone service are ideal because the available frequency ranges on the wires far exceed those required to carry a voice conversation. DSL requires some specialized equipment to ensure that voice and data are kept separate and are routed to the right place:

- Low-Pass Filters (LPFs) are placed on all phone jacks not used by a computer to prevent interference from high-frequency data signals.
- DSL modems are the interface from the phone line to the computer.
- DSL Access Multiplexers (DSLAMs) aggregate hundreds of signals from homes and are the access point to the Internet.

DSL Standards

There are several international DSL standards, all of which are supported by DSL providers. They are listed in the following table.

DSL Type	Speed	Distance Limit
Full-rate ADSL	384 kbps to 8 Mbps downlink and up to 1.024 Mbps uplink	18,000 ft
G.lite	1.544 to 6 Mbps downlink and 640 kbps uplink	18,000 ft
Very high data rate DSL (VDSL)	12.96 to 52.8 Mbps for both downlink and uplink	4,500 ft
IDSL	11 kbps for both downlink and uplink	18,000 ft
ISDN DSL (IDSL)	768 kbps for both downlink and uplink	22,000 ft
High Data Rate DSL (HDSL)	1.544 or 2.048 Mbps for both downlink and uplink	12,000 ft
G.SHDSL	192 kbps to 2.36 Mbps for both downlink and uplink	28,000 ft

DSL Limitations and Advantages

Advantages:

- DSL offers speeds up to and exceeding T1 for a fraction of the cost.
- DSL supports data and voice.
- DSL is an "always-on" technology.
- DSL service providers can add circuits as needed.

Limitations:

- DSL availability is limited.
- The telephone company must install DSL equipment.
- DSL has some distance limitations, and the signals cannot be amplified.

DSL Summary

- DSL operates at Layer 1 of the OSI model.
- DSL is a modem technology that uses existing twisted-pair telephone lines to transport both voice and data.
- The two types of DSL are asymmetric and symmetric. Asymmetric DSL provides higher downstream data rates than upstream. Symmetric DSLs' upstream and downstream rates are equal.
- Although DSL has high data rates, it is distance-limited.

Cable Modems

Cable Basics

Cable uses the same basic principles as DSL in that the bandwidth needed to accomplish the primary function (providing TV programming) is only a fraction of the available bandwidth on the wire, or in this case, cable.

Like DSL, cable modems provide "always-on" connectivity. This gives you the convenience of not having to dial up with every use, but it does make a system more vulnerable to hackers (which is why routers and firewalls should be installed behind a cable modem). Cable also offers speeds well over those of T1 (some claim up to 6 times T1 speed). Cable modems use quadrature amplitude modulation (QAM) to encode digital data into an analog signal to deliver 30 to 40 Mbps in one 6-MHz cable channel. A headend facility at the local cable office manages traffic flows and performs the following functions:

- Receives programming from networks
- Coverts signals and places them on the proper channel frequency
- Combines all channels into one broadband analog channel
- Broadcasts the combined analog signal to subscribers

Cable Limitations and Advantages

Advantages:

- Cable offers very high speeds in both upstream and downstream directions.
- Cable is fairly widespread in the U.S., so access is generally available.
- Many cable providers deploy hybrid-fiber coaxial (HFC) cable, which provides greater bandwidth and less noise than standard coaxial.

Limitations:

- Cable modems often require an overhaul of existing cable systems, which is very costly for small (customer base) providers.
- Cable is a shared medium, so as more people use the system, each gets less bandwidth.

Cable and the OSI Model

To be interoperable, cable systems must be standardized for different vendors. The following lists note the various cable standards for several layers of the OSI model.

The physical layer has the following standards:

- 64 and 256 QAM
- 6-MHz channels that operate with standard channels
- Supports both latency-sensitive and latency-insensitive data types.
- Uses cable modem terminal server (CMTS) to aggregate user traffic.

The data link layer provides the requirements that allow several users to share a single upstream data signal. Ranging is used to account for the delay differences between those close to the headend and those farther away. The MAC layer supports

- Timing and synchronization
- Bandwidth allocation
- Error detection, error handling, and error recovery
- Cable modem registration

At the application layer, cable modems support standard applications such as HTTP, FTP, e-mail, and many others.

Cable Modem Summary

- Cable modems put data signals on the same cable as television signals. Cable offers leased-line speeds and "always-on" connections.
- Cable is already installed throughout much of the U.S.
- Cable modems access a shared medium, so the more users (or TV channels), the less available bandwidth.
- Cable systems comprise many different technologies and standards. Vendors must be interoperable.

Operating and Configuring a Cisco IOS Device

Basic Operation of Cisco IOS Software

Cisco IOS enables network services in switches and routers. It provides the following features:

- Carries network protocols and functions
- Connectivity
- Security
- Scalability
- Reliability

The Cisco IOS command-line interface (CLI) can be accessed through a console connection, modem connection, or Telnet session. These connections are called EXEC sessions.

Starting a Switch

When a Catalyst switch is started for the first time, a default configuration is loaded. Three main operations are performed during normal startup:

Step 1 A power-on self test (POST) checks the hardware.

Step 2 A startup routine initiates the operating system.

Step 3 Software configuration settings are loaded.

Initial Startup Procedure

Step 1 Before you start the switch, verify the following:

- All network cable connections are secure.
- A terminal is connected to the console port.
- A terminal application is selected.

Step 2 Attach the switch to the power source to start the switch (there is no on/off switch). Observe the boot sequence.

System Status LED
Port Mode LED
Mode Button
Port Status LEDs
Redundant Power System LED

LEDs on the front panel of the switch provide information on switch status during startup, normal operation, and fault conditions. Pressing the mode button (shown in the figure, which shows a Catalyst 1900) toggles through the LED display modes:

- Port status
- Bandwidth utilization
- Full-duplex support

The following table details switch LED status indications for the Catalyst 1900.

Catalyst 1900 Switch LEDs

LED	Status
System	Green—System powered and operational Amber—System malfunction
Redundant power supply (RPS)	Green—RPS operational Amber—RPS installed but not operational Flashing amber—The internal power supply and RPS have power, and the internal power supply is powering the switch
Port status (STAT)	Green—Link present Flashing green—Activity Alternating green and amber—Link fault Amber—Port not forwarding
Bandwidth utilization (UTL)	1 to 8 LEDs on—0.1 to <6 Mbps 9 to 16 LEDs on—6 to <120 Mbps 17 to 24 LEDs on—120 to 280 Mbps
Full duplex (FDUP)	Green—Ports are configured in full-duplex mode Off—Ports are half-duplex

For the Catalyst 2900 series, the LED indicators are slightly different.

Catalyst 2900 Switch LEDs

LED	Status
System LED	Green—System powered and operational Amber—System malfunction; one or more POST errors
Redundant power supply (RPS)	Green—RPS operational Flashing green—RPS connected but is powering another device Amber—RPS installed but not operational Flashing amber—The internal power supply and RPS have power and are powering the switch
Port status (STAT)	Green—Link present Flashing green—Link present with traffic activity Alternating green and amber—Link fault Amber—Port not forwarding
Bandwidth utilization (UTL)	Green—Bandwidth utilization displayed over the amber LED on a logarithmic scale Amber—Maximum backplane utilization since the switch was powered on Green and amber—Depends on the model
Full duplex (FDUP)	Green—Ports are configured in full-duplex mode Off—Ports are half-duplex

Getting Help

Several commands built into IOS provide help when you enter configuration commands:

- ? displays a list of commonly used commands.
- -More- appears at the bottom of the screen when more information exists. Display the next available screen by pressing the Spacebar. Display the next line by pressing Enter. Press any other key to return to the user-mode prompt.
- s? lists all commands that start with s.
- show ? lists all variants of the show command.

- **show running-configuration** displays the currently active configuration in memory, including any changes made in the session that have not yet been saved.
- **show config** displays the last saved configuration.
- **show version** displays information about the system hardware and software.
- **show interfaces** displays information on connections and ports that connect with other devices.
- **show controller** displays the type of cable used on serial interfaces.

Starting a Switch Summary

- The Catalyst status LEDs are generally green when the switch is functioning and amber when there is a malfunction.
- Port LEDs are green during the POST. The power LED remains green when the test is complete. All other LEDs turn off after the test completes unless there is a malfunction.
- After a successful POST on a 1900, the Menu Console logon screen appears. From here you can enter three different modes: menu (M), command line (K), or IP configuration (I).
- After a successful POST on a 2950, the user is prompted to enter the initial configuration. An automatic setup program is available.
- The command-line interface includes several help commands, including **show**.

Starting a Router

When a Cisco router is started, it runs a POST to test the hardware. When the router is started for the first time, it does not have an initial configuration. The router prompts the user for a minimum of details. This basic setup is not intended for entering complex configurations or protocol features. The setup command gives you the following options:

- [0]—Go to the EXEC prompt without saving the created configuration.
- [1]—Go back to the beginning of setup without saving the created configuration.
- [2]—Accept the created configuration, save it to NVRAM, and exit to EXEC mode.

Default answers appear in square brackets ([ ]). Pressing Enter accepts the defaults. At the first setup prompt, you can enter no to discontinue the setup. The setup process can be aborted at any time by pressing Ctrl-C.

Access Levels

User EXEC level provides a limited number of basic commands.

```
Console

wg_ro_c con0 is now available
Press RETURN to get started

wg_ro_c>                          User-Mode Prompt
wg_ro_c>enable
wg_ro_c#                          Privileged-Mode Prompt
wg_ro_c#disable
wg_ro_c>
wg_ro_c>layout
```

Privileged EXEC (enable mode) level allows you to access all router commands. This level can be password-protected. The **enable** command allows access to this mode (**disable** exits to user mode).

Console Error Messages

When you enter an incorrect command, you receive one of three messages detailed in this table.

Error Message	Meaning	How to Get Help
% Ambiguous command: "show con"	Not enough characters were entered to define a specific command.	Reenter the command, followed by a question mark (?), with no space between the command and the question mark.
% Incomplete command.	Keywords or values are missing.	Reenter the command, followed by a space between the command and the question mark (?), with a space between the command and the question mark.
% Invalid input detected at '^' marker.	The command was entered incorrectly. The caret (^) marks the point of the error.	Enter a question mark (?) to display all the commands or parameters that are available in this mode.

History Buffer

A command history is available to review previously entered commands. This buffer defaults to ten lines, but can be configured to a maximum of 256 using the history size command:

    terminal history size lines   Sets the session command buffer size.
    history size line   Sets the buffer size permanently.
    show history   Shows command buffer contents.

CLI Editing Sequences

Cisco IOS allows for shortcuts to speed the editing process.

Command	Action
Ctrl-A	Moves the cursor to the beginning of the line.
Ctrl-E	Moves the cursor to the end of the line.
Esc-B	Moves the cursor back one word.
Esc-F	Moves the cursor forward one word.
Ctrl-B	Moves the cursor back one character.
Ctrl-F	Moves the cursor forward one character.
Ctrl-D	Deletes a single character.
Backspace	Removes one character to the left of the cursor.
Ctrl-R	Redisplays a line.
Ctrl-U	Erases from the cursor to the beginning of the line.
Ctrl-W	Erases a word.
Ctrl-Z	Ends configuration mode and returns to the EXEC.
Tab	Completes a partially entered (unambiguous) command.
Ctrl-P or ↑	Recalls commands, beginning with the most recent.
Ctrl-N or ↓	Returns the more recent commands in the buffer.

Starting a Router Summary

- The startup configuration routine option appears when no valid configuration exists in NVRAM.
- The setup configuration dialog can be accessed by entering the **setup** command in privileged mode.
- The **?** command displays the available commands in a given mode.
- Enhanced editing mode includes a set of keyboard shortcuts to simplify using the command-line interface.
- The command history feature lets you see a list of previously entered commands.

Configuring the Router

From privileged EXEC mode, the **configure terminal** command provides access to global configuration mode. From global configuration mode, you can access specific configuration modes:

- **Interface**—Configures operations on a per-interface basis.
- **Subinterface**—Configures multiple virtual interfaces.
- **Controller**—Supports commands that configure controllers (such as E1 and T1).
- **Line**—Configures the operation of a terminal line.
- **Router**—Configures IP routing protocols.
- **IPX-router**—Configures the Novell network layer protocol.

Assigning a Router Name Example

The **hostname** command names a router (or a switch).

```
Router> enable
Router# configure terminal
Router(config)# hostname Dallas
```

Configuring a Serial Interface Example

```
Router# configure terminal
Router(config)# interface s1
Router(config-if)# clock rate 64000
Router(config-if)# bandwidth 64
Router# show interface serial 1
```

Note: Unambiguous abbreviations of commands are allowed. Abbreviations of delimiters are not allowed. For example, a clock rate of 64000 cannot be abbreviated as 64. The bandwidth command overrides the default bandwidth. The bandwidth entered has no effect on the line's actual speed.

Major Command/Subcommand Relationship

Commands that indicate a process or interface that will be configured are called major commands. Major commands cause the CLI to enter a specific configuration mode:

```
User EXEC Commands - Router>
ping
show (limited)
enable
etc...

Privileged EXEC Commands - Router#
all User EXEC commands
debug commands
reload
configure
etc...

        Global Configuration Commands - Router(config)#
        hostname
        enable secret
        ip route
        interface                    Interface Commands - Router(config-if)#
                    ethernet         ip address
                    serial           ipx address
                    bri              encapsulation
                    etc...           shutdown / no shutdown
                                     etc...

        router                       Routing Engine Commands - Router(config-router)#
                    ospf             network
                    igrp             version
                    etc...           auto-summary
                                     etc...

        line                         Line Commands - Router(config-line)#
                    console          password
                    etc...           login
                                     modem commands
                                     etc...
```

Major commands have no effect unless they are immediately followed by a subcommand that supplies the configuration entry.

```
Router(config)# interface serial 0
Router(config-if)# shutdown

Router(config)# router rip
Router(config-router)# network 10.0.0.0
```

Configuring Router Password Examples

```
Router(config)# line console 0
Router(config-line)# login
Router(config-line)# password homer

Router(config)# line vty 0 4
Router(config-line)# login
Router(config-line)# password bart
```

The numbers 0 through 4 in the line vty command specify the number of Telnet sessions allowed in the router. You can also set up a different password for each line by using the line vty port number command.

```
Router(config)# enable password apu
Router(config)# enable secret flanders
Router(config)# service password-encryption
```

The no enable command disables the privileged EXEC mode password.

The no enable secret command disables the encrypted password.

Note: When the enable secret password is set, it is used instead of the enable password.

Configuring the Router Via the CLI Summary

• Entering the configure terminal command from enable mode places you in global configuration mode. From here, you have access to the interface, subinterface, controller, line, router, and IPX-router configuration modes.
• You must save your running configuration to NVRAM with the copy running-config startup-config command. Failing to save your configuration to NVRAM causes your configurations to be lost if your router is reloaded.
• Router security is achieved by password-protecting various access modes.
• Interface type and numbers must be defined when the interface command is used.
• Use the show interface command to verify configuration changes.

Managing Your Network Environment

Discovering Neighbors with CDP

CDP is a proprietary tool that enables access to protocol and address information on directly connected devices.

CDP runs over the data link layer, allowing devices running different network layer protocols (such as IP and IPX) to learn about each other.

CDP summary information includes device identifiers, address lists, port identifiers, and platform.

CDP runs over all LANs, Frame Relay, ATM, and other WANs employing Subnetwork Access Protocol (SNAP) encapsulation. CDP starts by default on bootup and sends updates every 60 seconds.

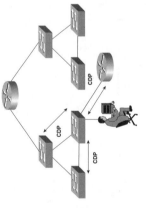

show cdp shows you the CDP output.

cdp enable enables CDP on an interface.

no cdp enable disables CDP on an interface.

cdp run allows other CDP devices to get information about your device.

no cdp run disables CDP on a device.

show cdp neighbors displays the CDP updates received on the local interfaces.

show cdp neighbors detail displays updates received on the local interfaces. This command displays the same information as the show cdp entry * command.

show cdp entry displays information about neighboring devices.

show cdp traffic displays information about interface traffic.

show cdp interface displays interface status and configuration information.

Discovering Neighbors with CDP Summary

- CDP gathers information on directly connected devices.
- CDP passes packets of information between neighboring devices.
- The **show cdp neighbors** command yields the following information for adjacent devices: attached interfaces, hardware platform, and remote port ID.
- The **show cdp entry *** command yields some Layer 3 protocol information, such as IP addresses.

Getting Information About Remote Devices

Telnet is an underlying TCP/IP protocol for accessing remote computers. Telnet allows connections and remote console sessions from one device to one or more other remote devices.

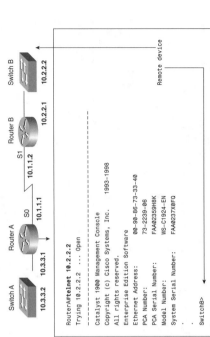

```
RouterA#telnet 10.2.2.2
Trying 10.2.2.2 ... Open

Catalyst 1900 Management Console
Copyright (c) Cisco Systems, Inc.    1993-1998
All rights reserved.
Enterprise Edition Software
Ethernet Address:      00-90-86-73-33-40
PCA Number:            73-2239-06
PCA Serial Number:     FAA02359H8K
Model Number:          WS-C1924-EN
System Serial Number:  FAA0237X0FQ
.
.
SwitchB>
```

Telnet Procedure

To establish a Telnet session, use the telnet or connect command. Both a router's IP address and host name (when DNS or the host entry is present) can be used as an argument.

Router Boot Flowchart

```
RouterA# telnet 10.2.2.2
RouterB# connect RouterA
RouterA# show sessions
```

Note: **show sessions** displays a list of hosts to which you are connected.

Suspending/Resuming Sessions

Pressing Ctrl-Shift-6 followed by x suspends the current session.

resume or pressing **Enter** resumes the last active session.

resume session# reconnects to a specific session. Use the show session command to find the session number.

A Telnet session can be ended with the **exit**, **logout**, **disconnect**, and **clear** commands.

Ping/Trace

Connectivity can be verified using the ping command. **ping** also tells you the minimum, average, and maximum times for packets that make the round trip to the target system and back. You can assess the path's reliability using this command.

```
Router## ping 10.1.1.10
Type escape sequence to abort.
Sending 5, 100-byte ICMP Echos to 10.1.1.10, timeout is 2 seconds:
!!!!!
Success rate is 100 percent (5/5), round-trip min/avg/max = 4/4/4 ms
```

The **trace** command can be used to view the actual routes that packets take between devices.

```
Router# trace 10.1.1.10
Type escape sequence to abort.
Tracing the route to 10.1.1.10

1 10.1.1.10 4 msec 4 msec 4 msec
Router#
```

Getting Information About Remote Devices Summary

- Telnet allows remote connections to distant devices.
- You open a Telnet session by entering the **telnet** or **connect** command followed by the IP address or host name of the target device.
- The **show sessions** command displays a list of connected hosts, their IP addresses, the byte counts, the idle time, and the session name.
- Use the **show user** command to list all active Telnet sessions.
- To reestablish a suspended Telnet session, press **Enter**, use the **resume** command (for the most recent session), or use the **resume session number** command (use **show session** to get session numbers).
- The **ping** and **trace** commands can be used to obtain information about network devices and to check for connectivity.

Altering the Configuration Register

Before changing the configuration register, use the show version command to determine the current image. The last line contains the register value. Changing this value changes the location of the IOS load (and many other things). A reload command must be used for the new configuration to be set. The register value is checked only during the boot process.

Configuration Register Boot Field Value	Meaning
0x0	Use ROM monitor mode (manually boot using the b command).
0x1	Automatically boot from ROM (provides IOS subset).
0x2 to 0xF	Examine NVRAM for boot system commands (0x2 is the default if router has Flash).

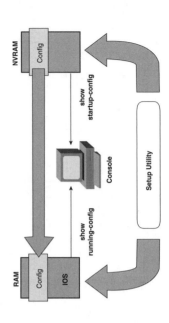

Router Boot Sequence and Verification

When a router is booted up, it goes through the following sequence:

Step 1   The router checks its hardware with a Power-On Self Test (POST).

Step 2   The router loads a bootstrap code.

Step 3   The Cisco IOS software is located and loaded using the information in the bootstrap code.

Step 4   The configuration is located and loaded.

After this sequence completes, the router is ready for normal operation. In RAM:

```
wg_ro_c# show running-config
Building configuration...

Current configuration:
!
version 12.0
!
--More--
```

Router Components

The major router components are as follows:

- **RAM**—Random Access Memory contains key software (IOS).
- **ROM**—Read-Only Memory contains startup microcode.
- **NVRAM**—Nonvolatile RAM stores the configuration.
- **Configuration register**—Controls the boot-up method.
- **Interfaces**—The interface is the physical connection to the external devices. Physical connections can include Token Ring and FDDI.
- **Flash memory**—Flash contains the Cisco IOS software image. Some routers run the IOS image directly from Flash and do not need to transfer it to RAM.

When IOS is loaded, the router must be configured. Configs in NVRAM are executed. If one does not exist in NVRAM, the router initiates an auto-install or setup utility. The auto-install routine downloads the config file from a TFTP server..

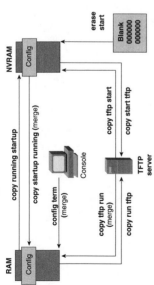

There are other sources of configs. The IOS copy commands are used to move configurations from one component or device to another. The syntax is

copy object source destination

For example:

copy running-config startup-config

Note: When a configuration is copied into RAM, it merges with the existing configuration in RAM. It does not overwrite the existing configuration.

The **show running-config** and **show startup-config** commands are useful troubleshooting aids. These commands allow you to view the current configuration in RAM or the startup configuration commands in NVRAM.

In NVRAM:

```
wg_ro_c# show startup-config
Using 1359 out of 32762 bytes
!
version 12.0
!
--More--
```

You know that you are looking at the startup config file when you see a message at the top telling you that NVRAM has been used to store the configuration.

You know that you are looking at the current config file when you see the words "Current configuration" at the top of the display.

Troubleshooting is aided with the **show** and **debug** commands. The following table details the differences between the two.

Characteristics	show	debug
Processing Load	Static	Dynamic
	Low overhead	High overhead
Primary Use	Gather facts	Observe processes

Key Features of IFS

The Cisco IOS File System (IFS) feature provides an interface to the router file systems. The Universal Resource Locator (URL) convention allows you to specify files on network devices.

URL Prefixes for Cisco Network Devices

- Bootflash—Boot Flash memory.
- Flash—This prefix is available on all platforms.
- Flh—Flash load helper log files.
- ftp—File Transfer Protocol (FTP) network server.
- Nvram—NVRAM.
- Rcp—Remote copy protocol (rcp) network server.
- slot0—First PCMCIA Flash memory card.
- slot1—Second PCMCIA Flash memory card.
- System—Contains the system memory and the running configuration.
- Tftp—Trivial File Transfer Protocol (TFTP) network server.

How to Manage IOS Images

It is always prudent to retain a backup copy of your IOS software image in case the software system in your router becomes corrupted.

IOS Upgrade Example

```
wg_ro_a# show flash
wg_ro_a# copy flash tftp
wg_ro_a# copy tftp flash
```

When using the copy flash command, you must enter the IP address of the remote host and the name of the source and destination system image file.

The router prompts you for the IP address of the remote host and the name of the source and destination system image file.

Router Boot Sequence and Verification Summary

The major router components are RAM, ROM, Flash memory, NVRAM, the configuration register, and the interfaces.

The four major areas of microcode contained in ROM are bootstrap code, POST code, ROM monitor, and a mini IOS.

The router configuration can come from NVRAM, a terminal, or a TFTP server.

You can back up your software image on the network server by using the copy flash [location] command.

General Concepts

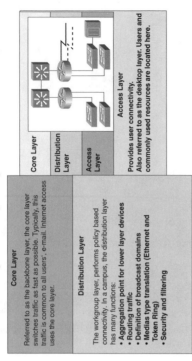

Bridge   Switch   Router   Access Server   ISDN Switch   Multilayer Switch

Personal Computer   File Server   Data Service Unit/ Channel Service Unit   Modem   Network Switch

WAN Cloud   VLAN   Hub   Network Cloud or Broadcast Domain

Ethernet   Fast Ethernet   Serial Line   Circuit Switched Line

Defining Networks

Several different types of users access the network from many locations:

- **Main office**—Most corporate information is located here. Everyone is connected to the LAN.
- **Branch office**— Remote sites with a separate LAN access the main office via the WAN.
- **Telecommuters**—
  Employees who work out of their homes using ISDN, cable, or DSL.
- **Mobile users**—Connect from multiple locations.

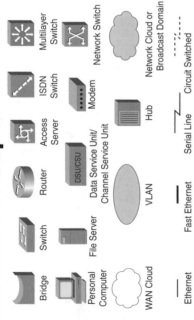

Hierarchical Model

Cisco uses a hierarchical network model for network design. High traffic loads create a need for efficient routing and switching techniques.

Core Layer

Referred to as the backbone layer, the core layer switches traffic as fast as possible. Typically, this traffic is common to all users; e-mail. Internet access uses the core layer.

Distribution Layer

The workgroup layer, performs policy based connectivity. In a campus, the distribution layer has many functions:

- **Aggregation point for lower layer devices**
- **Routing traffic**
- **Definition of broadcast domains**
- **Medias type translation (Ethernet and Token Ring)**
- **Security and filtering**

Access Layer

Provides user connectivity. Also referred to as the desktop layer. Users and commonly used resources are located here.

Defining Networks Key Points

Cisco uses a hierarchical network model. The three layers are the access layer, the distribution layer, and the core layer for network design.

- The access layer provides user connectivity to the network.
- The distribution layer is responsible for performing routing, filtering, and WAN access.
- The core layer is responsible for fast switching services.

OSI Model

The OSI model is a standardized framework for network functions and schemes. It breaks otherwise-complex network interactions into simple elements, which lets developers modularize design efforts. This method allows many independent developers to work on separate network functions, which can be applied in a "plug and play" manner.

Protocol Data Units (PDUs) are used to communicate between layers.

Encapsulation is the method of adding headers and trailers. As the data moves down the stack, the receiving device strips the header, which contains information for that layer (de-encapsulation).

OSI Model Summary

- The OSI model provides a standardized method of creating and implementing network standards and schemes.

- The OSI model allows "plug-and-play" applications, simplified building blocks, and modularized development.

- The OSI model has seven layers. Mnemonics are useful for remembering the layers and their functions (PDNTSPA).

- Encapsulation is the process of adding layer-specific instructions and information (for the receiving device) as headers and trailers.

- De-encapsulation is the reverse of encapsulation.

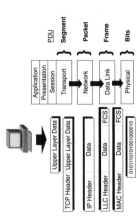

Application		
Presentation		
Session		
Transport		Segment
Network		Packet
Data Link		Frame
Physical		Bits

Upper Layer Data		
TCP Header	Upper Layer Data	
IP Header	Data	
LLC Header	Data	FCS
MAC Header	Data	FCS
01011101010001000010		

PDU

OSI MODEL		
Application	User interface.	Telnet HTTP
Presentation	Encryption and other processing.	ASCII/EBCDIC JPEG/MP3
Session	Manages multiple applications.	Operating systems Scheduling
Transport	Provides reliable or best-effort delivery and some error correction.	TCP UDP SPX
Network	Provides logical addressing used by routers and the network hierarchy.	IP IPX
Data Link	Creates frames from bits of data. Uses MAC addresses to access endpoints. Provides error detection but no correction.	802.3 802.2 HDLC Frame Relay
Physical	Specifies voltage, wire speed, and cable pin-outs.	EIA/TIA V.35

Lower (Data Link) Layers

Physical Layer Functions

- Media type
- Connector type
- Signaling type

What the Physical Layer Specifies

- Voltage levels
- Data rates
- Maximum transmission rates and distances
- Physical connectors' pin-outs

10Base2—Thin Ethernet
10Base5—Thick Ethernet

10BaseT—Twisted Pair

Host

Hub

Hosts

Type	Name	Distance	Carrier
10BASE2	Thinnet	To 185 m	Coaxial
10BASE5	Thicknet	500 m	Coaxial
10BASE-T	Ethernet	100 m	Twisted-pair

Collision/Broadcast Domains

All stations on an Ethernet segment are connected to the same wire. Therefore, all devices receive all signals. When devices send signals at the same time, a collision occurs. A scheme is needed to detect and compensate for collisions.

- **Collision domain**—A group of devices connected to the same physical medium such that if two devices access the medium at the same time, a collision results. Ethernet devices use a method called CSMA/CD (Carrier Sense Multiple Access Collision Detect) when sending bits. When a collision occurs, both stations resend the signal after a random period. Collisions increase with the number of stations.

- **Broadcast domain**—A group of devices on the network that receive one anothers' broadcast messages.

- **Hub**—A device that allows the concentration of many devices into a single segment. Hubs have the following characteristics:

  —Hubs are physical layer devices.

  —Hubs do not manipulate or view traffic.

  —Hubs do not create separate collision domains.

Data Link Layer Functions

- Performs physical addressing
- Provides support for connection-oriented and connectionless services
- Provides for frame sequencing and flow control

Two sublayers perform the data link functions:

Media Access Control (MAC) sublayer (802.3)—Responsible for how data is sent over the wire. The MAC address is a 48-bit address expressed as 12 hex digits.

MAC defines:

- Physical addressing
- Network topology
- Line discipline
- Error notification
- Orderly delivery of frames
- Optional flow control

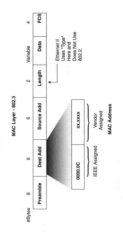

| | 802.2 | | Frame Relay |
| Ethernet | 802.3 | HDLC | |

Data Link / Physical

EIA/TIA-232 v.35

MAC Layer - 802.3

#Bytes	8	6	6	2	Variable	4
	Preamble	Dest Add	Source Add	Length	Data	FCS

Ethernet II Uses "Type" Here and Does Not Use 802.2

| 0000.0C | xx.xxxx |
| IEEE Assigned | Vendor Assigned |

MAC Address

Logical Link Control (LLC) sub-layer (802.2)—Responsible for identifying and encapsulating different protocol types. There are two types of LLC frames: Service Access Point (SAP) and Subnet-work Access Protocol (SNAP). SNAP is used to support non-802 protocols.

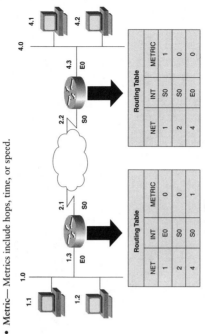

802.2 (SNAP)

1	1	1 or 2	3	2	Variable
Dest SAP AA	Source SAP AA	Ctrl 03	OUI ID	Type	Data

Or

802.2 (SAP)

1	1	1 or 2	Variable
Dest SAP	Source SAP	Ctrl	Data

MAC Layer - 802.3

Preamble	Dest add	Source add	Length	Data	FCS

Data Link Layer Devices

Bridges and Layer 2 switches function at the data link layer.

ASICs allow switches to operate at gigabit speeds. When a bridge or switch receives a frame, it processes the frame as follows: If the destination device is

- On the same segment, the bridge blocks the frame from going out other ports. This is known as filtering.
- On a different segment, the bridge forwards the frame to the appropriate segment.
- Unknown to the bridge, the bridge forwards the frame to all segments except the one on which it was received. This is called flooding.

For every frame that traverses a bridge, the bridge gleans the MAC address of the sending device and stores it for future forwarding decisions.

The purpose of Layer 2 devices is to reduce collisions. They have the following characteristics:

- Each segment defines a collision domain.
- All devices connected to the same bridge or switch belong to the same broadcast domain.

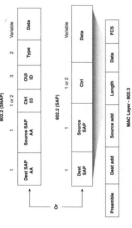

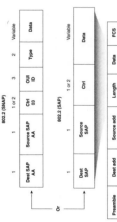

Network Layer Functions

Network traffic must often span devices that are not locally attached or that belong to separate broadcast domains. Two pieces of information are needed to do this.

- A logical address associated with the source and destination stations
- A path through the network to reach the desired destinations

Router Operation at the Network Layer

Routers operate by gathering and trading data on different networks and selecting the best path to those networks. Routing tables contain the following information:

- IP network addresses—32-bit addresses (this varies for other protocols).
- Interface—The port used to reach a given destination.
- Metric— Metrics include hops, time, or speed.

Routing Table

NET	INT	METRIC
1	E0	0
2	S0	0
4	S0	1

Routing Table

NET	INT	METRIC
1	S0	1
2	S0	0
4	E0	0

Transport Layer Functions

A logical connection (session) must be established to connect two devices in a network. The transport layer

- Allows end stations to multiplex multiple upper-layer segments into the same data streams.

- Provides reliable data transport between end stations (for TCP).

Lower Layers Summary

- The physical layer specifies the media type, connectors, signaling, voltage level, data rates, and distances required to interconnect network devices.
- Hubs are used to allow several end stations to communicate as if they were on the same segment.
- A collision occurs when two stations transmit at the same time.
- Hubs have a single collision domain and a broadcast domain.
- The data link layer determines how data is transported.
- Bridges and Layer 2 switches function at the data link layer.
- All devices connected to a bridge or Layer 2 switch belong to the same broadcast domain.
- All devices connected to a single segment of a bridge or Layer 2 switch belong to the same collision domain.
- The network layer defines how to transport traffic between devices that are not locally attached.
- The transport layer defines session setup rules between two end stations.
- Routers use routing tables to navigate paths to distant networks.

Assembling and Cabling Cisco Devices

LAN Specifications and Connections

The term Ethernet encompasses several LAN implementations. Physical layer implementations vary, and all support various cabling structures.

There are three main categories:

- **Ethernet (DIX) and IEEE 802.3**—Operate at 10 Mbps over coaxial cable, UTP, or fiber.
- **100 Mbps Ethernet (Fast Ethernet IEEE 802.3u)**—Operates over UTP or fiber.
- **1000 Mbps Ethernet**—Gigabit Ethernet that operates over fiber and copper.

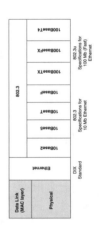

Fast Ethernet can be used throughout the campus environment. The following table gives examples of each campus layer.

	Ethernet 10BaseT Position	Fast Ethernet Position
Access Layer	Provides connectivity between the end-user device and the access switch.	Gives high-performance PCs and workstations 100 Mbps access to the server.
Distribution Layer	Not typically used at this layer.	Provides connectivity between access and distribution layers. Provides connectivity from the distribution to core layers. Provides connectivity from the server block to the core layer.
Core layer	Not typically used at this layer.	Provides interswitch connectivity.

This table compares cable and connecter specifications. Fast Ethernet requires unshielded twisted-pair (UTP) Category 5 (or higher) cabling.

	10Base5	10BaseT	100BaseTX	100BaseFX
Medium	50-ohm coaxial (thick)	EIA/TIA Category 3, 4, 5, UTP 2 pair	EIA/TIA Category 5 UTP 2 pair	62.5/125 micron multimode fiber
Maximum segment length	500 meters	100 meters	100 meters	400 meters
Topology	Bus	Star	Star	Point-to-point
Connector	AUI	ISO 8877 (RJ-45)	ISO 8877 (RJ-45)	Duplex media interface connector (MIC) ST

An RJ-45 connector is used with UTP cabling. The two types of connections are straight-through and crossover. Straight-through cables are typically used to connect different devices, such as switch-to-router connections.

Crossover cables are typically used to connect similar devices, such as switch-to-switch connections. The primary exception to this rule is switch-to-hub connections, which use a crossover cable.

Some device ports are marked with an X. In general, use a straight-through cable when only one of the ports is marked.

LAN Specifications and Connections Summary

- Ethernet has several LAN specifications, including IEEE 802.3 (10 Mbps), IEEE 802.3u (100 Mbps), and Gigabit Ethernet 802.3ae (1000 Mbps).
- UTP category 5 or higher is required for Fast Ethernet.
- Straight-through cables are typically used to connect different device types, such as a router and a switch. The exception is a switch-to-hub connection, which requires a crossover cable.
- Crossover cables are typically used to connect similar devices, such as a switch and a switch.

Pin	Wire Pair T is Tip R is Ring
1	Pair 2 T2
2	Pair 2 R2
3	Pair 3 T3
4	Pair 1 R1
5	Pair 1 T1
6	Pair 3 R3
7	Pair 4 T4
8	Pair 4 R4

The RJ-45 Connector

Cable 10 BaseT/100BaseT Crossover

Hub/Switch Pin Label	Hub/Switch Pin Label
1 RD+	1 RD+
2 RD-	2 RD-
3 TD+	3 TD+
4 NC	4 NC
5 NC	5 NC
6 TD-	6 TD-
7 NC	7 NC
8 NC	8 NC

Crossover Cable
Some Wires on Cable Ends Are Crossed.

WAN Specifications and Connections

There are several ways to carry traffic across the WAN. The implementation depends on distance, speed, and the type of service required. Connection speeds typically vary from 56 kbps to T1/E1 (1.544/2.048 Mbps, but can be as high as 10 Gbps). WANs use serial communication for long-distance communication. Cisco routers use a proprietary 60-pin connector, and the network end of the cable must match the service hardware.

Cabling Routers for Serial Connectors

When cabling routers, you need to determine if you need a data terminal equipment (DTE) connector or a data circuit-terminating equipment (DCE) connector.

- DTE—the endpoint of the user's device on the WAN link.
- DCE—the point where responsibility for delivery of data passes into the hands of the ISP.

If you connect routers back-to-back, one of the routers is a DTE, and the other is a DCE.

Router Ports

Routers can have fixed or modular ports.
With fixed ports, each port has a port type and number, such as "Ethernet 0." With modular ports, each port has a port type, slot number, and port number, such as "serial 1/0."

Configuring Devices

You must establish a connection via a console port to configure a Cisco device. Some devices use a rollover cable to connect a console port to a PC. To set up the connection, do the following:

Step 1   Cable the device using a rollover cable. You might need an adapter for the PC.

Step 2 Configure the terminal emulation application with the following COM port settings: 9600 bps, 8 data bits, no parity, 1 stop bit, and no flow control.

WAN Specifications and Connections Summary

- WANs use serial transmission for long-distance communication.
- Cisco routers use a proprietary 60-pin connector on serial ports.
- A DTE/DCE is the point where the service provider assumes responsibility for the WAN. A DCE provides clocking.
- Routers have either fixed or modular ports. The syntax you use to configure each interface depends on the type of port.
- Rollover cables are used to set up a console connection.

Operating and Configuring a Cisco IOS Device

Basic Operation of Cisco IOS Software

Cisco IOS enables network services in switches and routers. It provides the following features:

- Carries network protocols and functions
- Connectivity
- Security
- Scalability
- Reliability

The Cisco IOS command-line interface (CLI) can be accessed through a console connection, modem connection, or Telnet session. These connections are called an EXEC sessions.

Starting a Switch

When a Catalyst switch is started for the first time, a default configuration is loaded. Three main operations are performed during normal startup:

- A power-on self test (POST) checks the hardware.
- A startup routine initiates the operating system.
- Software configuration settings are loaded.

Initial Startup Procedure

Step 1 Before you start the switch, verify the following:
All network cable connections are secure.
A terminal is connected to the console port.
A terminal application is selected.

Step 2 Attach the switch to the power source to start the switch (there is no on/off switch).

Step 3 Observe the boot sequence.

LEDs on the front panel of the switch provide information on switch status during startup, normal operation, and fault conditions. Pressing the mode button (shown in the figure, which shows a Catalyst 1900), toggles through the LED display modes:

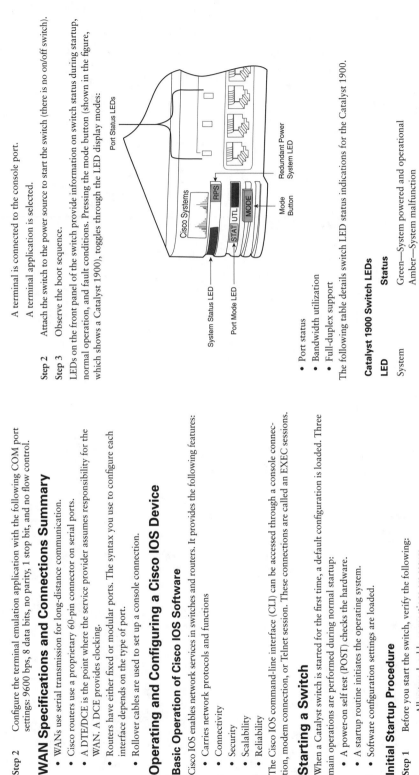

- Port status
- Bandwidth utilization
- Full-duplex support

The following table details switch LED status indications for the Catalyst 1900.

Catalyst 1900 Switch LEDs

LED	Status
System	Green—System powered and operational Amber—System malfunction

Redundant power supply (RPS)	Green—RPS operational Amber—RPS installed but not operational Flashing amber—The internal power supply and RPS have power, and the internal power supply is powering the switch
Full duplex (FDUP)	Green—Ports are configured in full-duplex mode Off—Ports are half-duplex

For the Catalyst 2900 series, the LED indicators are slightly different.

Catalyst 2900 Switch LEDs

LED	Status
System LED	Green—System powered and operational Amber—System malfunction; one or more POST errors
Redundant power supply (RPS)	Green—RPS operational Flashing green—RPS connected but is powering another device Amber—RPS installed but not operational Flashing amber—The internal power supply and RPS have power and are powering the switch
Port status (STAT)	Green—Link present Flashing green—Link present with traffic activity Alternating Green and amber—Link fault Amber—Port not forwarding
Bandwidth utilization (UTL)	Green—Bandwidth utilization displayed over the amber LED on a logarithmic scale Amber—Maximum backplane utilization since the switch was powered on Green and amber—Depends on the model
Full duplex (FDUP)	Green—Ports are configured in full-duplex mode Off—Ports are half-duplex

Getting Help

Several commands built into IOS provide help when you enter configuration commands:

- **?**—displays a list of commonly used commands.
- **More**—appears at the bottom of the screen when more information exists. Display the next available screen by pressing the Spacebar. Display the next line by pressing Enter. Press any other key to return to the user-mode prompt.
- **s?**—lists all commands that start with s.
- **show**—lists all variants of the show command.
- **show running-configuration**—displays the currently active configuration in memory, including any changes made in the session that have not yet been saved.
- **show config**—displays the last saved configuration.
- **show version**—displays information about the system hardware and software.
- **show interfaces**—displays information on connections and ports that connect with other devices.
- **show controller**—displays the type of cable used on serial interfaces.

Starting a Switch Summary

- The Catalyst status LEDs are generally green when the switch is functioning and amber when there is a malfunction.
- Port LEDs are green during the POST. The power LED remains green when the test is complete. All other LEDs turn off after the test completes unless there is a malfunction.
- After a successful POST on a 1900, the Menu Console logon screen appears. From here you can enter three different modes: menu (M), command line (K), or IP configuration (I).
- After a successful POST on a 2950, the user is prompted to enter the initial configuration. An automatic setup program is available.
- The command-line interface includes several help commands, including **show**.

Starting a Router

When a Cisco router is started, it runs a POST to test the hardware. When the router is started for the first time, it does not have an initial configuration. The router prompts the user for a minimum of details. This basic setup is not intended for entering complex configurations or protocol features. The setup command gives you the following options:

- Go to the EXEC prompt without saving the created configuration.

% Invalid input detected at '^' marker.	The command entered incorrectly. The caret (^) marks the point of the error.	Enter a question mark (?) to display all the commands or parameters that are available in this mode.

History Buffer

A command history is available to review previously entered commands. This buffer defaults to ten lines but can be configured to a maximum of 256 using the history size command:

- terminal history size lines—Sets the session command buffer size.
- history size line—Sets the buffer size permanently.
- show history—Shows command buffer contents.

CLI Editing Sequences
Cisco IOS allows for shortcuts to speed the editing process:

Command	Action
Ctrl-A	Moves the cursor to the beginning of the line.
Ctrl-E	Moves the cursor to the end of the line.
Esc-B	Moves the cursor back one word.
Esc-F	Moves the cursor forward one word.
Ctrl-B	Moves the cursor back one character.
Ctrl-F	Moves the cursor forward one character.
Ctrl-D	Deletes a single character.
Backspace	Removes one character to the left of the cursor.
Ctrl-R	Redisplays a line.
Ctrl-U	Erases from the cursor to the beginning of the line.
Ctrl-W	Erases a word.
Ctrl-Z	Ends configuration mode and returns to the EXEC.
Tab	Completes a partially entered (unambiguous) command.
Ctrl-P or ↑	Recalls commands, beginning with the most recent.

- Go back to the beginning of setup without saving the created configuration.
- Accept the created configuration, save it to NVRAM, and exit to EXEC mode.

Default answers appear in square brackets ([ ]). Pressing Enter accepts the defaults. At the first setup prompt, you can enter no to discontinue the setup. The setup process can be aborted at any time by pressing Ctrl-C.

Access Levels

User EXEC level provides a limited number of basic commands.

Privileged EXEC (enable mode) level allows you to access all router commands. This level can be password-protected. The enable command allows access to this mode (disable exits to user mode).

```
                                  Console

wg_ro_c con0 is now available
Press RETURN to get started
wg_ro_c>                            User-Mode Prompt
wg_ro_c>enable
wg_ro_c#
wg_ro_c#disable                     Privileged-Mode Prompt
wg_ro_c>
wg_ro_c>layout
```

Console Error Messages
When you enter an incorrect command, you receive one of three messages:

Error Message	Meaning	How to Get Help
% Ambiguous command: "show con"	Not enough characters were entered to define a specific command.	Reenter the command, followed by a question mark (?), with no space between the command and the question mark.
% Incomplete command.	Keywords or values are missing.	Reenter the command, followed by a question mark (?), with a space between the command and the question mark.

Ctrl-N or ↓	Returns the more recent commands in the buffer.

Starting a Router Summary

- The startup configuration routine option appears when no valid configuration exists in NVRAM.
- The setup configuration dialog can be accessed by entering the setup command in privileged mode.
- The ? command displays the available commands in a given mode.
- Enhanced editing mode includes a set of keyboard shortcuts to simplify using the command-line interface.
- The command history feature lets you see a list of previously entered commands.

Configuring the Router

From privileged EXEC mode, the configure terminal command provides access to global configuration mode. From global configuration mode, you can access specific configuration modes:

- Interface—Configures operations on a per-interface basis.
- Subinterface—Configures multiple virtual interfaces.
- Controller—Supports commands that configure controllers (such as E1 and T1).
- Line—Configures the operation of a terminal line.
- Router—Configures IP routing protocols.
- IPX-router—Configures the Novell network layer protocol.

Assigning a Router Name Example

The hostname command is used to name a router (or a switch).

```
Router>enable
Router#configure terminal
Router(config)#hostname Dallas
```

Configuring a Serial Interface Example

```
Router#configure terminal
Router(config)#interface s1
Router(config-if)#clock rate 64000
Router(config-if)#bandwidth 64
Router#show interface serial 1
```

Notes:

Unambiguous abbreviations of commands are allowed.

Abbreviations of delimiters are not allowed. For example, a clock rate of 64000 cannot be abbreviated as 64.

The bandwidth command overrides the default bandwidth. The bandwidth entered has no effect on the line's actual speed.

Major Command/Subcommand Relationship

Commands that indicate a process or interface that will be configured are called major commands. Major commands cause the CLI to enter a specific configuration mode:

```
User EXEC Commands - Router>
 ping
 show (limited)
 enable
 etc...

Privileged EXEC Commands - Router#
 all User EXEC commands
 debug commands
 reload
 configure
 etc...

        Global Configuration Commands - Router(config)#
         hostname
         enable secret
         ip route

         interface  ethernet       Interface Commands - Router(config-if)#
                    serial           ip address
                    bri              ipx address
                    etc...           encapsulation
                                     shutdown / no shutdown
                                     etc...

         router  rip               Routing Engine Commands - Router(config-router)#
                 ospf                network
                 igrp                version
                 etc...              auto-summary
                                     etc...

         line  vty                 Line Commands - Router(config-line)#
               console               password
               etc...                login
                                     modem commands
                                     etc...
```

Major commands have no effect unless they are immediately followed by a subcommand that supplies the configuration entry.

```
Router(config)#interface serial 0
Router(config-if)#shutdown
```

Configuring Router Password Examples

```
Router(config)#router rip
Router(config-router)#network 10.0.0.0
```

```
Router(config)#line console 0
Router(config-line)#login
Router(config-line)#password homer
```

```
Router(config)#line vty 0 4
Router(config-line)#login
Router(config-line)#password bart
```

The numbers 0 through 4 in the line vty command specify the number of Telnet sessions allowed in the router. You can also set up a different password for each line by using the line vty port number command.

```
Router(config)#enable password apu
Router(config)#enable secret flanders
Router(config)#service password-encryption
```

The no enable command disables the privileged EXEC mode password.

The no enable secret command disables the encrypted password.

Note: When the enable secret password is set, it is used instead of the enable password.

Configuring the Router Via the CLI Summary

- Entering the configure terminal command from enable mode places you in global configuration mode. From here, you have access to the interface, subinterface, controller, line, router, and IPX-router configuration modes.

- You must save your running configuration to NVRAM with the copy running-config startup-config command. Failing to save your configuration to NVRAM causes your configs to be lost if your router is reloaded.

- Router security is achieved by password-protecting various access modes.

- Interface type and numbers must be defined when the interface command is used.

- Use the show interface command to verify configuration changes.

Managing Your Network Environment

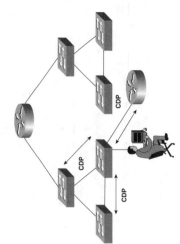

Discovering Neighbors with CDP

CDP is a proprietary tool that enables access to protocol and address information on directly connected devices. CDP runs over the data link layer, allowing devices running different network layer protocols (such as IP and IPX) to learn about each other. CDP summary information includes device identifiers, address lists, port identifiers, and platform.

CDP runs over all LANs, Frame Relay, ATM, and other WANs employing Subnetwork Access Protocol (SNAP) encapsulation. CDP starts by default on bootup and sends updates every 60 seconds.

- show cdp—shows you the CDP output.
- cdp enable—enables CDP on an interface.
- no cdp enable—disables CDP on an interface.
- cdp run—allows other CDP devices to get information about your device.
- no cdp run—disables CDP on a device.
- show cdp neighbors—displays the CDP updates received on the local interfaces.
- show cdp neighbors detail—displays updates received on the local interfaces. This command displays the same information as the show cdp entry * command.
- show cdp entry—displays information about neighboring devices.
- show cdp traffic—displays information about interface traffic.
- show cdp interface—displays interface status and configuration information.

Discovering Neighbors with CDP Summary

- CDP gathers information on directly connected devices.
- CDP passes packets of information between neighboring devices.
- The **show cdp neighbors** command yields the following information for adjacent devices: attached interfaces, hardware platform, and remote port ID.
- The **show cdp entry *** command yields some Layer 3 protocol information, such as IP addresses.

Getting Information About Remote Devices

```
RouterA#telnet 10.2.2.2
Trying 10.2.2.2 ... Open

Catalyst 1900 Management Console
Copyright (c) Cisco Systems, Inc.    1993-1998
All rights reserved.
Enterprise Edition Software
Ethernet Address:       00-90-86-73-33-40
PCA Number:             73-2239-06
PCA Serial Number:      FAA02359HBK
Model Number:           WS-C1924-EN
System Serial Number:   FAA0237X0FQ
.
.
SwitchB>
```

Telnet is an underlying TCP/IP protocol for accessing remote computers. Telnet allows connections and remote console sessions from one device to one or more other remote devices.

Telnet Procedure

To establish a Telnet session, use the **telnet** or **connect** command. Both a router's IP address and host name (when DNS or the host entry is present) can be used as an argument.

```
RouterA#telnet 10.2.2.2
RouterB#connect RouterA
RouterA#show sessions
```

Note: **show sessions** displays a list of hosts you are connected to.

Suspending/Resuming Sessions

Pressing Ctrl-Shift-6 followed by x suspends the current session.

resume or pressing Enter resumes the last active session.

resume session# reconnects to a specific session. Use the show session command to find the session number.

A Telnet session can be ended with the **exit**, **logout**, **disconnect**, and **clear** commands.

Ping/Trace

Connectivity can be verified using the **ping** command. **ping** also tells you the minimum, average, and maximum times for packets that make the round trip to the target system and back. You can assess the path's reliability using this command.

```
Router#ping 10.1.1.10
Type escape sequence to abort.
Sending 5, 100-byte ICMP Echos to 10.1.1.10, timeout is 2 seconds:
!!!!!
Success rate is 100 percent (5/5), round-trip min/avg/max 4/4/4 ms
```

The trace command can be used to view the actual routes that packets take between devices.

```
Router#trace 10.1.1.10

Type escape sequence to abort.
Tracing the route to 10.1.1.10

  1 10.1.1.10 4msec 4msec 4msec
Router#
```

Getting Information About Remote Devices Summary

- Telnet allows remote connections to distant devices.
- You open a Telnet session by entering the **telnet** or **connect** command followed by the IP address or host name of the target device.
- The **show sessions** command displays a list of connected hosts, their IP addresses, the byte counts, the idle time, and the session name.
- Use the **show user** command to list all active Telnet sessions.

- To reestablish a suspended Telnet session, press Enter, use the **resume** command (for the most recent session), or use the **resume** *session number* command (use **show session** to get session numbers).

- The **ping** and **trace** commands can be used to obtain information about network devices and to check for connectivity.

Router Boot Sequence and Verification

When a router is booted up, it goes through the following sequence:

1. The router checks its hardware with a POST.
2. The router loads a bootstrap code.
3. The Cisco IOS software is located and loaded using the information in the bootstrap code.
4. The configuration is located and loaded.

After this sequence completes, the router is ready for normal operation.

In RAM:

```
wg_ro_c#show running-config
Building configuration...

Current configuration:
!
version 12.0
!
```

- - More - -

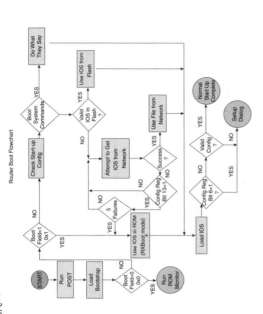

Router Boot Flowchart

Router Components

The major router components are as follows:

- **RAM**—Random Access Memory contains key software (IOS).
- **ROM**—Read-Only Memory contains startup microcode.
- **NVRAM**—Nonvolatile RAM stores the configuration.
- **Configuration register**—Controls the bootup method.
- **Interfaces**—Physical connections can include Token Ring and FDDI.

- **Flash memory**—Flash contains the Cisco IOS software image. Some routers run the IOS image directly from Flash and do not need to transfer it to RAM.

Altering the Configuration Register

Before changing the configuration register, use the **show version** command to determine the current image. The last line contains the register value. Changing this value changes the location of the IOS load (and many other things). The **reload** command must be used for the new configuration to be set. The register value is checked only during the boot process.

Configuration Register Boot Field Value	Meaning
0x0	Use ROM monitor mode (manually boot using the b command).
0x1	Automatically boot from ROM (provides a Cisco IOS subset).
0x2 to 0xF	Examine NVRAM for boot system commands (0x2 is the default if the router has Flash).

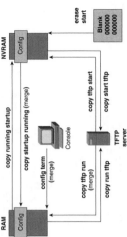

When IOS is loaded, the router must be configured. Configs in NVRAM are executed. If one does not exist in NVRAM, the router initiates an autoinstall or setup utility. The autoinstall routine downloads the config file from a TFTP server.

There are other sources of configs. The IOS copy commands are used to move configurations from one component or device to another. The syntax is **copy object source destination** For example:

```
copy running-config
startup-config
```

Note: When a configuration is copied into RAM, it merges with the existing configuration in RAM. It does not overwrite the existing configuration.

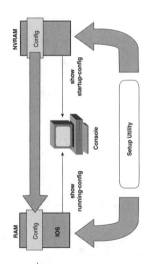

The **show running-config** and **show startup-config** commands are very useful troubleshooting aids. These commands allow you to view the current configuration in RAM or the startup configuration commands in NVRAM. In NVRAM:

```
wg_ro_c#show startup-config
Using 1359 out of 32762 bytes
!
version 12.0
!
--More--
```

You know that you are looking at the startup config file when you see a message at the top telling you that NVRAM has been used to store the configuration.

You know that you are looking at the current config file when you see the words "Current configuration" at the top of the display.

Troubleshooting is aided with the **show** and **debug** commands. The following table details the differences between the two.

Characteristics	show	debug
Processing Load	Low overhead	High overhead
Primary Use	Gather facts	Observe processes

Key Features of IFS

The Cisco IOS File System (IFS) feature provides an interface to the router file systems. The Universal Resource Locator (URL) convention allows you to specify files on network devices.

URL Prefixes for Cisco Network Devices

- **Bootflash**—Boots Flash memory.
- **Flash**—This prefix is available on all platforms.
- **Flh**—Flash load helper log files.
- **ftp**—File Transfer Protocol (FTP) network server.
- **Nvram**—NVRAM.
- **Rcp**—Remote copy protocol (rcp) network server.
- **slot0**—First PCMCIA Flash memory card.
- **slot1**—Second PCMCIA Flash memory card.
- **System**—Contains the system memory and the running configuration.
- **Tftp**—Trivial File Transfer Protocol (TFTP) network server.

How to Manage IOS Images

It is always prudent to retain a backup copy of your IOS software image in case the software system in your router becomes corrupted

IOS Upgrade Example

```
wg_ro_a#show flash
wg_ro_a#copy flash tftp
```

When using the **copy flash** command, you must enter the IP address of the remote host and the name of the source and destination system image file.

The router prompts you for the IP address of the remote host and the name of the source and destination system image file.

Router Boot Sequence and Verification Summary

- The major router components are RAM, ROM, Flash memory, NVRAM, the configuration register, and the interfaces.
- The four major areas of microcode contained in ROM are bootstrap code, POST code, ROM monitor, and a mini IOS.
- The router configuration can come from NVRAM, a terminal, or a TFTP server.
- You can back up your software image on the network server by using the **copy flash** [*location*] command.

Catalyst Switch Operations

Basic Layer 2 Switching (Bridging) Functions

Ethernet switching operates at OSI Layer 2, creating dedicated network segments and interconnecting segments. Layer 2 switches have three main functions:

- **MAC Address Learning**—Layer 2 switches must learn the MAC addresses of devices attached to each of their ports. The addresses are stored in a MAC database.
- **Forwarding and Filtering**— Switches determine which port a frame must be sent out to reach its destination. If the address is known, the frame is sent only on that port. If it's unknown, the frame is flooded to all ports except the one it originated from.
- **Loop Avoidance**—When the switched network has redundant links, the switch can prevent duplicate frames from traveling over multiple paths.

Bridging and Switching Comparison

Bridging	Switching
Software-based	Hardware (ASIC)-based
One spanning-tree instance per bridge	Many spanning-tree instances per switch
Usually up to 16 ports per bridge	More ports on a switch

Frame Transmission Modes

There are three primary frame switching modes:

- **Cut-through**—The switch checks the destination address and immediately begins forwarding the frame. This can decrease latency but can also transmit frames containing errors.
- **Store and forward**—The switch waits to receive the entire frame before forwarding. The entire frame is read, and a cyclic redundancy check (CRC) is performed. If the CRC is bad, the frame is discarded. Latency increases as a function of frame length.
- **Fragment-free (modified cut-through)**—The switch reads the first 64 bytes before forwarding the frame. 64 bytes is the minimum number of bytes necessary to detect and filter out collision frames. This is the default mode for the Catalyst 1900.

How Switches Learn Addresses

A switch uses its MAC address table when forwarding frames to devices. With an empty MAC address table, the switch must flood frames to all ports other than the one it arrived on. This is the least-efficient way to transmit data.

1. Initially, the switch MAC address table is empty.

2. Station A with the MAC address sends a frame to station C. When the switch receives this frame, it does the following:

   - Because the MAC table is empty, the switch must flood the frame to all other ports (except E0, the frame origin).
   - The switch notes the source address of the originating device and associates it with port E0 in its MAC address table entry.

3. The switch continues to learn addresses in this manner, continually updating the table. As the MAC table becomes more complete, the switching becomes more efficient, because frames are forwarded to specific ports rather than being flooded out all ports.

MAC Address Table

E0: 0260.8c01.1111

E3: 0260.8c01.4444

A 0260.8c01.1111
B 0260.8c01.3333
C 0260.8c01.2222
D 0260.8c01.4444

Broadcast and Multicast Frames

Broadcast and multicast frames are flooded to all ports other than the originating port. Broadcast and multicast addresses never appear as a frame's address, so the switch does not learn these addresses.

Basic Layer 2 Switching (Bridging) Functions Summary

- Ethernet switches are Layer 2 devices that increase a network's available bandwidth by creating separate network segments.
- Switches have three modes of frame transmission:
  - Cut-through: Only the destination address is checked before the frame is forwarded.
  - Store and forward: The entire frame is checked before forwarding.
  - Fragment-free: Only the first 64 bytes are checked before forwarding.
- Switches learn, store, and use MAC addresses to determine where a frame should be transmitted.
- A frame is forwarded to a specific port only when the destination address is known. Otherwise, it is flooded out all ports other than the one it was received on.

Redundant Topology Overview

A redundant topology has multiple connections to switches or other devices. Redundancy ensures that a single point of failure does not cause the entire switched network to fail. Layer 2 redundancy, however, can cause problems in a network, including broadcast storms, multiple copies of frames, and MAC address table instability.

Broadcast Storms

The flooding of broadcast frames can cause a broadcast storm (indefinite flooding of frames) unless there is a mechanism in place to prevent it.

An example of a broadcast storm is shown in the figure and can be described as follows:

1. Host X sends a broadcast frame, which is received by Switch A.

2. Switch A checks the destination and floods it to the bottom Ethernet link, Segment 2.

3. Switch B receives the frame on the bottom port and transmits a copy to the top segment.

4. Because the original frame arrives at Switch B via the top segment, Switch B transmits the frame a second time. The frame travels continuously in both directions.

Multiple Frame Transmissions

Most protocols cannot correctly handle duplicate transmissions. Protocols that use sequence numbering see that the sequence has recycled. Other protocols process the duplicate frame with unpredictable results. Multiple-frame transmissions occur as follows:

1. Host X sends a frame to Router Y. One copy is received over the direct Ethernet connection, Segment 1. Switch A also receives a copy.

2. Switch A checks the destination address. If the switch does not find an entry in the MAC address table for router Y, it floods the frame on all ports except the originating port.

3. Switch B receives the frame on segment 2 and forwards it to Segment 1.

Note that router Y has now received the same frame twice.

Database Instability

Database instability occurs when a switch receives the same frame on different ports. The following example shows how this occurs:

1. Host X sends a frame to Router Y. When the frame arrives at Switches A and B, they both learn the MAC address for Host X and associate it with Port 0.

2. The frame is flooded out port 1 of each switch (assuming that Router Y's address is unknown).

3. Switches A and B receive the frame on Port 1 and incorrectly associate host X's MAC address with that port.

This process repeats indefinitely.

Multiple Loops

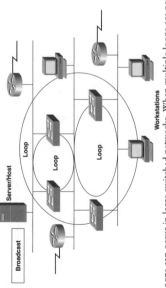

Multiple loops can occur in large switched networks. When multiple loops are present, a broadcast storm clogs the network with useless traffic. Packet switching is adversely affected in such a case and might not work at all. Layer 2 cannot prevent or correct broadcast storms.

Redundant Topology Summary

- A broadcast storm occurs when broadcast messages propagate endlessly throughout a switched network.
- Multiple transmissions of the same message cause errors in most protocols.
- A switch's MAC address table becomes unstable when the switch receives same frame on different ports.
- Layer 2 devices cannot recognize or correct looping traffic without help.

Spanning Tree Protocol

Spanning Tree Protocol prevents looping traffic in a redundant switched network by blocking traffic on the redundant links. If the main link goes down, spanning tree activates the standby path. Spanning Tree Protocol operation is transparent to end stations.

Spanning Tree Protocol was developed by DEC and was revised in the IEEE 802.1d specification. The two algorithms are incompatible. Catalyst switches use the IEEE 802.1d Spanning Tree Protocol by default.

Spanning-Tree Operation

Spanning Tree Protocol assigns roles to switches and ports so that there is only one path through the switch network at any given time. This is accomplished by assigning a single root bridge, root ports for nonroot bridges, and a single designated port for each network segment. On the root bridge, all ports are designated ports.

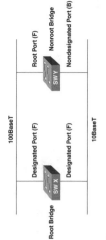

Link Speed	Cost (Reratify IEEE Spec)	Cost (Previous IEEE Spec)
10 Gbps	2	1
1 Gbps	4	1
100 Mbps	19	10
10 Mbps	100	100

On the root bridge, all ports are set to forwarding state. For the nonroot bridge, only the root port is set to forwarding state. The port with the lowest-cost path to the root bridge is chosen as the root port.

One designated port is assigned on each segment. The bridge with the lowest-cost path cost to the root bridge is the designated port. Nondesignated ports are set to blocking state (does not forward any traffic).

Selecting the Root Bridge

Switches running Spanning Tree Protocol exchange information at regular intervals using a frame called the bridge protocol data unit (BPDU). Each bridge has a unique bridge ID. The bridge ID contains the bridge MAC address and a priority number. The midrange value of 32768 is the default priority. The bridge with the lowest

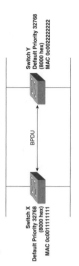

bridge ID is selected as the root bridge. When switches have the same priority, the one with the lowest MAC address is the root bridge. In the figure, Switch X is the root bridge.

Port States

Frames take a finite amount of time to travel or propagate through the network. This delay is known as propagation delay. When a link goes down, spanning tree activates previously blocked links. This information is sent throughout the network, but not all switches receive it at the same time. To prevent temporary loops, switches wait until the entire network is updated before setting any ports to forwarding state. Each switch port in a network running Spanning Tree Protocol is in one of the following states:

Blocking→Listening→Learning→Forwarding

The forward delay is the time it takes for a port to go to a higher state. It usually takes 50 seconds for a port to go from blocking state to forwarding state, but the timers can be adjusted.

Spanning-Tree Recalculation

When a link fails, the network topology must change. Connectivity is reestablished by placing key blocked ports in forwarding state.

In the following figure, if Switch X fails, Switch Y does not receive the BPDU. If the BPDU is not received before the MAXAGE timer expires, spanning tree begins recalculating the network. In the figure, Switch Y is now the root bridge. If Switch X comes back up, spanning tree recalculates the network, and switch X is once again the root bridge.

Time to Convergence

A network is said to have converged when all ports in a switched network are in either blocking or forwarding state after a topology change.

Rapid Spanning Tree

Rapid Spanning Tree Protocol (RSTP) significantly speeds up the recalculation process after a topology change occurs in the network. RSTP works by designating an alternative port and a backup port. These ports are allowed to immediately enter the forwarding state rather than passively waiting for the network to converge. Edge-port and link-type are new variables defined in RSTP.

Spanning Tree Protocol Summary

- Spanning Tree Protocol prevents loops in a redundant network.
- Spanning Tree Protocol assigns a root bridge, root ports for nonroot bridges, and designated ports for each segment. In a converged network, ports are in either forwarding or blocking state.
- BPDUs are exchanged every 2 seconds. The bridge ID is made up of the MAC address and priority. The bridge with the lowest bridge ID is the root bridge.
- The four port states are blocking, listening, learning, and forwarding.
- When a link fails, spanning tree adjusts the network topology to ensure connectivity.

Configuring the Catalyst Switch

An IP address must be assigned to a switch to use Telnet or Simple Network Management Protocol (SNMP).

A 32-bit subnet mask denotes which bits in the IP address correspond to the host portion and network portion of the address.

The default gateway is used when the switch must send traffic to a different IP network.

Configuring the IP Address

Before configuring the switch, you must identify its IP address, subnet mask, and default gateway. On the Catalyst 1900 switch, the ip address command is used to configure the switch's IP address and subnet mask. On the Catalyst 2950, you must configure each interface with an IP address and subnet mask.

```
SwitchA(config)#ip address 10.1.5.22 255.255.255.0
SwitchA (config)#ip default-gateway 10.1.5.44
```

Use the no ip address command to reset the IP address to the factory default of 0.0.0.0. Use the no ip default-gateway command to delete a configured default gateway and set the gateway address to the default value of 0.0.0.0.

The IP address, subnet mask, and default gateway settings can be viewed with the **show ip** command on the 1900.

Note that the 2950 uses the VLAN1 interface IP address as the switch IP address. Use the **show interface vlan** command to verify the IP address on each interface.

The **ip default-gateway** command can be used on both the 1900 and 2950. To delete a configured default gateway, use the **no ip default-gateway** command.

Duplexing

Duplexing is the mode of communication in which both ends can send and receive information. With Full Duplex, bidirectional communication can occur at the same time. Half-duplex is also bidirectional communication, but signals can flow in only one direction at a time. Simplex runs in a single direction only.

- Full duplex—Can send and receive data at the same time
  - —Collision-free
  - —Point-to-point connection only
  - —Uses a dedicated switched port with separate circuits
  - —Efficiency is rated at 100 percent in both directions
  - —Both ends must be configured to run in full-duplex mode
- Half duplex—CSMA/CD is susceptible to collisions
  - —Multipoint attachments
  - —Can connect with both half- and full-duplex devices
  - —Efficiency is typically rated at 50 to 60 percent
  - —The duplex setting must match on devices sharing a segment
- Simplex—Data is sent in one direction only and can never return to the source over the same link
  - —100% efficiency in one direction
  - —Satellite TV downlink is an example
  - —Not used very often in internetworking

Duplex Interface Configuration

The Catalyst 1900 can autonegotiate the duplex of an Ethernet connection. This mode is enabled when both speed and duplex flags are set to auto. The **show interfaces** command shows the current settings.

```
duplex {auto | full | full-flow-control | half}
```

For the 1900:

- **auto** sets autonegotiation.
- **full** sets full-duplex mode.
- **full-flow-control** sets full-duplex mode with flow control.
- **half** sets half-duplex mode.

The 2950 is the same, with the exception that there is no full flow control option on the 2950.

Managing MAC Addresses

MAC address tables contain three types of addresses:

- Dynamic addresses are learned by the switch and then are dropped when they are not in use.
- Permanent and static addresses are assigned by an administrator.

MAC Address Configuration

The **mac-address-table** global configuration command is used to associate a MAC address with a particular switched port interface. The syntax for the mac-address-table command is
mac-address-table {permanent | restricted static} {mac-address type module/port (src-if-list)}

You verify the MAC address table settings using the show mac-address-table command.
Note: The Catalyst 1900 can store up to 1024 MAC addresses in its MAC address table. As soon as the table is full, it floods all new addresses until one of the existing entries gets aged out.

- **mac-address-table permanent** —permanent MAC address.
- **no mac-address-table permanent** —deletes a permanent MAC address.
- **mac-address-table restricted static** —sets a restricted static address to an interface (1900 only).
- **no mac-address-table restricted static**—deletes a restricted static address (1900 only).

- **mac-address-table secure** —creates a secure address on the 2950.
- **src-if-list**—sets the restricted address to a port.

Port References (Catalyst 1900)

Different commands refer to the same ports in different ways.

- The **show running config** output refers to e0/1 as interface Ethernet 0/1.
- The **show spantree** output refers to e0/1 as port Ethernet 0/1.
- The **show vlan-membership** output refers to e0/1 as port 1.

Port References (Catalyst 2950)

The port references differ slightly on the 2950.

- The **show run** output refers to fa0/1 as interface FastEthernet 0/1.
- The **show spantree** output refers to fa0/1 as Interface Fa0.
- The **show vlan-membership** output refers to fa0/1 as portFa0/ 1.

Port Security

The port security feature is used to restrict the number of MAC addresses used on a switch or the use of a port to a specified group of users. The number of devices on a secured port can range from 1 to 132. The MAC addresses are either assigned by the administrator (statically assigned) or assigned automatically.

Address violations occur when a secured port receives a source address that is already assigned to another secured port or when a port exceeds its address table size limit. When a violation occurs, the action can be suspended, ignored, or disabled.

A suspended port is reenabled when a valid address is received. A disabled port must be manually reenabled. If the action is ignored, the switch port remains enabled. The 1900 uses the **port secure** command, and the 2950 uses the **port security max-mac-count** command.

```
SwitchA (config)#interface e0/1
SwitchA (config-if)#port secure max-mac-count 1
SwitchA (config-if)#exit
SwitchA (config)#address-violation ignore
SwitchA (config)#exit
SwitchA host#show mac-address-table security
```

The **no port secure** command disables addressing security and sets the maximum addresses on the interface to the default (132).

The **show** command yields a list of enabled ports and their security statuses. The action for an address violation can be **Suspend, Disable,** or **Ignore.** Use the **no address-violation** command to set the switch to its default value (suspend).

Configuring the Catalyst Switch Summary

- To configure global switch parameters (such as switch host name or IP address), use the **config term** command. To configure a particular port, use the **interface** command while in global config mode.
- MAC address table entries can be dynamic, permanent, or static.
- Switches are assigned IP addresses for network management purposes.
- A default gateway is used to reach a network with a different IP address.
- Use the various **show** commands to verify switch configuration.

VLANS

VLAN Operation Overview

The virtual LAN (VLAN) organizes physically separate users into the same broadcast domain.. The use of VLANs improves performance, security, and flexibility. The use of VLANs also decreases the cost of arranging users, because no extra cabling is required.

VLAN Characteristics

VLANs allow logically defined user groups rather than user groups defined by their physical locations. For example, you can arrange user groups such as accounting, engineering, and finance, rather than everyone on the first floor, everyone on the second floor, and so on.

- VLANs define broadcast domains that can span multiple LAN segments.
- VLANs improve segmentation, flexibility, and security.
- VLAN segmentation is not bound by the physical location of users.
- Each switch port can be assigned to only one VLAN.
- Only ports assigned to a VLAN share broadcasts, improving network performance.
- A VLAN can exist on one or several switches.

This figure shows a VLAN design. Note that VLANs are defined by user functions rather than locations.

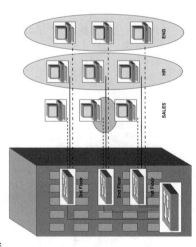

VLAN Operation

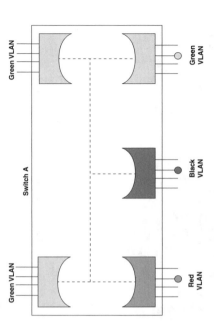

Each VLAN on a switch behaves as if it were a separate physical bridge. The switch forwards packets (including unicasts, multicasts, and broadcasts) only to ports assigned to the same VLAN from which they originated. This drastically cuts down on network traffic.

VLANs require a trunk or a physical connection for each VLAN to span multiple switches. Each trunk can carry traffic for multiple VLANs.

VLAN Assignment

A port can be assigned (configured) to a given VLAN. VLAN membership can be either static or dynamic.

- **Static assignment**—The VLAN port is statically configured by an administrator.

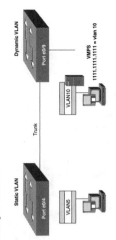

- **Dynamic assignment**—The switch uses a VMPS (VLAN Membership Policy Server). The VMPS is a database that maps MAC addresses to VLANs. A port can belong to only one VLAN at a time. Multiple hosts can exist on a single port only if they are all assigned to the same VLAN.

Trunking

The IEEE 802.1Q protocol is used to define VLAN topologies and to connect multiple switches and routers. Cisco supports 802.1Q trunking over Fast Ethernet and Gigabit Ethernet links. 802.1Q defines how to carry traffic from multiple VLANs over a single point-to-point link.

Inter-Switch Link (ISL)

ISL is a Cisco-proprietary protocol form of trunking designed to manage VLAN traffic between switches. ISL provides point-to-point links in full or duplex mode. ISL is performed with ASICs, which operate at wire speeds and enable VLANs to span the backbone.

ISL Tagging

ISL frame tagging multiplexes VLAN traffic onto a single physical path. It is used for connections between switches, routers, and network interface cards. A non-ISL-capable device treats ISL-encapsulated Ethernet frames as protocol errors if the frame size exceeds the maximum transmission unit (MTU). ISL tagging is a protocol-independent function that occurs at OSI Layer 2. ISL can be used to maintain redundant links and load-balance traffic.

VLAN Tag Added by Incoming Port

Inter-Switch Link Carries VLAN Identifier

VLAN Tag Stripped by Forwarding Port

ISL Encapsulation

ISL ports encapsulate each frame with a 26-byte ISL header and a 4-byte CRC. ASICs allow this to occur at wire speed (low latency). The number of VLANs supported depends on the switch. The Catalyst 1900 supports 64 VLANs with a separate spanning-tree instance per VLAN.

Per-VLAN Spanning Tree

Per-VLAN spanning tree is a method of giving different port assignments to the same physical port for different VLANs. The Cisco-proprietary version is called PVST+. PVST+ uses tunneling to allow several instances of STP on a single switch.

VLAN Operation Summary

- A VLAN is a broadcast domain that can span multiple physical LAN segments.
- VLANs improve performance, flexibility, and security by restricting broadcasts.
- VLANs only forward data to ports assigned to the same VLAN.
- VLAN ports can be assigned either statically or dynamically.
- The 802.1Q trunking protocol allows multiple VLANs to communicate over a single point-to-point link.
- ISL is a Cisco-proprietary protocol used to share and manage VLAN information across switches.
- ISL trunks encapsulate frames with an ISL header CRC.

Inter-VLAN Routing Summary

VLANs create Layer 2 segments. End stations in different segments (broadcast domains) cannot communicate with each other without the use of a Layer 3 device such as a router. Each VLAN must have a separate physical connection on the router, or trunking must be enabled on a single physical connection for inter-VLAN routing to work.

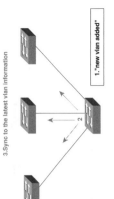

The figure shows a router attached to a switch. The end stations in the two VLANs communicate by sending packets to the router, which forwards them to the other VLAN. This setup is called "router on a stick."

Dividing Physical Interfaces into Subinterfaces

ISL trunking requires the use of subinterfaces. A subinterface is a logical, addressable interface on the router's physical Fast Ethernet port. A single port can have several subinterfaces (one per VLAN). The **encapsulation isl** *domain* command (in subinterface configuration mode) enables ISL. The *domain* parameter refers to the VLAN domain number.

In the figure, the FastEthernet 0 interface is divided into multiple subinterfaces (FastEthernet 0/1, FastEthernet 0/2, and so on).

Inter-VLAN Routing Summary

- "Router on a stick" is a router with a single connection to a switch. The router receives packets from one VLAN and forwards them to another VLAN.
- A subinterface is required to support ISL trunking.
- To configure "router on a stick," enable ISL on the switch port connecting to the router, enable ISL encapsulation on the router's FastEthernet subinterface, and then assign a network layer address to each subinterface.

Configuring a VLAN

VLAN Trunking Protocol (VTP) is a Layer 2 messaging protocol that distributes and synchronizes VLAN identification information throughout a switched network. VTP server updates are propagated to all connected switches in the network, which reduces the need for manual configuration (promotes scaling) and minimizes the risk of errors caused by duplicate names or incorrect VLAN types.

VTP Example

The VTP server notifies all switches in its domain that a new VLAN, named "ICND," has been added. The server advertises VLAN configuration information to maintain domain consistency.

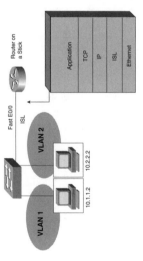

How VTP Works

Whenever there is a change to the VLAN database, the VTP server increments its configuration revision number and then advertises the new revision throughout the domain. When a switch receives the advertisement, it overwrites its configuration with the new information if the new revision number is higher than the one it already has. VTP cannot cross a Layer 3 boundary.

VTP Advertisements

VTP advertisements are flooded over the factory default VLAN (VLAN1) every 5 minutes or whenever there is a change. The **delete vtp** command resets the configuration number.

VTP Modes

VTP operates in server, client, or transparent mode. The default mode is server mode. VLAN configurations are not advertised until a management domain name is specified or learned.

VTP Pruning

VTP pruning improves bandwidth by restricting unnecessary traffic from flooding the entire domain.

By default, a trunk carries traffic for all VLANs in the VTP management domain. With VTP pruning enabled, update traffic from Station A is not forwarded to Switches 3, 5, and 6, because traffic for the red VLAN has been pruned on the links indicated on Switches 2 and 4.

vtp Command

```
vtp [server | transparent] [domain domain-name] [trap {enable | disable}]
password password] [pruning {enable | disable}]
```

- *domain-name*—can be specified or learned.
- **vtp trap**—Generates SNMP messages.
- *password*—Can be set for the VTP management domain. The password entered should be the same for all switches in the domain.
- **pruning**—VTP pruning on a server propagates the change throughout the domain.

On the 1900, the **vtp** command is used to specify VTP capabilities. The 2950 also uses the **vtp** command, but each of the corresponding parameters must be entered on a separate line in VLAN config mode. The **vlan database** command starts VLAN config mode.

VTP trunk Command

The **trunk** command is used to set a Fast Ethernet port to trunk mode. This command turns trunking on and off and sets the negotiation state. Although trunking and VTP do go hand in hand, they are not interdependent.

```
trunk [on | off | desirable | auto | nonegotiate]
```

- **desirable**—The port turns on trunking if the connected device is in the on, desirable, or auto state.
- **auto**—Enables trunking if the connected device is set to on or desirable.
- **nonegotiate**—The port is set to the permanent ISL trunk.

Configuring VTP on a 1900

```
SwitchA(config)#vtp transparent domain springfield
SwitchA (config)#int fa0/26
SwitchA (config-if)#trunk on desirable
SwitchA (config-if)#exit
SwitchA (config)#exit
SwitchA #show vtp
SwitchA #show trunk A
```

Configuring VTP on a 2950

```
SwitchA(config)#vlan database
SwitchA (vlan)#vtp server
SwitchA (vlan)#vtp domain shelbyville
SwitchA (vlan)#vtp password lovejoy
SwitchA (vlan)#vtp pruning
SwitchA (vlan)#snmp-server enable traps vtp
SwitchA (vlan)#exit
SwitchA #show vtp status
SwitchA #show interface Fa0/1 switchport
```

On the Catalyst 1900, the two Fast Ethernet ports are interfaces fa0/26 and fa0/27.

Configuring a VLAN on a 1900

```
SwitchA #config t
SwitchA (config)#vlan 7 name springfield
```

The TCP/IP protocol stack closely follows the OSI reference model. All standard Layer 1 and 2 protocols are supported (called the network interface layer in TCP/IP).

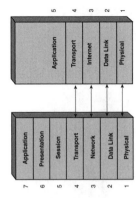

TCP/IP Datagrams

TCP/IP information is sent via datagrams. One message may be broken into a series of datagrams that are reassembled at the destination. Three layers are associated with the TCP/IP protocol stack:

- **Application layer**— Specifications exist for e-mail, file transfer, remote login, and other applications. Network management is also supported.
- **Transport layer**—Transport services allow multiple upper-layer applications to use the same data stream. TCP and UDP protocols exist at this layer, providing the following functions:
  —Flow control (through windowing)
  —Reliability (through sequence numbers and acknowledgments)
- **Internet layer**—Several protocols operate at the TCP/IP Internet layer:
  —IP provides connectionless, best-effort routing of datagrams.
  —ICMP provides control and messaging capabilities.
  —ARP determines the data link layer address for known IP addresses.
  —RARP determines network addresses when data link layer addresses are known.

```
SwitchA (config)#int fa0/26
SwitchA (config-if)#vlan-membership static 7
SwitchA (config-if)#trunk on
SwitchA (config-if)#exit
SwitchA (config)#exit
SwitchA #show vlan7
SwitchA #show vlan-membership
SwitchA #show spantree 7
```

Adding a VLAN on a 2950

```
SwitchA #vlan database
SwitchA (vlan)#vlan 7 name Springfield
SwitchA #exit
SwitchA #config t
SwitchA (config)#int fa0/1
SwitchA (config-if)#switchport access vlan 7
SwitchA (config-if)#exit
SwitchA #show vlan brief
SwitchA #show interface fa0/1 switchport
SwitchA #show spanning-tree vlan 7
```

Configuring a VLAN Summary

- VTP advertises and synchronizes VLAN configuration information.
- The three VTP modes are server (the default), client, and transparent.
- VTP messages include a configuration revision number. When a switch receives a higher configuration number, it overwrites its configuration with the newly advertised one.
- VTP pruning restricts flooded traffic to some trunk lines.
- VLAN 1 is the default VLAN configuration on the Catalyst 1900 switch.
- To configure a VLAN, you must enable VTP, create VLANs, and assign those VLANs to ports.

TCP/IP Overview

The TCP/IP suite of protocols is used to communicate across any set of interconnected networks. These protocols, initially developed by Defense Advanced Research Projects Agency (DARPA), are well-suited for communication across both LANs and WANs. The protocol suite includes Layer 3 and 4 specifications, as well as specifications for higher-layer applications such as e-mail and file transfer.

TCP

TCP is a connection-oriented, reliable protocol that is responsible for breaking messages into segments and reassembling them at the destination (resending anything not received). TCP also provides virtual circuits between applications.

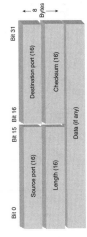

UDP

UDP is a connectionless, best-effort protocol used for applications that have their own error-recovery process. It trades reliability for speed. UDP is simple and efficient but unreliable. UDP does not check for segment delivery.

Connection-Oriented Services

A connection-oriented service establishes and maintains a connection during a transmission. The service first establishes a connection and then sends data. As soon as the data transfer is complete, the session is torn down.

Port Numbers

Both TCP and UDP can send data from multiple upper-layer applications at the same time. Port (or socket) numbers are used to keep track of different conversations crossing the network at any given time. Well-known port numbers are controlled by the Internet Assigned Numbers Authority (IANA). For example, Telnet is always defined by port 23. Applications that do not use well-known port numbers have them randomly assigned from a specific range.

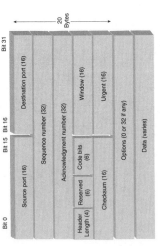

Port Number Ranges

- Numbers below 1024 are considered well-known ports.
- Numbers 1024 and above are dynamically assigned ports.
- Vendor-specific applications have reserved ports (usually greater than 1024).

How TCP Connections Are Established

End stations use control bits called SYNs (for synchronize) and Initial Sequence Numbers (ISNs) to synchronize during connection establishment.

Three-Way Handshake

The synchronization requires each side to send its own initial sequence number and to receive a confirmation of it in an acknowledgment (ACK) from the other side.

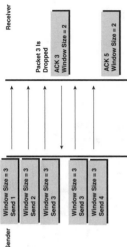

1. Host A sends a SYN segment with sequence number 100.
2. Host B sends an ACK and confirms the SYN it received. Host B also sends a SYN. Note that the ACK field in Host B is now expecting to hear sequence 101.
3. In the next segment, Host A sends data. Note that the sequence number in this step is the same as the ACK in Step 2.

TCP Windowing

Windowing ensures that one side of a connection is not overwhelmed with data it cannot process. The window size from one end station tells the other side of the connection how much it can accept at one time. With a window size of 1, each segment must be acknowledged before another segment is sent. This is the least-efficient use of bandwidth.

1. The sender sends three packets before expecting an ACK.
2. The receiver can handle only a window size of 2. So it drops packet 3, specifies 3 as the next packet, and specifies a window size of 2.
3. The sender sends the next two packets but still specifies its window size of 3.
4. The receiver replies by requesting packet 5 and specifying a window size of 2.

A TCP/IP session can have different window sizes for each node.

TCP Sequence and Acknowledgment Numbers

TCP uses forward reference acknowledgments. Each datagram is numbered so that at the receiving end TCP reassembles the segments into a complete message. If a segment is not acknowledged within a given time period, it is resent.

IP

IP provides connectionless, best-effort delivery routing of datagrams. The protocol field in the header determines the Layer 4 protocol being used (usually TCP or UDP).

Other Internet Layer Protocols

ICMP, ARP, and RARP are three protocols used by the Internet layer to IP. Internet Control Message Protocol (ICMP) is used to send error and control messages, such as destination unreachable, time exceeded, subnet mask request, echo, and others.

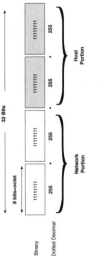

Address Resolution Protocol (ARP) is used to map a known IP address to a MAC sublayer address. An ARP cache table is checked when looking for a destination address. If the address is not in the table, ARP sends a broadcast looking for the destination station.

Reverse ARP

Reverse Address Resolution Protocol (RARP) is used to map a known MAC address to an IP address. Dynamic Host Configuration Protocol (DHCP) is a modern implementation of RARP.

TCP/IP Overview Summary

- The TCP/IP protocol suite includes Layer 3 and 4 specifications.
- UDP is connectionless (no acknowledgments). No software checking for segment delivery is done at this layer.
- TCP is a connection-oriented, reliable protocol. Data is divided into segments, which are reassembled at the destination. Missing segments are resent.
- Both TCP and UDP use port (or socket) numbers to pass information to the upper layers.
- The TCP "three-way handshake" is a synchronization process. Sequence numbers and acknowledgments (ACKs) are used to establish connections.

TCP/IP Address Overview

In a TCP/IP environment, each node must have a unique 32-bit logical IP address. Each IP datagram includes the source and destination IP addresses in the header.

Host and Network Address

Each company listed on the Internet is viewed as a single network. This network must be reached before an individual host within that company can be contacted. A two-part addressing scheme allows the IP address to identify both the network and the host.

- All the endpoints within a network share a common network number.
- The remaining bits identify each host within that network.

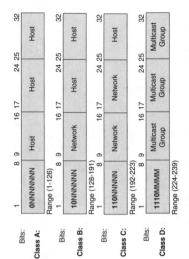

IP Address Classes

There are five classes of IP, A through E. Classes A, B, and C are the most common. Class A has 8 network bits and 24 host bits. Class B has 16 network bits and 16 host bits. Class C addresses allow for many more networks, each with fewer hosts (24 network bits and 8 host bits). This scheme was based on the assumption that the world would have many more small networks than large networks in the world. Class D is used for multicast purposes, and Class E addresses are used for research. The address range for all five classes is shown in the figure.

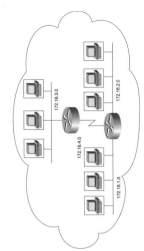

Implementing Subnet Planning

Without subnets, an organization operates as a single network. These flat topologies result in short routing tables, but as the network grows, the use of bandwidth becomes very inefficient (all systems on the network receive all the broadcasts on the network). Network addressing can be made more efficient by breaking the addresses into smaller segments, or subnets. Subnetting provides additional structure to an addressing scheme without altering the addresses.

In the figure, the network address 172.16.0.0 is subdivided into four subnets: 172.16.1.0, 172.16.2.0, 172.16.3.0, and 172.16.4.0. If traffic were evenly distributed to each end station, the use of subnetting would reduce the overall traffic seen by each end station by 75%.

In the next figure, networks A and B are connected by a router. Network B has a Class A address (10.0.0.0). The routing table contains entries for network addresses, not hosts within that network. In the figure, 172.16.0.0 and 10.0.0.0 refer to the wires at each end of the router.

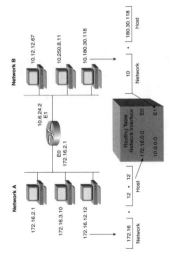

TCP/IP Address Summary

- In a TCP/IP environment, end stations each have a 32-bit logical IP address with a network portion and a host portion.
- The address format is known as dotted-decimal notation. The range is 0.0.0.0 to 255.255.255.255.
- There are five address classes: A, B, C, D, and E. They are suited to different types of users.
- The total number of available hosts on a network can be derived by using the formula $2^n - 2$, where n is the number of bits in the host portion.

Subnet Mask

A subnet mask is a 32-bit value written as four octets. In the subnet mask, each bit is used to determine how the corresponding bit in the IP address should be interpreted (network, subnet, or host). The subnet mask bits are coded as follows:

- Binary 1 for the network bits
- Binary 1 for the subnet bits
- Binary 0 for the host bits

IP Address — 172 | 16 | 0
Network / Host

Default Subnet Mask — 255 (11111111) | 255 (11111111) | 0 (00000000) | 0 (00000000)
Network / Host
Also Written as "/16" Where 16 Represents the Number of 1s in the Mask.

8-bit Subnet Mask — 255 | 255 | 255 | 0
Network / Subnet / Host
Also Written as "/24" Where 24 Represents the Number of 1s in the Mask.

Although dotted decimal is most common, the subnet can be represented in several ways:

- Dotted-decimal—172.16.0.0 255.255.0.0
- Bit count—172.16.0.0/16
- Hexadecimal—172.16.0.0 0xFFFF0000

The ip netmask-format command can be used to specify the format of network masks for the current session. Dotted-decimal is the default.

Default Subnet Masks

Each address class has a default subnet mask. The default subnet masks only the network portion of the address, the effect of which is no subnetting. With each bit of subnetting beyond the default, you can create 2^n-2 subnets. The following figures show the effect of increasing the number of subnet bits.

Address	Subnet Address	Number of Subnets	Comments
10.5.22.5/8	255.0.0.0	0	This is the default Class A subnet address. The mask includes only the network portion of the address and provides no additional subnets.
10.5.22.5/16	255.255.0.0	254	This Class A subnet address has 16 bits of subnetting, but only the bits in the second octet (those beyond the default) contribute to the subnetting.
155.13.22.11/16	255.255.0.0	0	In this case, 16 bits are used for subnetting, but because the default for a Class B address is 16 bits, no additional subnets are created.
155.13.10.11/26	255.255.255.192	1022	This case has a total of 26 bits of subnetting, but the Class B address can use only ten of them to create subnets. The result creates 1022 subnets (2^{10}-2).

How Routers Use Subnet Masks

To determine the subnet of the address, a router performs a logical AND operation with the IP Address and Subnet Mask. Recall that the host portion of the subnet mask is all 0s. The result of this operation is that the host portion of the address is removed and the router bases its decision only on the network portion of the address.

In the figure, the host bits are removed, and the network portion of the address is revealed. In this case, a 10-bit subnet address is used, and the network (subnet) number 172.16.2.128 is extracted.

172.16.2.160
255.255.255.192

	Network		Subnet	Host
	10101100	00010000	00000010	10100000
	11111111	11111111	11111111	11000000
	10101100	00010000	00000010	10000000

Network Number			
172	16	2	128

Broadcast Addresses

Broadcast messages are sent to every host on the network. There are three kinds of broadcasts:

- Directed Broadcasts—You can broadcast to all hosts within a subnet and to all subnets within a network. (170.34.2.255 sends a broadcast to all hosts in the 170.34.2.0 subnet.)
- Flooded broadcasts (255.255.255.255)—Are local broadcasts within a subnet.
- You can also broadcast messages to all hosts on all subnets within a single network. (170.34.255.255 sends a broadcast to all subnets in the 170.34.0.0 network.)

Identifying Subnet Addresses

Given an IP address and subnet mask, you can identify the subnet address, broadcast address, first usable address, and last usable address using this method:

1. Write down the 32-bit address and the subnet mask below that.
2. Draw a vertical line just after the last 1 bit in the subnet mask.
3. Copy the portion of the IP address to the left of the line. Place all 0s for the remaining free spaces to the right. This is the subnet number.
4. Copy the portion of the IP address to the left of the line. Place all 1s for the remaining free spaces to the right. This is the broadcast address.
5. Copy the portion of the IP address to the left of the line. Place all 0s in the remaining free spaces until you reach the last free space. Place a 1 in that free space. This is your first usable address.
6. Copy the portion of the IP address to the left of the line. Place all 1s in the remaining free spaces until you reach the last free space. Place a 0 in that free space. This is your last usable address.

					Host
174.24.4.176	174	24	4	176	Host
255.255.255.192	11111111	11111111	11111111	11000000	Mask
174.24.4.128	10101110	00011000	00000100	10000000	Subnet
174.24.4.191	10101110	00011000	00000100	10111111	Broadcast
174.24.4.129	10101110	00011000	00000100	10000001	First
174.24.4.190	10101110	00011000	00000100	10111110	Last

How to Implement Subnet Planning

Subnetting decisions should always be based on growth estimates rather than current needs.

To plan a subnet, follow these steps:

1. Determine the number of subnets and hosts per subnet required.
2. The address class you are assigned, and the number of subnets required, determine the number of subnetting bits used. For example, with a Class C address and a need for 20 subnets, you have a 29-bit mask (255.255.255.248). This allows for the Class C default 24-bit mask and 5 bits required for 20 subnets. (The formula 2^n-2 yields only 14 subnets for 4 bits, so 5 bits must be used.)
3. The remaining bits in the last octet are used for the host field. In this case, each subnet has 2^3-2, or 6, hosts.
4. The final host addresses are a combination of the network/subnet plus each host value. The hosts on the 192.168.5.32 subnet would be addressed as 192.168.5.33, 192.168.5.34, 192.168.5.35, and so forth.

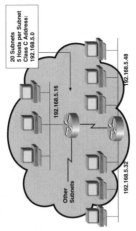

20 Subnets
5 Hosts per Subnet
Class C Address: 192.168.5.0

Other Subnets
192.168.5.16
192.168.5.32
192.168.5.48

Implementing Subnet Planning Summary

- Breaking networks into smaller segments (or subnets) improves network efficiency.

- A 32-bit subnet mask determines the boundary between the subnet host portions of the IP Address using 1s and 0s.
- A subnet defines a broadcast domain in a routed network.
- IOS supports directed, local network, and subnet broadcasts.
- Subnet planning should be based on future growth predictions rather than current needs.

Configuring the IP Addresses

An IP address must be assigned to a switch if you plan on using SNMP or plan on connecting to the switch via a web browser or Telnet. If the switch needs to send traffic to a different IP network, the traffic is routed to a default gateway.

Configuring a Switch IP Address

```
SwitchA>enable
SwitchA#config term
SwitchA(config)#ip address 10.2.5.10  255.255.255.0
SwitchA(config)#ip default-gateway 10.2.5.2
SwitchA(config)#exit
SwitchA#show ip
```

The no ip address command resets the address to the default (0.0.0.0).

Each unique IP address can have a host name associated with it. A maximum of six IP addresses can be specified as named servers.

Domain Name System (DNS) is used to translate names into addresses. If a system sees an address it does not recognize, it refers to DNS. DNS is enabled by default with a server address of 255.255.255.255. The ip domain-lookup and no ip domain-lookup commands turn DNS on and off, respectively.

Router IP Host Names

When names are used to denote route destinations, they must be translated to addresses. Routers must be able to associate host names with IP addresses to communicate with other IP devices. The ip host command manually assigns host names to addresses.

Configuring the Switch IP Address Summary

- The ip address command sets the IP address and subnet mask.
- The ip name-server command defines which hosts can provide the name service.

- DNS translates node names into addresses.
- The show hosts command displays host names and addresses.

NAT and PAT

Network Address Translation (NAT) was initially developed by Cisco as an answer to the diminishing number of IP addresses. When the IP address scheme was originally developed, it was believed that the address space would not run out. The combination of the PC explosion and the emergence of other network-ready devices quickly ate up many of the available addresses.

An additional (and equally important) benefit of NAT is that it hides private addresses from public networks, making communication more secure from hackers.

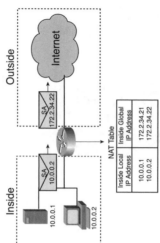

- NAT is configured on a router, firewall, or other network device.
- Static NAT uses one-to-one private-to-public address translation.
- Dynamic NAT matches private addresses to a pool of public addresses on an as-needed basis. The address translation is still one-to-one.

Port Address Translation (PAT) is a form of dynamic address translation that uses many (private addresses) to few or one (public address). This is called overloading and is accomplished by assigning port numbers as shown in the figure.

- Because the port number is 16 bits, PAT can theoretically map 65,536 sessions to a single public address.
- PAT continues to look for available port numbers. If one is not found, PAT increments the IP address (if available).

Configuring NAT

```
RouterA>enable
RouterA#config term
RouterA(config)#ip nat inside source static 10.0.0.1 172.33.42.15
RouterA(config)#interface ethernet 0
RouterA(config-if)#ip nat inside
RouterA(config-if)#exit
RouterA(config)#interface 0/1
RouterA(config-if)#ip nat outside
```

For dynamic NAT, a pool of addresses is used for the inside and outside addresses.

Configuring PAT

```
RouterA>enable
RouterA#config term
RouterA(config)#acess-list 99 permit 10.0.0.1
RouterA(config)#ip nat inside source list 99 interface fa0/1 overload
RouterA(config)#interface ethernet 0
RouterA(config-if)#ip nat inside
RouterA(config-if)#exit
RouterA(config)#interface fa 0/1
RouterA(config-if)#ip nat ouside
RouterA(config-if)#exit
RouterA(config)#exit
```

The **clear ip nat translation** command clears all dynamic translation tables.

The **clear ip nat translation inside global-ip local-ip** command clears a specific entry from a dynamic translation table.

The **clear ip nat translation outside local-ip global-ip** command clears a specific outside translation address.

The **show nat translations** command lists all active translations.

The **show nat statistics** command shows all translation statistics.

Determining IP Routes

Routing Overview

Routing is the process of getting packets and messages from one location to another.

Key Information a Router Needs

A router needs the following key information:

- **Destination address—** The destination (typically an IP address) of the information being sent. This includes the subnet address.

- **Sources of information—** Where the information came from (typically an IP address).

- **Possible routes—** Likely routes to get from source to destination.

- **Best route—** The best path to the intended destination.

- **Status of routes—** Known paths to destinations.

Network Protocol	Destination Network	Exit Interface
Connected	10.120.2.0	E0
Learned	172.16.1.0	S0

Routed Protocol: IP

A router is constantly learning about routes in the network and storing this information in its routing table. The router uses its table to make forwarding decisions. The router learns about routes in one of two ways:

- Manually (routing information entered by the network administrator)
- Dynamically (a routing process running in the network)

Identifying Static and Dynamic Routes

A router uses static or dynamic routes when forwarding packets.

- **Static** routes are manually entered by the network administrator. These routes must be manually updated whenever there is a topology change.

- **Dynamic** routes are learned by the router. Unlike static routes, topology changes are learned without administrative intervention and are automatically propagated throughout the network.

Examining Static Routes

Static routes specify the path that packets take, allowing precise control over a network's routing behavior. Static routes are sometimes used to define a "gateway of last resort". This is where a packet is routed if no other suitable path can be found. Static routes are also used when routing to a stub network. A stub network is a network accessed by a single route. Often, static routes are the only way on to or off of a stub network.

Examining Static Route Configuration

The `ip route` command is used to configure a static route in global configuration mode. This command manually creates routing table entries. This table entry does not accept dynamic changes as long as the path is active.

`ip route network [mask] {address | interface}[distance] [permanent]`

- *mask* and *address* are the IP address of the next-hop router.

- *interface* is the interface to the destination network. It must be a point-to-point interface.

- *distance* is optional. It defines the administrative distance.

- **permanent** is optional. It specifies that the route will not be removed, even if the interface shuts down.

A default route is a special type of static route. Use a default router when the route is not known or when storing the needed information is unfeasible.

Routing Overview Summary

- Routing is the process of sending packets from one location to another across an internetwork. A router needs to know the destination address, initial possible routes, and best path to route packets.
- Routing information is stored in the router's routing table.
- Static routes are user-defined, and dynamic routes are learned by the router running a routing protocol.
- Use the **ip route** command to configure a static route.
- A default route is used for situations in which the route is not known or when it is unfeasible for the routing table to store sufficient information about the route.

Dynamic Routing Overview

Routing protocols are used to determine paths between routers and to maintain routing tables. Dynamic routing uses routing protocols to disseminate knowledge throughout the network. A routing protocol defines communication rules and interprets network layer address information. Routing protocols describe the following:

- Routing update methods
- Information contained in updates
- When updates are sent
- Paths to other routers

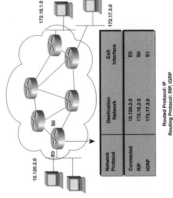

Network Protocol	Destination Network	Exit Interface
Connected	10.120.2.0	E0
RIP	172.16.2.0	S0
IGRP	172.17.3.0	S1

Routed Protocol: IP
Routing Protocol: RIP, IGRP

Autonomous Systems

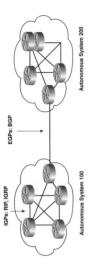
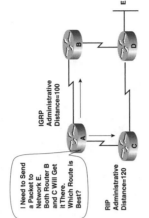

An autonomous system refers to a group of networks under a common administrative domain. Interior Gateway Protocols (IGPs) such as RIP and IGRP exchange routing information within an autonomous system. Exterior Gateway Protocols (EGPs) are used to connect between autonomous systems. A Border Gateway Protocol (BGP) is an example of an EGP.

Ranking Routes with Administrative Distance

Several routing protocols can be used at the same time in the same network. When there is more than a single source of routing information, the router uses an administrative distance value to rate the trustworthiness of each routing information source. The administrative distance metric is an integer from 0 to 255. In general, a route with a lower number is considered more trustworthy and is more likely to be used.

Default Distance Values

Route Source	Default Distance
Connected interface	0
Static route address	1
EIGRP	90
IGRP	100

How Information Is Discovered with Distance Vectors

Network discovery is the process of learning about non-directly connected destinations. As the network discovery proceeds, routers accumulate metrics and learn the best paths to various destinations. In the example, each directly connected network has a distance of 0. Router A learns about other networks based on information it receives from Router B. Router A increments the distance metric for any route learned by Router B. For example, Router B knows about the networks to Router C, which is directly connected. Router B then shares this information with Router A, which increments the distance to these networks by 1.

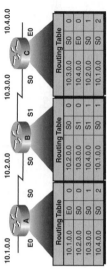

10.1.0.0	10.2.0.0	10.3.0.0	10.4.0.0

	Routing Table			Routing Table			Routing Table	
E0	S0	S0	S1	S0	S0	E0
10.1.0.0	E0	0	10.2.0.0	S0	0	10.3.0.0	S0	0
10.2.0.0	S0	0	10.3.0.0	S1	0	10.4.0.0	E0	0
10.3.0.0	S0	1	10.4.0.0	S1	1	10.2.0.0	S0	1
10.4.0.0	S0	2	10.1.0.0	S0	1	10.1.0.0	S0	2

Examining Distance Vector Routing Metrics

Distance vector routing protocols use routing algorithms to determine the best route. These algorithms generate a metric value for each path through the network. The smaller the metric, the better the path. Metrics can be calculated based on one or more characteristics of a path.

Commonly Used Metrics

- **Hop count**—The number of times a packet crosses a router boundary.
- **Ticks**—Delay on a data link using IBM PC clock ticks (~ 55 ms).
- **Cost**—An arbitrary value based on a network administrator-determined value. Usually bandwidth, monetary cost, or time.
- **Bandwidth**—A link's data capacity.
- **Delay**—The amount of time required to reach the destination.
- **Load**—Network activity.
- **Reliability**—The bit-error rate of each network link.
- **MTU**—Maximum Transmission Unit). The maximum message length allowed on the path.

OSPF	110
RIP	120
External EIGRP	170
Unknown	255

Routing Protocol Classes

There are three basic routing protocol classes:

- **Distance vector**—Uses the direction (vector) and distance to other routers as metrics. RIP and IGRP are both distance vector protocols.
- **Link-state**—Also called shortest path first, this protocol re-creates the topology of the entire network.
- **Balanced hybrid**—Combines the link-state and distance vector algorithms.

How Distance Vector Protocols Route Information

Routers using distance vector-based routing share routing table information with each other. This method of updating is called "routing by rumor." Each router receives updates from its direct neighbor. In the figure, Router B shares information with Routers A and C. Router C shares routing information with Routers B and D. In this case, the routing information is distance vector metrics (such as the number of hops). Each router increments the metrics as they are passed on (incrementing hop count, for example).

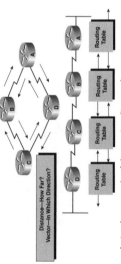

Distance accumulation keeps track of the routing distance between any two points in the network, but the routers do not know the exact topology of an internetwork.

hybrid routing provides faster convergence while limiting the use of resources such as bandwidth, memory, and processor overhead. Cisco's Enhanced IGRP is an example of a balanced hybrid protocol.

Dynamic Routing Overview Summary

- Routing protocols use the network layer address to forward packets to the destination network.
- An autonomous system is a collection of networks under a common administrative domain.
- More than one routing protocol may be used at the same time.
- Administrative distance is used to rate the trustworthiness of each information source.
- Distance vector, link-state, and balanced hybrid are the most common Interior Gateway Protocols (IGPs).
- Distance-vector-based algorithms send copies of routing tables. As network discovery proceeds, routers accumulate metric information used to determine the best path to distant networks.
- A link-state routing algorithm, also known as shortest path first, sends network topology information rather than metrics.
- Balanced hybrid routing combines aspects of both distance vector and link-state protocols.

Distance Vector Routing

Any topology change in a network running a distance vector protocol triggers an update in the routing tables. The topology updates follow the same step-by-step process as the initial network discovery.

Link-State Routing

The link-state-based routing algorithm (also known as shortest path first [SPF]) maintains a database of topology information. Unlike the distance vector algorithm, link-state routing maintains full knowledge of distant routers and how they interconnect. Network information is shared in the form of Link State Advertisements (LSAs).

Link-state routing provides better scaling than distance vector routing for the following reasons:

- Link-state sends only topology changes. Distance vector sends complete routing tables.
- Link-state updates are sent less often than distance vector updates.
- Link-state uses a two-state hierarchy (areas and autonomous systems), which limits the scope of route changes.
- Link-state supports classless addressing and summarization.
- Link-state routing converges fast and is robust against routing loops, but it requires a great deal of memory and strict network designs.

Balanced Hybrid Routing

Balanced Hybrid routing combines aspects of both distance vector and link-state protocols. Balanced hybrid routing uses distance vectors with more accurate metrics, but unlike distance vector routing protocols, it updates only when there is a topology change. Balanced

Updating routing tables

A router compares the information contained in the update to its current table. If the update contains information about a better route to a destination (a smaller total metric), the router updates its own routing table. As always, the distance metric is incremented by 1 greater than the neighbor it received the update from. During updates, the router sends its entire routing table to each of its adjacent neighbors. The table includes the total path cost (defined by its metric) and the logical address of the first router on the path to each destination network. In the figure, Router B is one unit of cost from Router A. Therefore, it adds 1 to all costs reported by Router A.

How Routing Loops Occur in Distance Vector Protocols

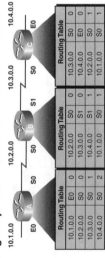

During updates, routing loops can occur if the network has inconsistent routing entries. Slow convergence on a new configuration is one cause of this phenomenon. The network is converged when all routers have consistent routing tables. The following example illustrates how a routing loop occurs. Before a network failure, all routers have correct tables. The figure uses hop count as a cost metric, so the cost of each link is 1. Router C is directly connected to network 10.4.0.0, with a distance of 0. Router A's path to network 10.4.0.0 is through Router B, with a hop count of 2.

If network 10.4.0.0 fails, Router C detects the failure and stops routing packets to that network. At this point, Routers A and B still do not know of the failure. Router A's table still shows a valid path to 10.4.0.0 through Router B. If Router B sends out its normal update to Routers A and C, Router C sees a valid path to 10.4.0.0 through Router B and updates its routing table to reflect a path to network 10.4.0.0 with a hop count of 2 (remember, it must add 1 to the hop count). Now Router C sends an update back to Router B, which then updates Router A. Router A detects the modified distance vector to network 10.4.0.0 and recalculates its own distance vector to 10.4.0.0 as 4. With each update, the incorrect

information continues to bounce between the routers. Without some mechanism to prevent this, the updates continue. This condition, called counting to infinity, continuously loops packets around the network.

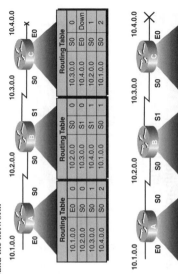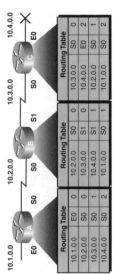

Some distance vector routing algorithms have a time-to-live (TTL) value, but the routing loop problem can occur with this limit. You can avoid this by defining infinity as some maximum number. If you set this value, the routing loop continues until the metric value exceeds the maximum allowed value. As soon as this happens, the network is unreachable.

Eliminating Routing Loops Through Split Horizon

Split horizon is one way to eliminate routing loops and speed up convergence. The idea behind split horizon is that it is never useful to send information about a route back in the direction from which the update came. If the router has no valid alternative path to the network, it is considered inaccessible. Split horizon also eliminates unnecessary routing updates, thus speeding convergence.

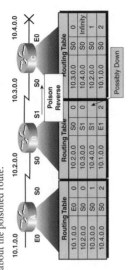

Route Poisoning

Route poisoning (part of split horizon) also eliminates routing loops caused by inconsistent updates. Route poisoning basically sets a route to "unreachable" and locks the table (using hold-down timers) until the network has converged.

Example of Route Poisoning

The figure provides the following example. When network 10.4.0.0 goes down, router C "poisons" its link to network 10.4.0.0 with an infinite cost (marked as unreachable).

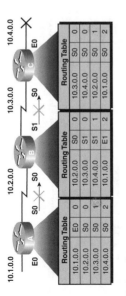

Router C is no longer susceptible to incorrect updates about network 10.4.0.0 coming from neighboring routers that might claim to have a valid alternative path. After the hold-down timer expires (which is just longer than the time to convergence), Router C begins accepting updates again.

Poison Reverse

When Router B sees the metric to 10.4.0.0 jump to infinity, it sends a return message (overriding split horizon) called a poison reverse back to Router C, stating that network 10.4.0.0 is inaccessible. This message ensures that all routers on that segment have received information about the poisoned route.

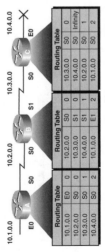

Avoiding Routing Loops with Triggered Updates

A triggered update is sent immediately in response to a change in the network. The router detecting the change immediately sends an update message to adjacent routers, which then generate their own triggered updates. This continues until the network converges. There are two problems with triggered updates:

- The update message can be dropped or corrupted.
- The updates do not happen instantly. A router can issue a regular update before receiving the triggered update. If this happens, the bad route can be reinserted into a router that received the triggered update.

Solution—Hold-down timers dictate that when a route is invalid, no new route with the same or a worse metric will be accepted for the same destination for a period of time. This allows the triggered update to propagate throughout the network.

Characteristics of Hold-down Timers

- They prevent regular update messages from inappropriately reinstating a route that might have gone bad.
- They force routers to hold any changes for a period of time.

- The hold-down period should be calculated to be just greater than the period of time it takes for updates to converge.

Hold-down Implementation Process

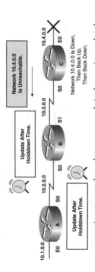

1. When a router receives an update that a network is down, it marks the route as inaccessible and starts a holddown timer.

2. If an update is received from a neighboring router with a better metric, the router removes the timer and users the new metric.

3. If an update is received (before the hold-down timer expires) with a poorer metric, the update is ignored.

4. During the hold-down period, routes appear in the routing table as "possibly down."

Distance Vector Routing Summary

- Distance vector routing protocols maintain routing information by updating routing tables with neighboring routing tables.
- Defining a maximum count prevents infinite loops.
- Split horizon solves routing loops by preventing routing updates from being sent back in the same direction from which they came.
- Route poisoning sets downed routes to infinity to make them unreachable.
- A triggered update is sent immediately in response to a change. Each router receiving a triggered update sends its own until the network converges.
- Hold-down timers prevent regular update messages from reinstating failed routes.
- More than one loop-preventing solution can be implemented on networks with multiple routes.

Enabling Routing Information Protocol (RIP)

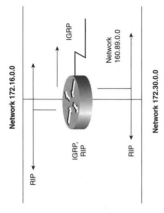

To enable a dynamic routing protocol, you must do the following:

Step 1   Select a routing protocol (such as RIP or IGRP).

Step 2   Assign IP network numbers.

Assign network/subnet addresses and the appropriate subnet mask to interfaces. The **network** command starts the routing protocol. The **network** command also specifies a directly connected network and advertises that network.

Routing Information Protocol (RIP)

Cisco devices support two versions of RIP: RIP Version 1 (RFC 1058), and an enhanced version, RIP Version 2 (RFC 1723), a classless routing protocol.

Key RIP characteristics are as follows:

- RIP is a distance vector routing protocol.
- Hop count is used as the metric for path selection (the maximum is 15).
- Routing updates broadcast every 30 seconds (the default).
- It can load-balance over six equal-cost paths (the default is 4).
- Only one network mask can be used for each classful network (RIPv1).
- RIPv2 permits variable-length subnet masks on the internetwork.
- It performs triggered updates (RIPv2 only).
- RIPv2 supports simple route authentication.

A classless routing protocol allows routers to summarize information about several routes to cut down on the quantity of information carried by the core routers. With **ip classless** configured, packets received with a unknown subnet of a directly attached network are sent to the next hop on the default route.

With **Classless Interdomain Routing (CIDR)**, several IP networks appear to networks outside the group as a single, larger entity. Classless routing also allows different masks on different parts of a network.

Defining Paths

Load balancing occurs when a router uses several paths to reach the same destination, improving bandwidth efficiency. The maximum number of parallel paths allowed must be defined. With RIP, all paths must be equal-cost. Load balancing can be disabled by setting the maximum number of paths to 1.

Configuring RIP

```
RouterA>enable
RouterA#config term
RouterA(config)#router rip
RouterA(config-router)#network 10.3.2.0
RouterA(config-router)#exit
RouterA(config)#exit
RouterA#show ip protocols
```

- **show ip protocols**—Used to see if a router is delivering bad routing information.
- **show ip route**—Shows RIP routing tables.
- **debug ip rip**—Displays RIP routing updates (no debug all disables).

Note: The **network** command specifies the autonomous system and starts the routing protocol in the specified network. The **network** command also allows the router to advertise that network.

Enabling Routing Information Protocol (RIP) Summary

- To configure a dynamic routing protocol, select a protocol, assign a network number, and assign network addresses for each interface.
- RIP, a distance vector routing protocol, uses hop count as a route-selection metric. RIP can load-balance across equal-cost paths.
- The **ip classless** command prevents the router from dropping packets destined for unknown subnets of directly connected networks.

Enabling Interior Gateway Routing Protocol (IGRP)

IGRP is a distance vector routing protocol with sophisticated metrics and improved scalability, allowing better routing in larger networks. IGRP uses delay and bandwidth as routing metrics (reliability and load are optional). IGRP has a default maximum hop count of 100 hops (RIP's maximum is 15 hops), which can be reconfigured to 255 hops.

IGRP can load-balance across six unequal paths, increasing the available bandwidth and providing route redundancy.

IGRP Metrics

IGRP achieves greater route selection accuracy than RIP with the use of a composite metric. The path that has the smallest metric value is the best route. IGRP's metric includes bandwidth, delay, reliability (based on keepalives), loading (bits per second), and MTU (maximum transmission unit). Performance can be significantly affected by adjusting IGRP metric values.

Paths of Different Metrics

IGRP allows load balancing over unequal paths. If two unequal paths are used and one path is four times better than the other, the better path will be used four times as often. The variance command allows you to define the amount of load balancing by specifying a metric range for multiple paths.

Configuring IGRP

```
RouterA>enable
RouterA#config term
RouterA(config)#router igrp 100
RouterA(config-router)#network 170.8.0.0
RouterA(config-router)#variance 1
RouterA(config-router)#traffic-share balanced
RouterA(config-router)#exit
RouterA(config)#exit
RouterA#show ip protocols
```

The syntax for the router igrp command includes the autonomous system number. All routers within an autonomous system must use the same system number.

- The default value of variance is 1 (equal-cost load balancing).
- The traffic-share balanced command distributes traffic proportionally to the ratios of the metrics.
- Use show ip protocols to verify the IGRP protocol configuration.

- Use show ip route to display the contents of the IP routing tables.

Enabling Interior Gateway Routing Protocol (IGRP) Summary

- IGRP has increased scalability and a more sophisticated routing metric than RIP. IGRP can load-balance over unequal paths.
- IGRP's routing metric is a composite of bandwidth, delay, reliability, loading, and MTU.
- The debug ip igrp configuration commands display routing and transaction information for troubleshooting purposes.

Enabling Enhanced Interior Gateway Routing Protocol (EIGRP)

EIGRP is an enhanced version of Cisco-proprietary IGRP. EIGRP scales well, converges quickly, and works with several media types.

- In some cases, EIGRP convergence is instantaneous, because alternative routes are stored and updated.
- EIGRP is very resource-efficient, sending only hello packets to neighboring routers.
- EIGRP supports automatic route summarization, but unlike other interior protocols, EIGRP allows manual configuration to reduce routing table size.
- EIGRP uses the same metrics and load-balancing features as IGRP but converges more quickly and uses less overhead.

Configuring EIGRP

```
RouterA>enable
RouterA#config term
RouterA(config)#router eigrp 100
RouterA(config-router)#network 170.8.0.0
RouterA(config-router)#exit
RouterA(config)#exit
```

```
RouterA#show ip eigrp neighbors
RouterA#show ip eigrp topology
RouterA#show ip route eigrp
RouterA#show ip protocols
RouterA#show ip eigrp traffic
```

The show ip eigrp neighbors command shows routers discovered using EIGRP. The show ip eigrp topology command displays the topology table.

The show ip route eigrp command displays the EIGRP entries in the routing table. The show ip protocols command shows the state of the active routing process. The show ip eigrp traffic command displays the number of EIGRP packets sent and received. To analyze the packets sent and received by EIGRP, use the debug ip eigrp command.

Enabling Open Shortest Path First (OSPF)

OSPF is an interior gateway protocol based on link state rather than distance vectors.

- OSPF was developed in the 1980s as an answer to RIP's inability to scale well in heterogeneous internetworks.

- OSPF is an open-standard protocol and is open to the public domain.

- OSPF forwards link-state advertisements (LSA) rather than routing tables.

- OSPF uses a hierarchical network to separate networks (autonomous systems) into manageable areas. Routing can occur between areas, but overhead data is kept within each area.

Configuring OSPF

```
RouterA>enable
RouterA#config term
RouterA(config)#router ospf 100
RouterA(config-router)#network 170.8.0.0 area 1
RouterA(config-router)#exit
RouterA(config)#exit
RouterA#show ip protocols
```

The show ip protocols command verifies that OSPF is configured. The show ip route command displays all known routes. The show ip ospf interface command displays the area ID and adjacency information. To analyze the OSPF events, use the debug ip ospf command.

Variable-Length Subnet Masks (VLSMs)

VLSMs were developed to allow multiple levels of subnetting in an IP network. This allows network administrators to overcome the limitations of fixed-sized subnets within a network and in effect subnet a subnet. VLSMs are available only on certain routed protocols, such as EIGRP and OSPF.

The primary benefit of VLSMs is more efficient use of IP addresses.

Without VLSMs, you are confined to a fixed number of subnets, each with a fixed number of hosts.

With VLSMs, you can have multiple subnets, with a varying number of hosts. Adding subnets works the same way as normal subnets.

Access Lists and Their Applications

As a network grows, it becomes more important to manage the increased traffic going across the network. Access lists help limit traffic by filtering traffic based on packet characteristics. Access lists define a set of rules that routers use to identify particular types of traffic. Access lists can be used to filter both incoming and outgoing traffic on a router's interface. An access list applied to a router specifies only rules for traffic going through the router. Traffic originating from a router is not affected by that router's access lists. (It is subject to access lists within other routers as it passes through them.)

Packet Filtering

Access lists can be configured to permit or deny incoming and outgoing packets on an interface. By following a set of conventions, the network administrator can exercise greater control over network traffic by restricting network use by certain users or devices.

Applications of an IP Access List

To establish an access list, you must define a sequential list of permit and deny conditions that apply IP addresses or IP protocols. Access lists only filter traffic going through the router; they do not filter traffic originated from the router. Access lists can also filter Telnet traffic into or out of the router's vty ports.

Access List Type		Number Range/Identifier
IP	Standard	1-99
	Extended	100-199
	Named	Name (Cisco IOS 11.2 and later)
IPX	Standard	800-899
	Extended	900-999
	SAP filters	1000-1099
	Named	Name (Cisco IOS 11.2 F and later)

Other Access List Uses

- Access lists allow finer granularity of control when defining priority and custom queues.
- Access lists can be used to identify "interesting traffic," which triggers dialing in dial-on-demand routing (DDR).
- Access lists filter and in some cases alter the attributes within a routing protocol update (route maps).

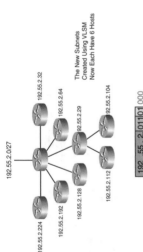

192.55.2.0/27
192.55.2.32
192.55.2.64
192.55.2.29
92.55.2.104
192.55.2.224
192.55.2.192
192.55.2.128
192.55.2.112

The New Subnets
Created Using VLSM
Now Each Have 6 Hosts

192	.55	.2	011	01	000

Network   Subnet   VLSM   Host

Note that VLSMs can only be added to subnets that do not already have hosts assigned to them.

Route Summarization with VLSMs

In large networks, it is impractical for a router to maintain tables with hundreds of thousands of routes. Route summarization (also called route aggregation or supernetting) reduces the number of entries in a routing table by representing blocks of address using a single summary address. Route summarization is accomplished by using a wire address and masks of the higher-level subnet to represent all routers using a lower-level (VLSM) router. Route summary addresses are most efficient when they are based on the largest number of common bits.

Route summarization can also isolate topology changes, because the routing changes are propagated only to the router that accesses the rest of the network. All other routers use a summary address.

Classless routing schemes such as RIPv2, IS-IS, EIGRP, and OSPF support route summarization using subnets and VLSMs. Classful routing protocols such as RIPv1 and IGRP automatically summarize at network boundaries and are unable to perform additional summarization.

Types of Access Lists

There are two general types of access lists:

- Standard access lists check packets' source addresses. Standard IP access lists permit or deny output for an entire protocol suite based on the source network/subnet/host IP address.

- Extended IP access lists check both source and destination packet addresses. Extended lists specify protocols, port numbers, and other parameters, allowing admins more flexibility and control.

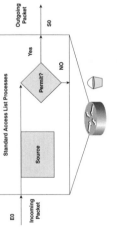

Standard	Extended
Filter based on source	Filter based on source and destination
Permit or deny the entire TCP/IP protocol suite	Specify a specific IP protocol and port number
Range: 1 to 99	Range: 100 to 199

Access List Process Options

- **Inbound access lists**—Incoming packets are processed before they are sent to the outbound interface. If the packet is to be discarded, this method reduces overhead (no routing table lookups). If the packet is permitted, it is processed in the normal way.

- **Outbound access lists**—Outgoing packets are processed by the router first and then are tested against the access list criteria.

Permit or Deny Process

Access list statements are operated on one at a time from top to bottom.

As soon as a packet header match is found, the packet is operated on (permitted or denied), and the rest of the statements are skipped. If no match is found, the packet is tested against the next statement until a match is found or the end of the list is reached. An implicit deny statement is present at the end of the list (all remaining packets are dropped). Unless there is at least one permit statement in an access list, all traffic is blocked.

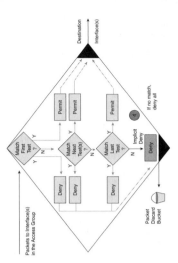

Guidelines for Implementing Access Lists

- Be sure to use the correct numbers for the type of list and protocols you want filter.

- You can use only one access list per protocol, per direction, per interface. A single interface can have one access list per protocol.

- Put more-specific statements before more-general ones. Frequently occurring conditions should be placed before less-frequent conditions.

- Additions are always added to the end of the access list. You cannot selectively add or remove statements in the middle of an access list. You can delete in the middle of a named extended access list.

- Without an explicit permit, any statement at the end of a list of packets not matched by other statements is discarded. Every access list should include at least one permit statement.

- An interface with an empty access list applied to it allows (permits) all traffic. Create your statements before applying the list to an interface.
- Access lists filter only traffic going through the router.

Protocol Access List Identifiers

The access list number entered by the administrator determines how the router handles the access list. The arguments in the statement follow the number. The types of conditions allowed depend on the type of list (defined by the access list number). Conditions for an access list vary by protocol. You can have several different access lists for any given protocol, but only one protocol is allowed on any access list (one protocol, per direction, per interface).

TCP/IP Packet Tests

For TCP/IP packets, access lists check the packet and upper-layer headers for different items (depending on the type of access list, standard or extended).

Standard IP access lists are assigned the range of numbers 1 to 99. Extended IP access lists use the range 100 to 199.

After a packet is checked for a match with the access list statement, it is either permitted to an interface or discarded.

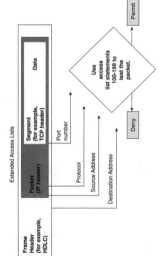

Wildcard Masking

It is not always necessary to check every bit within an address. Wildcard masking identifies which bits should be checked or ignored. Admins can use this tool to select one or more IP addresses for filtering.

Wildcard masking is exactly the opposite of subnet masking:

- A wildcard mask bit 0 means check the corresponding bit value.
- A mask bit 1 means do not check (ignore) that corresponding bit value.

To specify an IP host address within a permit or deny statement, enter the full address followed by a mask of all 0s (0.0.0.0).

To specify that all destination addresses are permitted in an access list, enter 0.0.0.0 as the address, followed by a mask of all 1s (255.255.255).

Abbreviated Commands in Wildcard Masking

Abbreviations can be used instead of entering an entire wildcard mask.

Check all addresses—To match a specific address, use host: 172.30.16.29 0.0.0.0 can be written as host 172.30.16.29.

Ignore all addresses—Use the word any to specify all addresses: 0.0.0.0 255.255.255.255 can be written as any.

Access Lists and Their Applications Summary

- Access lists filter packets as they pass through the router.
- The two general types of IP access lists are standard and extended. Standard filters based on only the source address, and extended filters based on source and destination addresses as well as specific protocols and numbers.
- Access lists can be set to either inbound or outbound. For inbound access lists, the packets are processed first and then are routed to an outbound interface (assuming that the filter passes them). In outbound access lists, the packets are sent to the interface and then are checked.
- If a packet meets a permit statement's criteria, it is forwarded. If a packet meets a deny statement's criteria, it is immediately discarded.
- More-restrictive statements should be at the top of the list.
- Only one access list per interface, per protocol, per direction is allowed.
- Every access list should have at least one permit statement.
- For IP, standard access lists use the number range 1 to 99, and extended access lists use 100 to 199. For IPX, standard access lists use 800 to 899, and extended access lists use 900 to 999.
- Wildcard masking is used to filter single IP addresses or blocks of addresses.

Access List Configuration

Principles of Configuring Access Lists

Access lists are processed from top to bottom, making statement ordering critical to efficient operation. Always place specific and frequent statements at the beginning of an access list. Named access lists allow the removal of individual statements (but no reordering). To reorder statements, the whole list must be removed and re-created with the proper statement ordering. A text editor should be used to create lists. Remember that all access lists end with an implicit deny any statement.

Access List Syntax

The syntax for standard and extended IP access lists is
access-list *access-list-number* [permit | deny] *source* [*mask*]

access-list *access-list-number* [permit | deny] *protocol source source-wildcard* [operator port] *destination destination-wildcard* [*operator port*] [established] [log]

operator port can be less than, greater than, equal to, or not equal to a port number.

- **established** (used for inbound TCP only) allows only established connections to pass packets.
- **log** sends a logging message to the console.

After the statements are added, they are applied to an access group using the following syntax:
ip access-group *access-list-number* [in | out]

Configuring Extended IP Access Lists

```
RouterA>enable
RouterA#config term
RouterA(config)#access-list 101 deny tcp 172.16.4.0 0.0.0.255 172.16.3.0
0.0.0.255 eq 21
RouterA(config)#interface ethernet 0
RouterA(config-if)#access group 101 in RouterA(config)#exit
RouterA#show ip interface
```

Named Access Lists

Named IP access lists (Cisco IOS software Release 11.2 or greater) allow alphanumeric strings as identifiers rather than numbers. Named access lists can be standard or extended. Named IP access lists also allow you to delete individual statements from an access list.

Named access lists can be used when more than 99 standard or extended access lists are configured on any router. Duplicate names are not allowed on any one router, but you can use the same name on two different routers.

Guidelines for Placing Access Lists

Extended IP access lists can block traffic from leaving the source and should be as close as possible to the source of the traffic to be denied.
Standard IP access lists block traffic at the destination and should be as close as possible to the destination of the traffic to be denied.

Virtual Terminal Access Lists

In addition to physical ports, devices also have virtual ports (called virtual terminal lines). There are five such virtual terminal lines, numbered vty 0 through vty 4. Standard and extended access lists do not prevent router-initiated Telnet sessions.

Router#

Physical Port (e0) (Telnet)

Virtual Ports (vty 0 Through 4)

e0

Virtual terminal access lists can block vty access to the router or block access to other routers on allowed vty sessions. Restrictions on vty access should include all virtual ports, because users can connect via any vty port. The syntax for a vty access list is

```
line vty {vty# | vty-range}
access-class {IP access list #} in
```

After the vty statements are added, they are assigned to the router with the following command:

```
access-class access-list-number {in | out}
```

Specifying **in** prevents incoming Telnet connections, and **out** prevents Telnet connections to other routers from the vty ports.

Access List Configuration Summary

- Here are some general guidelines for configuring access lists:
  —All access lists end with an implicit deny.
  —More-specific tests should precede more-general tests.
  —Frequently used tests should precede infrequent tests.
- Standard IP access lists filter based on source addresses only.
- Extended IP access lists filter based on source and destination addresses, protocols, and ports.
- The **access-list** command assigns statements to a list. The **access-group** command assigns an access list to an interface.
- Named access lists allow you to identify access lists with alphanumeric strings rather than numbers. You can delete entries from a named access list.

- Extended access lists should be close to the destination of the traffic to be denied.
- Standard access lists should be close to the source.
- Access lists can be used to control virtual terminal (vty) access to or from a router.

WAN Concepts and Terminology

WANs connect networks, users, and services across a broad geographic area. Companies use the WAN to connect company sites for information exchange.

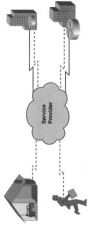

Service Provider

Three WAN Connection Types

WAN services are generally leased from service providers on a subscription basis. There are three main types of WAN connections (services):

- **Leased line**—A leased line (or point-to-point dedicated connection) provides a preestablished connection through the service provider's network (WAN) to a remote network. Leased lines provide a reserved connection for the client but are costly. Leased-line connections typically are synchronous serial connections with speeds up to 45 Mbps (T3).

Synchronous Serial

- **Circuit switch**—Circuit switching provides a dedicated circuit path between sender and receiver for the duration of the call. Circuit switching is used for basic telephone service or Integrated Services Digital Network (ISDN). Circuit-switched connections are best for clients that require only sporadic WAN usage.

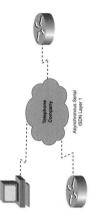

Telephone Company

Asynchronous Serial
ISDN Layer 1

Physical Parameters for WAN Connections

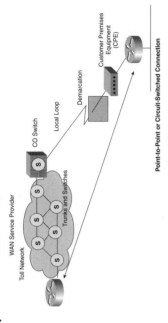

Point-to-Point or Circuit-Switched Connection

A WAN service provider assigns your organization the parameters required for making the WAN link connection.

- **Customer Premises Equipment (CPE)**—Located on the subscriber's premises and includes both equipment owned by the subscriber and devices leased by the service provider.
- **Demarcation (or demarc)**—Marks the point where CPE ends and the local loop begins. Usually it is located in the telecommunications closet.
- **Local loop (or last mile)**—The cabling from the demarc into the WAN service provider's central office.
- **Central office (CO)**—A switching facility that provides a point of presence for WAN service. The central office is the entry point to the WAN cloud, the exit point from the WAN for called devices, and a switching point for calls.
- **Toll network**—A collection of trunks inside the WAN cloud.

- **Packet switch**—With packet switching, devices transport packets using virtual circuits (VCs) that provide end-to-end connectivity. Programmed switching devices provide physical connections. Packet headers are used to identify the destination. Packet switching offers leased line-type services over shared lines, but at a much lower cost. Packet-switched networks typically use serial connections with speeds ranging from 56 kbps to T3 speeds.

Other WAN Connections

- **Digital Subscriber Line (DSL)**—DSL delivers high bandwidth over existing telephony copper lines. There are four varieties of DSL:
  —Asymmetric digital subscriber line (ADSL)
  —High data rate digital subscriber line (HDSL)
  —Symmetric digital subscriber line (SDSL)
  —Very-high data rate digital subscriber line (VDSL)
  DSL does not use the entire bandwidth available on the twisted pair, leaving room for a voice channel.
- **Cable**—Broadband cable uses a coaxial cable to transport the data.

WAN Cabling

The router end of the cable connects to the DB-60 port on a serial WAN interface card (using a DB-60 connector) or another connector. The connector on the other end of the serial cable is specified by the standard used.

DTE or DCE port configuration

The ports on either end of a WAN connection are specified as DTE (data terminal equipment) or data communications equipment (DCE). DCE converts user data into the service provider's preferred format. The port configured as DTE requires external clocking from the CSU/DSU or other DCE device.

Layer 2 Encapsulation Protocols

- **High-Level Data Link Control (HDLC)**—The default encapsulation type on point-to-point dedicated links and circuit-switched connections. HDLC should be used when communicating between Cisco devices.

- **Point-to-Point Protocol (PPP)**—Provides connections between devices over several types of physical interfaces, such as asynchronous serial, HSSI, ISDN, and synchronous. PPP works with many network layer protocols, including IP and IPX. PPP uses PAP and CHAP for basic security.
- **X.25/Link Access Procedure, Balanced (LAPB)**—Defines connections between DTE and DCE for remote terminal access. LAPB is a data link layer protocol specified by X.25.
- **Frame Relay**—The industry-standard switched data link layer protocol. Frame Relay (based on X.25) can handle multiple virtual circuits. Asynchronous Transfer Mode (ATM): The international standard for cell relay using fixed-length (53-byte) cells for multiple service types. Fixed-length cells allow hardware processing, which greatly reduces transit delays. ATM takes advantage of high-speed transmission media such as E3, T3, and SONET.

WAN Concepts and Terminology Summary

- WANs connect devices across broad geographic regions. Companies use WANs to connect various sites.
- Leased line or point-to-point connections provide a dedicated connection.

- Circuit-switched connections provide a dedicated circuit path for the duration of the call. Circuit switching is best for sporadic WAN usage.
- Packet-switched connections use virtual circuits to provide end-to-end connectivity.
- The five serial standards supported by Cisco devices are EIA/TIA-232, EIA/TIA-449, V.35, X.21, and EIA/TIA-530.
- Typical WAN protocols include HDLC, PPP, SLIP, and ATM.

Configuring HDLC and PPP Encapsulation

HDLC is a data-link protocol used on synchronous serial data links. HDLC cannot support multiple protocols on a single link, because it lacks a mechanism to indicate which protocol it is carrying.

The Cisco version of HDLC uses a proprietary field that acts as a protocol field. This field makes it possible for a single serial link to accommodate multiple network-layer protocols. Cisco's HDLC is a point-to-point protocol that can be used on leased lines between two Cisco devices. PPP should be used when communicating with non-Cisco devices.

Cisco HDLC

Flag	Address	Control	Proprietary	Data	FCS	Flag

To change the encapsulation back to HDLC from some other protocol, use the following command from interface configuration mode:

```
Router(config-if)#encapsulation hdlc
```

PPP Encapsulation

PPP uses a Network Control Protocol (NCP) component to encapsulate multiple protocols and the Link Control Protocol (LCP) to set up and negotiate control options on the data link.

Figure labels: IP, IPX, Many Others, Protocols, Layer 3, Network Layer — IPCP, IPXCP, Network Control Protocol — PPP — Authentication, Other Options, Link Control Protocol, Data Link Layer — Synchronous or Asynchronous Physical Media, Physical Layer

- **Authentication options**—Are Password Authentication Protocol (PAP) and Challenge Handshake Authentication Protocol (**CHAP**).
- **Compression options**—Increase the effective throughput on PPP connections.
- **Error detection**—The quality and magic number options help ensure a reliable, loop-free data link.
- **Multilink**—Is available in Cisco IOS software Release 11.1 and later. It improves throughput and reduces latency between peer routers.
- **PPP callback**—Is available in Cisco IOS software Release 11.1. PPP callback offers enhanced security. After making the initial DDR call, the router requests that it be called back and then terminates its call.

Establishing a PPP Session

The three phases of PPP session establishment are link establishment, authentication, and the network protocol phase.

- **Link establishment**—Each PPP device sends LCP packets to configure and test the data link. Options such as maximum receive unit, compression, and link authentication are negotiated here. Default values are assumed when no figures are present.
- **Authentication (optional)**—After the link is established, the peer may be authenticated.
- **Network layer protocol**—NCP packets are used to select and configure network-layer protocols. After they are configured, the network layer protocols can begin sending datagrams over the link.

Configuring HDLC and PPP Encapsulation Summary

- HDLC is the default protocol on serial data links for Cisco devices. Cisco's proprietary HDLC supports multiprotocol environments.
- PPP encapsulates Layer 3 data over point-to-point links.
- LCP options for PPP define authentication, passwords and challenge handshakes, compression, error detection, and multilink parameters.
- The three PPP session establishment phases are link establishment, authentication, and network layer configuration.

ISDN BRI Concepts

Integrated Services Digital Network (ISDN) is a collection of standards that define an integrated voice/data architecture over the Public Switched Telephone Network (PSTN). ISDN

PPP Configuration Options

Cisco routers using PPP encapsulation include the LCP options shown in the table.

Feature	How It Operates	Protocol
Authentication	Requires a password; performs challenge handshake	PAP CHAP
Compression	Compresses data at source; reproduces data at destination	Stacker or protocol
Error detection	Monitors data dropped on link; avoids frame looping	Magic Number
Multilink	Load balancing across multiple links	Multilink Protocol (MP)

standards define both the hardware and call setup schemes. ISDN provides the following benefits:

- **Multiple traffic feeds**—Voice, video, telex, and packet-switched data are all available over ISDN.
- **Fast call setup**—ISDN uses out-of-band (D, or delta channel) signaling for call setup. ISDN calls can often be set up and completed in less than 1 second.
- **Fast bearer channel services (64 kbps per channel)**—With multiple B channels (two B channels with BRI), ISDN offers 128 kbps. Leased lines usually provide only 56 kbps in North America.

ISDN Standard Access Methods

- **Basic Rate Interface (BRI)**—BRI has two bearer channels (64 kbps each) and one delta channel (16 kbps). BRI is sometimes written as 2B+D. The B channels are used for digitized voice and high-speed data transport. The D channel is used for signaling. The D channel can also be used for low-rate packet data (such as alarms). D channel traffic is transported using the LAPD data-link-level protocol.

Channel	Capacity	Mostly Used For
B	64 kbps	Circuit-switched Data (HDLC, PPP)
D	16/64 kbps	Signaling information (LAPD)

- **Primary Rate Interface (PRI)**—In North America and Japan, PRI has 23 B channels and one D channel (all channels are 64 kbps). In Europe, PRI has 30 B channels and one D channel.

ISDN Call Setup

The D channel initiates the call by establishing a path between switches and passing the called number. Local switches use the SS7 signaling protocol to complete the path and pass the called number to the terminating ISDN switch. When the destination receives the setup

information, it uses the D channel to tell the ISDN switch that it is available. The B channel is now connected end-to-end and can carry conversation or data.

ISDN Functions

Customer premises equipment (CPE) is used to connect to the ISDN switch. The ISDN standards define functions (devices) that act as transition points between reference-point interfaces. With BRI you must determine whether you need a transition device (NT1) between the router and the service provider's ISDN switch. Connectors labeled as BRI U are built into NT1. Connectors marked BRI S/T require an external NT1.

Caution: Insert the cable running from an ISDN BRI port into only an ISDN BRI jack or switch. ISDN BRI uses voltages that can seriously damage non-ISDN devices.

ISDN Device Types and Reference Points

- TE1—Terminal endpoint 1. Devices have a native ISDN interface.
- NT2—Network termination 2. Aggregates and switches all ISDN lines at a customer service site using a customer switching device.
- NT1—Network termination 1. Converts BRI signals into a form used by the ISDN digital line. An NT1 terminates the local loop.
- TE2—Terminal endpoint 2. A device that requires a TA.
- TA—Terminal adapter. Converts EIA/TIA-232, V.35, and other signals into BRI signals.
- R—A connection point between a non-ISDN-compatible device and a terminal adapter.
- S—The connection point into the customer switching device (NT2). Enables calls between customer equipment.
- T—The outbound connection from the NT2 to the ISDN network. This reference point is electrically identical to the S interface.
- U—The connection point between NT1 and the ISDN network.

Determining the Router ISDN Interface

Cisco routers might not have a native ISDN terminal, and those with terminals might not have the same reference point. To avoid damaging equipment, you should evaluate each router carefully.

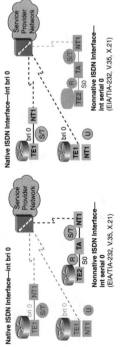

Native ISDN Interface—int bri 0

Native ISDN Interface—int bri 0

Nonnative ISDN Interface—int serial 0 (EIA/TIA-232, V.35, X.21)

Nonnative ISDN Interface—int serial 0 (EIA/TIA-232, V.35, X.21)

Connectors labeled BRI have a native ISDN interface built in (your router is a TE1). A router might also have a built-in NT1 (BRI U interfaces). If your router interface is labeled BRI, you must use an external TA device.

Warning: Never connect a router with a U interface to an NT1. It will most likely ruin the interface!

ISDN Switch Types

Service providers use several different types of switches for their ISDN services. Before connecting a router to an ISDN service, you must be aware of the switch types used at the central office. This information must be specified during router configuration to allow ISDN service.

Service Provider Identifiers (SPIDs)

SPIDs are assigned by your service provider to identify your switch at the central office. Your switch must be identified before a connection can be made (during call setup). SPIDs might or might not be required, depending on the switch type you are connecting to. The syntax for configuring a SPID on your switch is as follows:

```
isdn [spid1 | spid2] spid-number [ldn]
```

- [spid1 | spid2] specifies the SPID as either the first or second B channel.
- *spid-number* is the number assigned by the ISDN service provider.
- *ldn* is an optional local dial number.

ISDN BRI Concepts Summary

- ISDN standards define a digital architecture for integrated voice/data capability using the PSTN. ISDN provides multiple user traffic feeds, fast call setup, and fast data transfer rate.
- ISDN protocols include the E-series protocol for the telephone network and ISDN; the I-series protocol for ISDN concepts, aspects, and interfaces; and the Q-series protocol for switching and signaling.
- ISDN BRI has two 64-kbps B channels and one 16-kbps D channel.
- ISDN PRI has 23 B channels and one D channel.
- Reference points define connection points between functions.
- SPID numbers are required to access the ISDN network.

Dial-on-Demand Routing Overview

Dial-on-demand routing (DDR) refers to an as-needed connection service over the PSTN. DDR is typically used for low-volume, periodic connections and can offer a substantial savings over traditional WAN connections. DDR is well-suited for telecommuters, satellite offices sending sales transactions or order requests, and automated customer order systems.

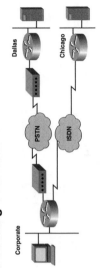

DDR Process

DDR uses the concept of "interesting traffic" to determine when a dialup connection should be made. Interesting traffic is defined in a router lookup table. The router locates the next-hop router and any dialing instructions (located in a dialer map). If the link is not already up, the router initiates a connection and traffic is sent. After a link is enabled, the router transmits both interesting and uninteresting traffic. The call is terminated if no more additional interesting traffic is sent within a specified time period.

Defining Static Routes for DDR

Static routes are required for DDR, because you want to maintain control over which routes are used to reach each destination. These routes must be manually configured on all participating routers because static routes have no routing updates. To manually configure a route, use the following command:

```
ip route [network prefix] [prefix mask] {address | interface} [distance]
[permanent]
```

- *network prefix* is the address of the destination network.
- *address | interface* is the address and interface of the next-hop router.
- *permanent* sets the static condition.

```
ip route 10.10.0.0  255.255.0.0  10.1.0.2
ip route 10.20.0.0  255.255.0.0  10.1.0.2
```

Network Prefix and Prefix Mask

```
ip route 10.40.0.0  255.255.0.0  10.1.0.1
```

Specify Address of Next Hop Router

Specifying Interesting Traffic for DDR

Interesting packets are determined by the network administrator and can be defined by protocol type, source address, or destination host. Use the following command to define interesting packets:

```
dialer-list dialer-group protocol protocol-name {permit | deny | list
access-list-number}
```

- *dialer-group* maps the dialer list to an interface.
- *list access-list-number* assigns an access list to the dialer group.

Other important DDR commands are **dialer-group**, which links interesting traffic created in the dialer list to the interface, and **dialer map**, which defines one or more DDR numbers.

Dial-on-Demand Routing Summary

- DDR refers to dynamic connections made over dialup facilities on an as-needed basis.
- DDR is best suited for low-volume, periodic connections.
- To configure legacy DDR, define static routes (ip route command), specify interesting traffic (dialer-list command), and configure the dialer information (dialer-group command).
- All participating routers must have static routes defined to reach the remote networks.
- To use a DDR circuit as a backup for another WAN interface type, a floating static route is used.

Frame Relay Overview

Frame Relay is a connection-oriented Layer 2 protocol that allows several data connections (virtual circuits) to be multiplexed onto a single physical link. Frame Relay relies on upper-layer protocols for error correction. Frame Relay specifies only the connection between a router and a service provider's local access switching equipment.

A connection identifier is used to map packets to outbound ports on the service provider's switch. When the switch receives a frame, a lookup table is used to map the frame to the correct outbound port. The entire path to the destination is determined before the frame is sent.

Frame Relay Stack

The bulk of Frame Relay functions exist at the lower two layers of the OSI reference model. Frame Relay is supported on the same physical serial connections that support point-to-point connections. Cisco routers support the EIA/TIA-232, EIA/TIA-449, V.35, X.21, and EIA/TIA-530 serial connections. Upper-layer information (such as IP data) is encapsulated by Frame Relay and is transmitted over the link.

	OSI Reference Model		Frame Relay
7	Application		
6	Presentation		
5	Session		
4	Transport		
3	Network		IP/IPX/AppleTalk, etc.
2	Data Link		Frame Relay
1	Physical		EIA/TIA-232, EIA/TIA-449, V.35, X.21, EIA/TIA-530

Frame Relay Terms

- **VC (virtual circuit)**—A logical circuit between two network devices. A VC can be permanent (PVC) or switched (SVC). PVCs save bandwidth (no circuit establishment or teardown) but can be expensive. SVCs are established on-demand and are torn down when transmission is complete. VC status can be active, inactive, or deleted.

- **DLCI (Data-Link Connection Identifier)**—Identifies the logical connection between two directly connected sets of devices.

- **CIR (Committed Information Rate)**—The minimum guaranteed data transfer rate agreed to by the Frame Relay switch.

- **Inverse ARP**—Routers use Inverse ARP to discover the network address of a device associated with a VC.

- **LMI (Local Management Interface)**—A signaling standard used to manage the connection between the router and the Frame Relay switch. LMIs track and manage keepalive mechanisms, multicast messages, and status. LMI is configurable (in Cisco IOS software Release 11.2 and later), but routers can autosense LMI types by sending a status request to the Frame Relay switch. The router configures itself to match the LMI type response. The three types of LMIs supported by Cisco Frame Relay switches are Cisco (developed by Cisco, StrataCom, Northern Telecom, and DEC), ansi Annex D (ANSI standard T1.617), and q933a (ITU-T Q.933 Annex A).

- **FECN (Forward Explicit Congestion Notification)**—A message sent to a destination device when a Frame Relay switch senses congestion in the network.

- **BECN (Backward Explicit Congestion Notification)**—A message sent to a source router when a Frame Relay switch recognizes congestion in the network. A BECN message requests a reduced data transmission rate.

Dynamic Mapping with Inverse ARP

To correctly route packets, each DLCI must be mapped to a next-hop address. These addresses can be manually configured or dynamically mapped using Inverse ARP. After the address is mapped, it is stored in the router's Frame Relay map table.

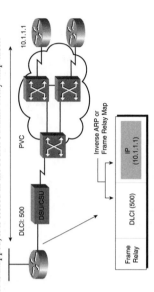

LMI Signaling Process

1. The router connects to a Frame Relay switch through a channel service unit/data service unit (CSU/DSU).

2. The router sends a VC status inquiry to the Frame Relay switch.

3. The switch responds with a status message that includes DLCI information for the usable PVCs.

4. The router advertises itself by sending an Inverse ARP to each active DLCI.

5. The routers create map entries with the local DLCI and network layer address of the remote routers. Static maps must be configured if Inverse ARP is not supported.

6. Inverse ARP messages are sent every 60 seconds.

7. LMI information is exchanged every 10 seconds.

Frame Relay Overview Summary

- Frame Relay is a connection-oriented Layer 2 protocol that allows several data connections (virtual circuits) to be multiplexed onto a single physical link.

- Cisco routers support Frame Relay on EIA/TIA-232, EIA/TIA-449, V.35, X.21, and EIA/TIA-530 serial connections.

- Local DLCI addresses can be dynamically mapped using Inverse ARP or manually configured using static Frame Relay maps.
- LMI signaling is used by Frame Relay switches to manage connections and maintain status between the devices. The supported LMI types are cisco, ansi, and q933a.

Configuring Frame Relay

The three commands used to configure basic Frame Relay on a router select the Frame Relay encapsulation type, establish the LMI connection, and enable Inverse ARP. The commands used are

```
encapsulation frame-relay [cisco | ietf]
frame-relay lmi-type {ansi | cisco | q933i}
frame-relay inverse-arp [protocol] [dlci]
```

Configuring Basic Frame Relay

```
RouterA>enable
RouterA#config term
RouterA(config)#int ser 1
RouterA(config-if)#ip address 10.16.0.1    255.255.255.
RouterA(config-if)#encapsulation frame-relay cisco
RouterA(config-if)#frame-relay lmi-type    cisco
RouterA(config-if)#bandwidth 64
RouterA(config-if)#frame-relay inverse-arp ip 16
RouterA(config-if)#exit
RouterA(config)#exit
RouterA#
```

Verifying Frame Relay Operations

The following commands can be used to verify and display Frame Relay information:

- **show interface**—Displays Layer 1 and Layer 2 status, DLCI information, and the LMI DLCIs used for the local management interface.
- **show frame-relay lmi**—Displays LMI traffic statistics (LMI type, status messages sent, and invalid LMI messages).
- **show frame-relay pvc**—Displays the status of all configured connections, traffic statistics, and BECN and FECN packets received by the router.
- **show frame-relay map**—Displays the current map entries for static and dynamic routes. The frame-relay-inarp command clears all dynamic entries.

Static Frame Relay Map Configuration

A router's address-to-DLCI table can be defined statically when Inverse ARP is not supported. These static maps can also be used to control broadcasts. To statically configure the map table, use the following command:

```
frame-relay map protocol protocol-address dlci [broadcast] [ietf | cisco |
payload-compress packet-by-packet]
```

- *protocol* specifies bridging or logical link control.
- **broadcast** is an optional parameter used to control broadcasts and multicasts over the VC.
- **payload-compress** is an optional Cisco-proprietary compression method.

The frame interface *dlci* command also statically maps a local DLCI to a configured Layer 3 protocol on a subinterface. The difference is that map statements are used in multipoint Frame Relay configurations and the frame interface *dlci* command is used in point-to-point subinterface configurations.

Frame Relay Topology

Frame Relay is a nonbroadcast multiaccess (NBMA) connection scheme. This means that although Frame Relay interfaces support multipoint connections by default, broadcast routing updates are not forwarded to remote sites. Frame Relay networks can be designed using star, full-mesh, and partial-mesh topologies.

A star topology, also known as a hub-and-spoke configuration, is the common network topology. Remote sites are connected to a central site, which usually provides services. Star topologies require the fewest PVCs, making them relatively inexpensive. The hub router provides a multipoint connection using a single interface to interconnect multiple PVCs.

In a **full-mesh** topology, all routers have virtual circuits to all other destinations. Although it is expensive, this method provides redundancy, because all sites are connected to all

Full Mesh

Partial Mesh

Star (Hub and Spoke)

other sites. Full-mesh networks become very expensive as the number of nodes increases. The number of links required in a full-mesh topology that has n nodes is $(n * (n-1))/2$.

In a partial-mesh topology, not all sites have direct access to all other sites. Connections usually depend on the traffic patterns within the network.

Configuring Frame Relay Summary

- The frame-relay, frame-relay lmi-type, and frame-relay inverse-arp commands are used to configure Frame Relay.
- The frame-relay map command is used to configure static address-to-DLCI tables.
- The three WAN topologies used to interconnect remote sites are star, partial mesh, and full mesh.

Configuring Frame Relay Subinterfaces

Frame Relay provides NBMA connectivity between sites, which means that although remote locations can reach each other, routing update broadcasts are not forwarded to all locations. Frame Relay networks use split horizon to prevent routing loops. With split horizon activated, if a remote router receives an update on an interface with multiple PVCs, the router cannot forward that broadcast to routers on other PVCs on the same interface.

Routing Update Replication

When several DLCIs terminate in a single router, that router must replicate all routing updates and service advertisements on each DLCI. These updates consume bandwidth, cause latency variations, and consume interface buffers, which leads to higher packet loss rates.

Broadcast traffic and virtual circuit placement should be considered when designing Frame Relay networks to avoid negatively impacting critical user data.

Resolving Reachability Issues in Frame Relay

Reachability issues can be solved by configuring subinterfaces on the router. These logically assigned interfaces let the router forward broadcast updates in a Frame Relay network. Subinterfaces are logical subdivisions of a physical interface. Routing updates received on one subinterface can be sent out another subinterface without violating split horizon rules. By configuring virtual circuits as point-to-point connections, the subinterface acts similar to a leased line. It is also possible (and sometimes recommended) to turn off split horizon to solve this problem.

Subinterface Configuration

Subinterfaces can be configured as either point-to-point or multipoint. With point-to-point, one PVC connection is established with another physical interface or subinterface on a remote router using a single subinterface. With multipoint, multiple PVC connections are established with multiple physical interfaces or subinterfaces on remote routers on a single subinterface. All interfaces involved use the same subnet, and each interface has its own local DLCI.

To select a subinterface, use the following command:

```
interface serial-number.subinterface-number {multipoint | point-to-point}
```

To configure a subinterface, use the following command:

```
frame-relay interface-dlci dlci-number
```

The range of subinterface numbers is 1 to 4294967293. The number that precedes the period (.) must match the physical interface number to which this subinterface belongs.

The *dlci-number* option binds the local DLCI to the Layer 3 protocol configured on the subinterface, as evidenced by the **show frame map** command. This is the only way to link an LMI-derived PVC to a subinterface (LMI does not know about subinterfaces).

Configuring Basic Frame Relay

```
RouterA>enable
RouterA#config term
RouterA(config)#int ser0
RouterA(config-if)#ip address 172.10.122.30
RouterA(config-if)#encapsulation frame-relay cisco
RouterA(config-if)#interface serial0.3 point-to-point
RouterA(config-if)#frame-relay interface-dlci 120
RouterA(config-if)#exit
RouterA(config)#exit
RouterA#
```

The **frame-relay interface-dlci** *dlci* command is required for all point-to-point configurations and multipoint subinterfaces for which Inverse ARP is enabled. Do not use this command on physical interfaces.

Configuring Frame Relay Subinterfaces

- Split horizon does not allow routing updates received on one interface to be forwarded out the same interface.
- Routing updates received on one subinterface can be sent out another subinterface configured on the same physical interface.
- Virtual circuits can be configured as point-to-point connections allowing subinterfaces to act like leased lines.
- Subinterfaces can be configured to support point-to-multipoint or point-to-point connection types.
- A physical interface is always a multipoint interface.

Notes

Notes

Notes

Notes

Notes

Notes

Notes

Notes

Notes

Notes

Notes

Notes

Notes

Notes

Notes

Notes

Notes

Notes